PHOTO: LOLA YA BONOBO SANCTUARY

Vanessa Woods is a feature writer for the Discovery Channel. She has written for a large number of publications including *New Scientist*, *BBC Wildlife* and *Australian Geographic*. In 2003, Vanessa won the Australasian Science award for journalism. She is currently studying the psychology of bonobos and chimpanzees in Africa.

Vanessa Woods

It's Every Monkey for Themselves

A true story
of sex, love and
lies in the jungle

ALLEN&UNWIN

First published in 2007

Allen & Unwin
83 Alexander Street
Crows Nest NSW 2065
Australia
Phone: (61 2) 8425 0100
Fax: (61 2) 9906 2218
Email: info@allenandunwin.com
Web: www.allenandunwin.com

Cataloguing-in-Publication entry is available
from the National Library of Australia.

ISBN 978 1 74114 859 6

Set in 10.5/14 pt Galliard by Bookhouse, Sydney

10 9 8 7 6 5 4 3 2 1

For my mother and her chicken wing.
And for my sister, the most beautiful girl in the world.

Acknowledgements

i owe this book to Brian, who gave me an ending and a new beginning. Thanks to Heather Catchpole, Helen Woods, Tanya Patrick, Sean Kahl, Sam Spurr and Anna Wallace whose love got me through Costa Rica alive and well enough to write the book. Thanks to Rose Gill for giving me the strength to write in the first place, and for helping me to grow up.

Thanks to everyone at Allen & Unwin, especially Catherine Milne and Jo Paul, who saw potential through the mess, and to Alexandra Nahlous and Susin Chow who helped me clean it up.

And finally, to my monkey buddies out there, you know who you are—especially you, Brad.

Al-pha [**al**-f*uh*] — *adjective*

8. a. (esp. of animals) having the highest rank of its sex in a dominance hierarchy: the alpha female.

Dictionary.com Unabridged (v 1.0.1) Based on the *Random House Unabridged Dictionary*, © Random House, Inc. 2006

Contents

chapter 1
Monkey blind

the sun had risen six times on Cielo Forest and I still did not know the monkeys. The monkey in front of me bit the head off an enormous caterpillar, flicked away the intestines, and chewed on the luminous green body.

'You are so disgusting,' I muttered, but I didn't know who I was talking to. Its white fluffy face had a reddish birthmark under the right side of the lip. Maybe Murder. Or Scandal.

The monkey licked some bubbling green froth from the decapitated caterpillar with its little pointed tongue. Maybe it was Mayhem. Apparently Mayhem was a pretty monkey, whatever the hell that meant. They all looked the same to me. And they were all ugly.

The project director, Diane, came up behind me and we stood together in silence, watching the monkey finish off the caterpillar.

'Do you know who this is?' she asked.

'Murder?'

'Mayhem.'

Fuck.

Clamouring through the tropical forests of Costa Rica, the monkeys of Cielo were used to people staring at them and swearing. The monkey known as Mayhem was sitting so close to me, if I reached out I could snatch the squirming caterpillar from her tight little fists. It was the twenty-sixth caterpillar I had seen her eat that morning. The tree was crawling with them, and nearly every leaf drooped with the weight of a caterpillar on the underside. The rest of the monkeys were stuffing caterpillars in their mouths like marshmallows. But not Mayhem. She carefully turned over a leaf and picked up a fat morsel laced with a row of bright blue diamonds. She poked the velvety skin to test for juiciness and delectability, then tore off the head and started chewing. She flicked her wrist expertly, and the caterpillar's poisonous intestines landed on the collar of my white shirt. It joined four or five other black slimy stains. As I stood beneath the tree, scrutinising Mayhem's face, intestines and caterpillar body parts fell around me like rain. They made small thuds as they hit the ground. Some of them were still moving.

If you had asked me what I was doing, trying to memorise a monkey's face by the way it ate caterpillars, I would have replied I was studying the behavioural ecology of capuchin monkeys.

But the truth was, I had no idea.

It wasn't my first trip away from home. After four years studying Marine Biology and English Literature at the University of New South Wales, I took off to Africa to count chimpanzees. The largest population of chimpanzees in the world was in the Congo, but they were rapidly being butchered and eaten. It was estimated that the second largest population of chimpanzees was in Uganda, but no one knew exactly how many there were or where they lived.

For four months I lived in the Ugandan jungle, working with eight Ugandans and one English girl. We slept in tents, shifted camp every three days, and walked between five and thirteen hours a day and ate beans and rice for every meal.

I found myself looking after infant chimpanzees rescued from the pet trade. I slept, showered and went to the toilet with a baby chimp hanging around my neck until three months later when I headed to Kenya for a zebra census.

For four months we surveyed the National Parks from Nairobi all the way to the Chelbe Desert on the Ethiopian border. I survived lions walking past my tent, an attempted clitoridectomy, and Ethiopian bandits holding a gun to my head.

But that was a long time ago. Years of wandering with no home, sleeping on everything from lice-ridden mattresses to dirt, and eating tempting dishes such as dead camel and grasshoppers, cured me of wanderlust. I was 24 when I took up the quiet life in a leafy suburb in Canberra, Australia, where everyone had a dog and a backyard. In preparation for my unborn children, I practised being an entertaining and educating mother by researching stories for a kid's television show called *Totally Wild* on Channel 10.

My partner in domestic bliss was Edward, a dark-haired economics student. He had a dry, quick wit, and loved to torment me. I adored him. We were all set up for marriage (even though he swore he'd never propose), and kids were right around the corner (even though he hated children). I knew the love of a good woman would change him, and I carried on my picture-perfect life, somewhat deluded, but happy.

Until one night I was woken by a rough hand on my shoulder.

'Vanessa, wake up.'

Edward had stumbled in, reeking of alcohol.

'Ed, what are you doing? Piss off.'

'I have something important to tell you.'

'Tell me in the morning.'

'We have to talk now.'

Everyone knows those words are the universal code for 'the shit is about to hit the fan'. I was wide awake instantly. Waiting.

He took a deep breath.

'I don't love you anymore.'

I opened and closed my mouth like a goldfish. I can still see his shadow against the blue of my window and hear my own deep breathing as the tears crawled up my throat.

'What are you talking about?'

'It's not working. Us. The kids thing. I don't love you.'

'You can't mean this. You're drunk.'

'I'm dead sober. I'm sorry.'

I can't remember the details. I remember begging, screaming, hitting him, before he passed out on the bed. Hours later, I sobbed myself to sleep beside him.

In the morning, I was hugging myself in the shower, still crying. The door opened and Edward ducked his head in.

'Morning, lover. Can I come in?'

I stared at him in disbelief. It wasn't possible. He couldn't crush my world then stand there like nothing had happened. His eyes were clear and painless.

'Why are you crying?'

'Get out,' I said, my heart spiralling down the drain with the dirty water. 'Just get out.'

The first alcoholic I'd lived with was my father. He left my mother when I was five. Besides alcoholism, the Vietnam War had left him with mild schizophrenia and manic depression. As a child I never knew what was wrong with my father. He was well educated and, most of the time, sophisticated and charming. When things were bad, he'd tell me he was sick, and I began to associate illness with catatonic stupors and violent outbursts of rage. I didn't find out about the mental institutions and rehabilitation centres until much later.

Edward was also well educated, sophisticated and charming. Considering my previous experience, it took longer than it should have for me to become suspicious. All the warning signs were there: drunken abuse in front of our embarrassed friends; bottles of gin in our room that would empty in a day. But this behaviour isn't really abnormal for university students and Edward was good at making me feel paranoid and overbearing. And then I just loved him so much I didn't want to believe it.

I had applied for the job in Costa Rica six months before the break-up, because Edward wanted to do his PhD in New York and I was looking for something I could do on the same continent. The monkey project had offered me the job but I hadn't accepted because I was waiting to see if I could get something a little closer to New York.

'That bastard,' said my best friend, Heather, when I went into work, my eyes red-rimmed and swollen. 'Throw him out.'

'I did.'

'Well make sure he's gone.'

I dialled home. Edward picked up on the first ring.

'Hello?'

'I want all your stuff gone by the time I get home.'

'You can't mean that.'

'Please,' I said, my voice breaking. 'Don't make this harder. Just leave.'

'I still don't get it—'

I hung up.

I half hoped he would still be there when I got home, convincing me I was overreacting, that he loved me, that he would stop. But he must have thought if he lay low for a while he could try to talk me out of it later. I never gave him a chance.

When I opened the door, blank spaces yawned from the shelves, the wardrobe and the floor. I didn't know who I was. I lay on our bed, the earth's gravity conspiring to suck me through the mattress to its molten core. I knew with the certainty that follows the destruction of first love that my life was over. At worst, the loss I had suffered would spread through my body like cancer, eating the remains of my youth until I was a shrivelled husk. At best, I would never be happy again.

A photo of me holding an orphan chimpanzee caught my eye. I remembered who I was when that photo was taken. I had just come out of the African jungle. I'd survived parasites and cannibals. I could have strangled a man with my thighs. I was fit, fresh and ready to take on the world. Most of all, I was smiling.

I booked my flight to Costa Rica the next day.

chapter 2

Wild
things

i arrived in Costa Rica with too much luggage. You would think with my previous African experience I would bring only what I needed to survive. Unfortunately, it was the opposite. Having suffered deprivation before, I didn't want to miss anything this time. In addition to two huge bags with half my wardrobe, I also couriered two boxes with a lifetime supply of Australian insect repellent, a flamingo-pink mosquito net, sparkling green eye shadow, a laptop and a guitar. I also brought a video camera, tapes, microphone and a tripod—because, unbeknownst to anyone on the monkey project, I was an international documentary maker.

My foray into filming began with my scientific connections at *Totally Wild*. While researching a story, I came across a scientist who sent people to Antarctica to measure the water temperature of the Southern Ocean. I signed up, and at the same time asked *Totally Wild* if I could film some segments for them. I didn't even know how to turn on a camera, but after a crash course in filming by a friend, and ten hours a day filming penguins for a month, I came back with six stories. They were a big hit. When I got the job in Costa Rica, I thought it would be a good idea if I did the same thing. I approached all the big TV networks and offered them exclusive, not-to-be-missed coverage of Costa Rican wildlife.

Luckily, I was too stupid to know it was a flooded market. Documentaries were a highly specialised field, and professionals spent years perfecting their craft. Not to mention the hundreds of film graduates ahead of me who were far more talented than I was.

Most of the networks said no. But Anita Goldring, the Senior Producer of the Disney Channel, a small dynamic woman, was amused and indulgent at my enthusiasm. She commissioned ten short segments for twice as much money as I'd asked for.

So there I was, May 2003, stepping off the bus at the station at Vacas, filmmaker, behavioural ecologist and collapsing with jetlag. It had taken 72 hours from the time I checked in my considerable luggage to hauling it off the bus. As I waited at the bus stop, I wondered what these people would be like. I had no idea what to expect. I had never seen a photo of anyone on the monkey project. I didn't know how many people there were, or how old they would be. I assumed they would be girls, since most primatology students were female.

I knew that in 1990 Diane, the project leader, arrived at Cielo Forest in Costa Rica to study capuchin monkeys. I read a couple of her papers. I learnt that capuchins had the largest brain in proportion to body size of all primates besides chimpanzees, and two female monkeys did something cool once and kicked out the alpha male. Diane had sent me a very scary field guide of what to expect from my year in Costa

Rica, including carnivorous wasps, killer bees, sleep deprivation, flash floods, forest fires, and snakes.

But that was about it.

Vacas was a one-horse town. There was one main street that turned off the Pan-American Highway, and on that street were the three main buildings; the bus station, the supermarket and the bakery. The bus station seemed to be the hub, as a small crowd was lounging on the benches talking in small groups. As soon as I got off the bus, everyone stopped and stared. It was like a scene in a Western movie when the newcomer walks into town. A guy with a moustache and a cowboy hat hawked and spat while looking at me, and an old woman with no teeth selling oranges shook her head and muttered.

After a few minutes of uncomfortable waiting, a young man drove up in a four-wheel drive the colour of an eggplant. He was girlish and slender with eyelashes so long they nearly stabbed my eyeballs. He introduced himself as Andreas and then was silent, except to say, 'Wow, you sure have a lot of luggage.'

As we loaded up the car, a hot, gusty wind blew across my face. I caught the faint smell of rotting mangoes. Feeling like a circus, I loaded my bags into the car and we drove a hundred metres down the road to the monkey house.

The monkey house was between the highway and the bus station. The houses along the street were as brightly painted as tropical birds. Flamingo pink. Peacock green. The monkey house was canary yellow. The second storey was stacked on precariously and looked like any minute it would slide down the first level's corrugated iron roof. All the windows had bars except one downstairs that was covered in a black cloth. I wondered if someone had died.

A pile of junk lying on the porch turned out to be tangled bicycles. A giant mango tree towered above the house. It must have been nearly a hundred years old, and the ground was carpeted with squashed fruit. The house was surrounded by a large yard, and two scrappy dogs were chasing what looked like an oversized rat around a grapefruit tree.

A long, gangly man was swinging in a hammock reading a book. He was handsome in a farmboy kind of way, with cornflower blue eyes and a short beard. He jumped up awkwardly and introduced himself.

'Hi, I'm Charles.'

He talked like Elvis. As I shook his hand, there were footsteps inside the house and a motherly giantess rushed through the door like a little girl. Her narrow eyes, broadly spaced, and vast cheeks made her look vaguely leonine.

'Wow, it's so great to meet you we've heard so much about you and we were so excited you were coming hi by the way my name is Sarah.'

She sounded a little desperate.

Inside, the place was dark and filthy. A layer of grime covered everything from the ping pong table to the books stacked along a wooden plank. I caught a whiff of stench to my right as I walked in. A jumbled row of hiking boots lay against the wall. On the inside, all the windows were covered with wire mesh, and the light strained through in broken rays. My new home.

I spent the next few hours unpacking. My couriered boxes had arrived, battered but intact. I lovingly lined up all my bottles of RID, smugly thinking how no Costa Rican mosquito was a match for Australian insect repellent. As the light faded outside, I sat at the dinner table, checking that my laptop had survived the flight.

There was the sound of a car pulling up in the drive. The rest of the group was home. I realised I would be working, eating and sleeping with these people for the next year. I was suddenly nervous. What if I didn't like them? What if they didn't like me?

The screen door screeched open and a file of young men walked in, followed by a dirty, plump girl. The four boys were stripped to the waist, their skin gleaming in the dull overhead light. Their machetes made a sinister clang as they threw them on the ground and started unlacing their boots. I tried to look unconcerned by their semi-nakedness as they walked past me into the kitchen, casually nodding or saying hello as though strange girls turned up at their dinner table all the time. Then I looked up and met the dark eyes of the most beautiful boy I had ever seen. He didn't smile.

'Hey,' he said, tossing his head back.

'Hey,' I said. I didn't smile either. Moody, I thought. Trouble. Probably a total asshole.

Needless to say, I fell for him instantly.

Diane came in a few minutes later to say hello. During the months she was in Vacas, she stayed in the house next door, called the 'pizza house', to preserve her peace of mind. The pizza house used to be a pizza restaurant, hence the name. It was much smaller than the monkey house and a large wasp nest hung from the porch. There were no plants in the garden and rickety stairs scaled the garden wall and connected the pizza house to the monkey house.

Diane had the face of a young girl, big eyes and soft lips, and her hair was a brown bouffant that defied gravity.

'Hi Vanessa. It's so nice to meet you.' I craned my neck, trying to see around the hairstyle. Did she do it like that every morning? It appeared that her hair was short and just sat in a pouf ball on her head. Amazing.

She smiled lopsidedly. 'I have to go. Enjoy your dinner.'

Dinner was the strangest event I had ever attended. It was silent. Everyone looked down at their plates and shovelled their food into their mouths. I kept waiting for someone to say something to me, like 'Who are you?' or 'Where do you come from?'

'So, when do you go out?' Andreas, the boy with the killer eyelashes, finally broke the silence. The plump girl was sitting next to him, and it was obvious by the way they moved in unison that they were a couple.

'Out?' Like on Saturday nights?

'Yeah, out with the monkeys.'

'Umm, I don't know. I just got here.'

He shrugged and nodded. Hello? I thought, what about, did you have a nice trip? Are you a lesbian psychopath? Didn't these people know about covering up awkward social silences with meaningless chit-chat? Obviously Andreas was the conversation initiator because, fifteen minutes later, he said, 'Anything happen with the monkeys today?'

The beautiful boy, whose name was Tristan, still looking at his food, said, 'Snow White killed a coati.'

The conversation, if that's what you could call it, made no sense to me. Why didn't they ask each other normal questions like, how was your day? Are you tired? How is your dinner? Why was the word 'monkey' in every fragment of conversation?

After dinner, Diane came back from the house next door.
'So, what time do we go out tomorrow?'

'Four thirty-five,' Andreas said, scraping his plate.

That was my first dinner at the monkey house.

As I was stacking my plate on the sink, a bug-eyed boy called
Billy came up to me. 'We're going to the bar tonight.' He
had an English accent. 'You should come.'

If the bar is going to be as riotous as dinner, I thought,
I'd rather get some rest. But I scolded myself for not giving
these people a chance.

'Sure.'

Las Tehas was a wooden shack just down the road from
the supermarket (I was later to find out that in Vacas,
everything was just down the road from the supermarket). A
string of coloured light bulbs hung outside the entrance and
someone had scrawled 'Las Tehas' in black paint above the
door. The interior was flooded with red light, like a brothel.

The bar was empty except for two old men, drinking at
separate tables, and a girl who looked twelve serving at the
bar. They stared at us as we walked in. I remembered that
the monkey project field guide said only prostitutes went to
bars. No one else with me seemed worried, so the field guide
must be outdated.

In the rustic setting, a high tech LCD projector was
beaming MTV onto a large screen. On it, Jon Bon Jovi was
larger than life in tight snakeskin pants and a billowing black
shirt. He was screaming 'Living on a Prayer' to a live audience.

Our party included Charles, Billy, Tristan, Ada (the plump
girl), Andreas and I. We all sat down and the dinner
phenomenon continued. Normally, when I went to a bar, it

was to talk to people. But no one said anything. Andreas and Ada sat together like synchronistic organisms, lifting their drinks at the same time with the same hand. Everyone watched the enormous TV. I was puzzled. Why would you rather watch Bon Jovi than talk to the person next to you?

I turned to Billy. He was one of those lollipop people with a round head too big for the rest of his body. He had an impish smile that made him look ready for mischief.

'It was a good phase, while it lasted,' I said.

'What?'

'Snakeskin leather pants.'

Billy smirked. He looked relieved to be talking.

'You'd look good in them.'

'So would you. Did you ever get around to buying them?'

'Close. I used to be in a rock band. I had some pretty tight pants.'

'Did you cover Bon Jovi?'

'Occasionally. More Creed, you know, Pearl Jam.'

From the corner of my eye, I saw Andreas turn to Tristan.

'So, who do you think will be the next alpha of Sin?'

Are you serious? I thought. They were talking about monkeys again. I resolutely drilled Billy on his theory of Michael Jackson's *Thriller* phase. So it went on for about an hour. Everyone else talking about monkeys, and me refusing to.

Billy got up to get a drink and I found the attractive but clearly dysfunctional Tristan sitting next to me.

'I want to know about Antarctica,' he demanded.

'Um,' I faltered. His eyes pinned me to my chair. I fluttered my wings helplessly. I knew this was the time to enchant him with tales of vast white emptiness, cragged icebergs and crystalline light that never faded.

'It was a bit like a chicken farm,' I said. 'There were a lot of penguins.'

He looked dissatisfied, then suspicious, as if I was making fun of him. I kicked myself under the table, and then, at a loss, I smiled. He didn't smile back. But he said, 'It sucks. Just when someone new and interesting comes, I have to leave.'

'What do you mean?'

'I'm leaving at the end of the month. Ada is too. Our year is up.'

I digested this. I felt disappointment, then relief. It was good he was leaving. Even from our brief encounter, it was obvious. The boy was nothing but trouble.

My first day with the monkeys came a few days later. The alarm woke me up in the dark. I stumbled around, trying not to step on my new room-mate, Sarah, and shining my torch into corners trying to find a matching pair of socks. I shoved everything I could think of into my day pack and went to get some breakfast.

In the kitchen, people were shuffling around, pouring cereal, digging in the food bins. No one spoke to each other.

'Good morning,' I said softly, to no one in particular. No one answered me. Apparently, like dinner, the mornings were silent.

We piled into the back of the eggplant Toyota. Two benches ran along each side, like an army truck. I was sandwiched between Charles and Sarah. I tried to remember the last time I had been in such intimate contact with complete strangers. I decided I never had been. The forest was a 25-minute drive from the house. We hurtled down the highway at breakneck speed. My pulse was racing because, for me, we were on the wrong side of the road. Costa Rica had the second highest number of road fatalities in the world, and the Costa

Ricans drove as though they were personally insulted they weren't number one. There seemed to be a mysterious third lane which straddled the white line in the middle of the road. Every time a pair of headlights flooded the darkness, I thought we were going to die.

After no less than ten near-death experiences, the car turned off the highway onto a dirt track. The road was pitted with potholes and deep rivulets eroded by rain. The car bravely rode over the least treacherous route, lurching and swaying. It was like being on a boat. I felt sick.

Shallow grooves on the road were littered with nesting nightjars. We swerved madly around these, presumably because no one wanted to extract a mashed bird from the tyres at 4 a.m. It did not help that the nightjars were camouflaged with the gravel, or that they only woke up when the car was practically on top of them.

The houses we passed were poorer than the ones in Vacas. Their faces were streaked with dirt and the paint was cracked and peeling. As we drove further along, the houses thinned out until they were replaced by pasture. There was a yelp and a growl, and a dog ran in front of the car.

'Watch out!' I yelled, shattering the sanctity of silence in the car. We swerved, and I hit my head on the window.

'Goddamn dog,' Andreas muttered.

'It does that every morning,' Sarah said.

I looked through the back window. The dog was chasing the car, barking with bared teeth like a hound guarding the gates of hell.

I was a nervous wreck by the time the car pulled up next to a palm tree. It was still dark. Diane, Tristan and Sarah jumped out of the car.

'You're with us today, Vanessa,' Diane said. I scrambled for my things. By the time I got out, Tristan had already taken

off. I followed slowly behind Sarah and Diane. We walked
through a field full of wispy branches partially lit by moonlight.
Thorns pulled at my sleeves as we passed. I wondered where
the jungle was, or whether the monkeys lived in the pasture,
like cows.

Then I saw it. It loomed above the pasture like a slum-
bering beast. As we approached, a faint glow of fireflies
hovered at the entrance. Diane and Sarah walked straight into
its jaws. I lingered on the outskirts, afraid. Then, worried I
would lose them, I plunged in.

It was like another world. The leaves shone in the
moonlight. Fireflies floated by like fairies. I was in the jungle
again. I breathed in the morning air, still wet with dew and
heavy with the smell of rotting leaves. I could just see the
flash of Diane's pink shirt in front of me. Her footsteps
crunching the leaves sounded loud and intrusive.

'Sarah,' I heard her say, 'why don't you go around the
pozza and try and cut them off at Quebrada Acacia?'

I scurried behind Diane. We wandered through the dense
forest without a trail or a path. When we reached a river, Diane
nimbly skipped across three rocks to the other side. I made
it to rock number one, but when one foot was on rock
number two, I became distracted by the large volume of
water rushing between my legs. The splash I made when I
fell was muffled by the river. Diane did not turn around.
I climbed out and hurried after her, dripping wet.

Ten minutes later, there were two eerie calls. Like an owl.
To my surprise, Diane arched her neck like a wolf and gave
one whoop in response. She turned to me.

'Let's go.'

We found Tristan sitting under a large tree. Its branches rustled as though it was possessed by a demon spirit.

'Are they there?' Diane asked him.

'Yup.'

Everyone stood around. I waited for them to do something dramatic. My wet pants were making puddles in my shoes. When I wriggled my toes, they made squelching noises in my socks.

'Now what do we do?'

Tristan looked at me, his eyes darker than the leaves that blended into the night.

'We wait.'

As the sky grew pink with dawn, the leaves high above our heads began to shake. There was a coughing sound.

'What's that?' I asked. Tristan gave me one of his half smirks.

'Puking.'

A puking monkey sounded bad. Was it okay? I thought. Was it sick? No one else looked concerned. For the next hour, the monkeys jumped from tree to tree. All I could see was the occasional black wriggling tail. We followed them from the river to a group of mango trees. They began to make little peeping noises.

'What are they doing now?'

'They're food peeps,' Diane said. 'The monkeys are eating. We should be able to see them soon.'

My first monkey jumped at me through the mango leaves, its teeth bared and threatening. My first thought was 'Wow, it's so close!' followed by 'Holy shit, it's so ugly!'

Forward thinking is not my strong point. Before I left Australia, I neglected to look up a single picture of capuchin monkeys. For some reason, I had capuchins mixed up with the cotton-topped tamarins I saw at Taronga Zoo. Tamarins are the size of a coffee cup and have little punk hairstyles, like gremlins. They looked so sweet and cute as they twittered and groomed one another, I thought studying them all day would be like watching cartoons.

The monkey that leapt from the branches was not a cotton-topped tamarin. Neither was it cute. It was frightening. Capuchin monkeys have a white face and a black cap on top of their heads. They were named after the capuchin monks, who wore dark hoods. The monkeys were also called organ grinder monkeys because they used to be dressed up in little hats and coats to play organs in the nineteenth century. They frequently star in movies, like the ghost monkey in *Pirates of the Caribbean*. Standing there, this hideous monkey threatening me and shaking a branch, I felt cheated. Diane came up beside me.

'It's because you're new,' she said. 'Calamity's threatening at you.'

'You mean they can tell us apart?'

Diane looked at me strangely.

'Of course. They recognise us as easily as we recognise them.'

It was then I noticed I had a problem. A friend of the stressed-out monkey had come and jumped on its back and was also threatening. They were stacked one on top of the other like a totem pole. They looked exactly the same. I looked at other monkeys in the group and stared hard at them. Just as I feared. Identical.

I stared at the monkey for what seemed like hours. How do you learn to recognise a monkey? I figured you just stared at it.

'When they jump on top of one another, it's called overlording. That's Sorrow on top of Calamity,' Diane explained.

Sorrow pushed out his lips so he looked like a duck. Then he squeaked. Calamity spun around in a pirouette and looked at Sorrow between his legs. They chased each other up and down the branch, grunting and squeaking. Then Sorrow jumped on top of Calamity.

'Another overlord?' I asked.

'No, that's sex.'

'But I thought they were both boys.'

'They are.'

Oh my god. The monkeys are gay.

'Lots of species have same-sex socio-sexual behaviour,' said Diane, seeing my face. We watched Sorrow thrusting away. My legs began to buckle and I was dizzy with exhaustion. I figured it must be nearly lunchtime. I checked my watch. It was 7:03 a.m. Eleven hours to go. I sidled up to Sarah.

'How do you make it through the day?' I asked, desperate to sit down.

'You get used to it,' she whispered back.

chapter 3
Grooming

So began my life as a monkey researcher.

My day started with the piercing shriek of the alarm that drilled into my head in the middle of the night. There is something about getting up before dawn that is unnatural. From the moment I opened my eyes, I was filled with enough rage to smother the world.

I threw on my field clothes that stank of the rotting layer of the forest floor, and shoved binoculars, hand-held computer called a PSION, dictaphone, water and a sandwich into my backpack. I had about five minutes to eat some Choc Crispies, before I put on my shoes and climbed into the car.

The walk into the forest was always different. There was a labyrinthine network of trails that never seemed to lead to the same spot. I tried to remember landmarks, like crooked trees or wombat-shaped rocks, but at 4:30 a.m. everything looked the same.

While my body was still in shock from being awake, we climbed hills and tramped through undergrowth. My worst fear was crossing rivers. My first fall was indicative of a natural clumsiness I'd forgotten I had. Every time I stared at the others leaping across rocks I could not even see, I knew I was about to get wet.

We usually had between ten and 30 minutes to rest before the monkeys woke up. The sky was neither the pink of the dawn or the blue of the day. It was a blazing white noise, a vast nothingness, and everything else was a dull black. It was at this time each morning, as the howler monkeys began their long broken cries across the treetops, that I would decide to quit and go home.

The more I thought about it, the more I was convinced that Edward was not the reason I came. People broke up all the time. They lied and cheated and betrayed each other. Running off to the jungle to get over it was a stupid thing to do. I could have cut my hair. Bought some big boots and stomped around for a while. Even though I fell asleep every night with the look in his eyes when I told him it was over, it wasn't enough to bring me here, was it? There must be another reason. A higher purpose for me scampering after pint-sized primates. But I couldn't think of one. And if there was no reason, no purpose, what the hell was I doing? I mentally packed my bags, changed my plane ticket, filmed some sloths and went home. A documentary maker but no monkey researcher. Wasn't that enough?

Then leaves began to rustle, someone puked and the monkeys woke up screaming. They hit one another, pulled tails, scratched and bit. They had sex and other monkeys screamed at the sex. The branches shook with early morning fury until, when the sky was whitewashed with light, the monkeys began to move. And for no reason at all, I followed them.

Monkeys never slept where they ate, so after everyone was wide awake, they began to hunt for food. In every season, trees came into fruit. Where they were, and how many, varied from month to month. In the rainy season, big juicy fruit, like figs or orange twist, burst from their flowers. In the dry season there was less. Desiccated fruit grew on skeletal trees and took half an hour of pounding to extract a few meagre seeds. The monkeys knew every fruiting tree in a 20-kilometre radius. Their primary objective in the morning was to get to one of them as rapidly as they could. This meant we had to move with them. Losing the monkeys first thing in the morning was a disaster because they could be anywhere by lunchtime. Which meant for the first few hours of the morning, when your body was telling you it was still asleep, you had to run. Fast.

When the sun began to burn brightly overhead, the monkeys slowed down and started foraging. This was when we began to work. A 'follow' was a period of ten minutes where you typed absolutely every movement of a monkey into the PSION. Every time the monkey scratched, ate a berry, screamed or threw up, you had to type it in. Because monkeys were hyperactive, you couldn't watch and type at the same time. So you had a spotter, who told you what was happening so you could concentrate on typing. If things got really hectic, you had to talk into a dictaphone then transcribe the data later. The problem for me was, you also had to type in who the monkey approached, who approached your monkey, and every interaction between them. A monkey could hit, bite, scream and grab another monkey in the space of a few seconds. It could also run up to six other monkeys and interact with all of them at the same time. Since they all looked the same to me, effectively I was useless.

We took data standing up. It was like being a check-out chick. We sat down occasionally but if you didn't stay right under your monkeys, when you looked up they were gone. After an hour, my legs ached. After three hours, I was nearly collapsing, looking longingly at every log and bare patch of ground. However, in my low-ranking position, I didn't have the option of sitting down, and had to wait for a more senior monkey watcher to take a break. By the end of the day, I was swaying on my feet. Sharp pains fired up my legs, and I thought about all the time I had spent in an office sitting down and not appreciating it.

Diane could recognise the monkeys like they were her children. I was told the average number of follows for a Diane day was 35, which is about six and a half hours of straight data-taking. This may not sound like much from dawn to dusk but when you factor in walking in and out of the forest, running up and down cliffs, losing the monkeys, finding them and losing them again, 35 lots of ten minutes were hard work. Also, for those ten minutes, you had to be able to see the monkeys at all times. If you missed something, or the monkeys ran up a tree where you couldn't see them, the follow had to be aborted.

In the late afternoon, the monkeys started to move quickly, looking for a thick-limbed tree to sleep in. Monkeys slept with their stomachs on the branch and all four limbs hanging over the sides. Leaving the monkeys at their sleeping tree was called 'putting the monkeys to bed'. When the squabbling and chattering settled down, you could safely leave them, knowing they'd be there the next morning.

We worked in the field for two days, then had one day at home called a 'Vacas day'. It was made clear to me from the beginning that this was NOT a rest day. Rest days, or 'vacation', came at the end of every month, where we had five days to do nothing or to travel around. Vacas days were for cleaning data, since the data you typed on the PSION was bound to be full of mistakes. Dictaphone data had to be typed out. Then there was washing, cleaning, cooking (if it was your turn) and, if you were lucky, maybe you had time to eat an ice cream while you were carrying five bags of groceries back to the house. Since I didn't have any data to clean, I was supposed to learn the codes for different monkey behaviour (in total there were more than two hundred), practise typing on the PSION (the keys were different to a normal keyboard), and help with household chores. At the end of a Vacas day I was often more tired than after a day in the field.

I had the same Vacas day as Manuel and Tristan. Manuel was the only Costa Rican on the team. He lived upstairs with his girlfriend, Angelina, an almond-eyed beauty, and her curly-haired daughter, Linda. I had taken Spanish for a year, but when I arrived I found I couldn't talk. The words mixed themselves up inside my head like Lotto balls and I couldn't spit them out in logical order. Manuel and Angelina didn't speak English, so while we smiled at each other, we couldn't actually communicate.

In the periphery of my exhaustion was Tristan. Tristan peeling off his shirt at the end of the day, skin glistening in the fading light. Tristan scrambling like a cat through thickets, perfectly poised and coming out clean at the other end. In his limbs was a coiled strength he was not yet aware of, though occasionally he would hold out an arm and rotate his wrist, as if trying to guess its capacity for destruction. He never made much noise, and I never saw him drop anything or trip. The only sound he made was the metallic ringing of his machete as he sliced through the jungle. Otherwise he was silent as a snake.

Despite my earlier resolution, I couldn't resist tempting him. It should have been easy. We were together all the time. I had no competition. I did my hair like Lara Croft and walked around the house with a sarong tied above my breasts. He didn't bite.

One morning we watched two monkeys. One was the alpha male, and he lay sprawled on his back with his eyes closed and his legs spread. Beside him a low-ranking female was picking the lice out of his crotch. This was called grooming, the monkey equivalent of kissing ass. The most important rule of grooming was that high-ranking monkeys did not groom low-ranking monkeys.

It was just past dawn and the group was still a shadow. They rustled the branches and leapt above our heads, high in the tree tops. As they leapt I asked him who they were because I thought he wouldn't be able to tell me. He named them one by one.

'Dopey, he has a lump in his tail. Sleepy, she has a mangled walk. Doc, chunky and aggressive. Happy . . . I can just tell by the shape of his head.'

The other monkey researchers were good, but they couldn't tell a monkey by the back of its head, 20 feet up in the dark. It put Tristan and I on different levels. The hierarchy in the monkey house depended on who knew the monkeys best. I was at the bottom and Tristan was at the top. The most I could imagine was me crouched beside him, picking the lice out of his crotch.

But not everyone liked him. He had two friends, Manuel and Charles. The three of them would huddle together at the table and talk in Spanish, or camp out in the forest to see what the monkeys did at night—although why you'd want to spend more than fourteen hours a day with them was beyond me. But while Manuel and Charles could diffuse into the group, Tristan did not talk to anyone else. He was guarded and suspicious. He rarely spoke, and when he did, his voice was almost a threat. He had a dampening effect on people, especially the girls. When he left the room, it was a little lighter. Sarah could barely stand him. As for Ada, she hid behind Andreas most of the time, and the two of them moved in gentle unison. But I noticed she would not make eye contact with Tristan, and whenever he spoke, she looked down at her hands.

The only female he had a positive effect on was Diane. She softened visibly when he was around. She laughed and talked more. Tristan carried all the heavy equipment, and ran after the monkeys so she could take her time catching up. They had intimate conversations about monkeys, leaning towards each other in a way that excluded everyone else.

He didn't have the same hostility towards me that he had towards the others. True, he had not smiled at me, even once, but he realised I was struggling and tried to help. He drew me maps of the forest, and spent hours teaching me how to recognise monkeys.

'You're concentrating too much on scars and spots,' he said when I misidentified Carnage, the alpha male, for the fourth time. 'You can tell who Carnage is just by watching him. See how he's slinking around like someone's out to get him? Well, over there, that's Loss. He wants to be the alpha male so he's just waiting for a weak moment before he attacks.

'And that one over there that's really cut up is Hector. He was alpha of this group for years, but he was beaten and now he's at the bottom. He's not really a threat so the other males just tolerate him, but they can throw him out anytime they want.

'The dark-eyed one is Murder. She became the alpha female of Sin really young because she was meaner than everyone else. She's a complete bitch and just struts around all the time.

'Murder's best friend is Assassin. If Murder starts fighting anyone, Assassin's there straightaway, and no one messes with them.'

Tristan went through the monkeys one by one, over and over. I tried my hardest to understand, but it was no good. How did a monkey slink look different from a monkey strut? Coming to the end of my first month, despair had lodged like a rock in my stomach. I was going to get fired.

The only part of the day I really enjoyed was the end, when I could go home and play my guitar. Not that I was any good. My guitar fad came upon me around the same time as my filming fad, which was when I went to Antarctica. I fell in with a bunch of 40-year-old French hoodlums. They played guitars, smoked and drank until 3 a.m., and I stayed up with them, singing and playing a rice shaker. On the boat trip home, I was made an honorary member of the group and one of them placed his sacred guitar in my hand.

'Vaneza,' said Jean, 'you 'ave got a good voice. But without guitar, it soundz like sheet.'

From then on I practised my three cords of the 4 Non Blondes song 'What's up?'. Three months later, I was still crap but I'd added some U2 and Ani DiFranco to my repertoire. I liked to play on the porch in the dark while everyone was unpacking and getting ready for dinner.

One night, I played a song to the two mangy dogs, Strider and Tucker. They belonged to the field manager who everyone called Princess because she could chase monkeys to hell and back without messing up her hair. Princess was in Europe with her Costa Rican boyfriend Carlos. The dogs kept escaping through a hole in the fence and bringing back dirty nappies to rip up in the front yard.

I already loved the mutts. They were knee high with the shaggy coats, limpid brown eyes and floppy ears of village dogs. They barked obsessively and ran around maniacally all day, their joy uncontainable as they dragged small garbage bags and other such delights through our backyard. They were friendlier to me than anyone else had been, and they never mentioned monkeys. While I tuned my guitar, Strider put his head in my lap.

I played a few songs, and closing my eyes I could imagine I was on a beach somewhere. A beach with a late sunrise and no monkeys. When I opened my eyes, Tristan was in a chair, watching me. A slight frown creased his eyes, as though I was a monkey he didn't recognise. He was leaning back, his hands folded across his stomach, one ankle crossed over the other. Although his limbs were relaxed and entwined, he looked like he could spring up and bite me. I smiled at him, nervous. He didn't smile back.

'You have a beautiful voice,' he said, and left.

After an eternity of trailing, useless and bored, behind Diane and Tristan, my monkey recognition was going nowhere. In a desperate attempt to expose me to different teaching styles, Diane scheduled me with Charles and Billy in Sin. The rest of the car took off for the other two monkey groups: Nirvana and Snow White.

It was just the three of us, and as soon as the car pulled away I knew something was different. Instead of charging off to find the monkeys and standing under them until they woke, Billy threw his backpack on the ground, laid his head on it and went to sleep.

'What are you doing?' I asked, horrified.

'Can't find the monkeys now,' Billy murmured. 'It's dark.'

Charles laughed softly behind me. 'Don't mind him. He wakes up with the sun.'

I hadn't spoken much to Charles. He was a country boy from Georgia who always wore lumberjack shirts tucked into his pants with a belt.

'So,' he said, 'what are you doing so far from home?'

It was the first time since I arrived that someone had asked me a question about myself.

'I don't know.'

He laughed.

'I'm not sure any of us do.'

'I wish I knew the monkeys. I can't seem to recognise them.'

'You will. When you start, you think you're so stupid and you're never going to get it. My girlfriend Lisa was so mad because I kept telling her I was quitting and coming home. And then one day their faces just sort of came into focus. It took ages, but then all of a sudden, when I was in the shower, Calamity appeared inside my head. Over and over, each day in the shower, there he was.'

His reassurance flooded me like hot chocolate. I was silent for a moment, appreciating my first real human interaction.

'So what do you like doing back home?' he said. I nearly collapsed in shock. I was having a non-monkey orientated conversation.

'Um, I like going to the beach.'

'I've heard the beaches are pretty cool in Australia.'

I had a wave of homesickness. A scream pierced the lightening sky.

'Shit,' Charles said, pronouncing it more like *Shi-et*. 'Billy, get up. The monkeys are moving.'

That day with Charles and Billy was nothing like any day I'd had so far. Tristan and Diane talked about the monkeys in hushed and reverent tones. They discussed monkey personalities and hierarchy like they were analysing the political state of the European Union. Charles and Billy spent most of the day yelling.

'Get out of that bush you little punk ass monkey,' Billy swore as Calamity disappeared into a viney entanglement.

'Goddamn!' Charles swore, throwing his cap on the ground like an angry umpire, when Calamity disappeared and they had to abort the follow.

While Tristan and Diane treated me like I was far too inexperienced to contribute to the sacred data collection, Billy acted as though he needed me.

'Holy shite, Vanessa, keep that monkey over there, Charles I've got him. Approaches five to—Vanessa where's your monkey—Scandal, it was Scandal, okay thanks Vanessa, I've got her again. Jesus fuck I hate Scandal follows.'

When we weren't doing monkey follows, Billy and Charles would try to help me recognise monkeys. You could tell which group a monkey was from by its name. The original monkeys in Sin were named after the seven deadly sins, and the new generation were given similar names like Calamity and Mayhem. The monkeys in Snow White were named after the seven dwarves and other cartoon characters, and Nirvana's monkeys had celestial names like Seraph and Paradise.

Sin was a straggly bunch with no real alpha. The old alpha, Hector, had been overthrown but no one had taken his place. Carnage and Loss, who might have been Hector's sons, were fighting for the alpha position, but so far no one was winning.

'Okay, this one here. This is Hector, see how his face looks like it's been through a blender? And this one over here? Angel. He's from Nirvana. Remember Skeletor, from He-Man? Well he looks like that, doesn't he Charles, wouldn't you say Skeletor?'

'You piece of shit, he don't look a damn thing like Skeletor. He looks like the Skeksies from the Dark Crystal.'

'You retard Southern asshole, I can't even begin to tell you how wrong you are.'

'Well you can kiss my ass with wrong, baby, because the only wrong around here is you.'

And so it went on. At around two o'clock, Billy threw his bag down under a tree and went to sleep.

'Billy, what are you doing?'

'Siesta. It's two.'

I stood around for a while, not sure of what to do. Then I dropped my bag and fell asleep next to him.

I woke up to a stinging on my arm. A tiny orange ant clenched my soft flesh in its pincers while it jabbed its abdomen viciously into my skin.

I brushed it off and at the same time another ant stung me on my wrist. I jumped up, brushing myself off. I saw a trail of ants coming from an acacia tree. On its trunk were fat thorns and in each thorn was an ant-sized hole. The acacia made a sugary syrup for the ants to eat. In return, the ants lived inside the thorns, killing all intruders. They even chewed up any seedlings that sprang up within a metre of the acacia, so the tree was surrounded by a geometrically perfect circle of clean ground. Not a blade of grass, not a stray bug disturbed the photosynthetic efforts of the little tree.

'Billy,' I said, nudging him. 'Wake up. You'll get bitten by ants.'

'No I won't,' he murmured, and went back to sleep. I looked around for Charles. He was nowhere in sight. I wasn't sure which way to go, but in the heat I didn't think the monkeys would stray far from the river.

After a while I came to a small waterfall. It dropped about a foot and spilled into a deep pool. The spray made the air cooler and thick flowering plants arched towards the rippling surface.

I was desperate for a swim. A lump the size of a grapefruit had puffed up where the ant had bitten me. I was caked in grime, and I stank. Seeing no one, I stripped down to my underwear and climbed in. It was like slipping into a cool, blissful sleep.

'What the bloody hell do you think you're doing?'

It was Billy. Charles was next to him and they were both staring at me. Panicking, I scrambled out and stood on the rocks, sodden and dripping in my underwear. I should have known their relaxed attitude to monkeys was too good to be true. They were going to tell Diane that I snuck off and went swimming. I was going to get fired. They climbed through the fence and came towards me.

'You're in big trouble,' said Billy.

They started taking off their shirts.

'I can't believe you didn't call us.'

As we basked on the rocks like lizards, I felt brave enough to ask a question that had been bothering me since I arrived.

'So, why's everyone so quiet at dinner?'

'Oh my god,' said Billy. 'Thank you so much. If I even open my mouth during supper, everyone looks at me like I put my wanker on the table.'

'Billy!'

'It's true!'

'But why is everyone so quiet?'

Charles looked thoughtful.

'I guess it's because we're all so tired after the field.'

'Well there are some people . . .' Billy began.

Charles cut him off.

'Billy, that's enough. She's only new. She'll figure it out soon enough.'

'Figure what out?' The secrecy was driving me crazy.

Charles shrugged. 'There's just some tension, that's all.'

'With Tristan?' I guessed.

Charles looked at me strangely.

'With everyone. You know how it is. A big group in a small house.'

Billy interrupted.

'Well Tristan is a trouble-maker.'

'Billy!'

'It's true. He's got a bad temper.'

Charles was Tristan's friend, and I could tell he was getting uncomfortable.

'What about Andreas and Ada?' I said to change the topic. As a couple they intrigued me; Andreas so feminine and slender, Ada so stocky and German. They hardly spoke to anyone, and just drifted along in their private universe.

'They got together a few months ago,' Charles replied.

'Do either of them ever talk?'

'Andreas's a riot when he comes out of himself. Ada's just really shy. They're good together really.'

'So what happens when Ada leaves for Germany at the end of the month?'

Charles shrugged.

'Maybe Andreas will go to Germany too. We don't know.'

I thought it was strange Andreas and Ada had isolated themselves to the point that no one knew what their plans were after she left.

'There was a bit of tension when they got together,' said Charles. 'Tristan didn't like it. He and Ada were friends,' he said hastily when he saw the look on my face. 'Then she and Andreas got together, and Tristan didn't think it was good for the group.'

'But why? Was he jealous?' Somehow I couldn't picture Tristan with the quiet dumpling German girl.

'No way. He just didn't like it. Then Tristan stopped talking to Ada, and Ada was really upset. It split the house in two. Andreas and Ada broke off from the group and stopped talking to people. It was weird.'

The monkey house was becoming more like *Alice in Wonderland* with every revelation. Nothing was as it seemed.

When we got home, Charles and Billy sat down at the table arguing about who was the stupidest monkey. I was laughing as I sat down with them. Tristan was in the kitchen, but he came out to see what all the noise was. The laughter seemed to relax him. He sat down next to me.

'They always do this,' he said. 'Sometimes they fight until they go to bed, then they start again in the morning. It can go on for days.'

'I like it.'

Without warning, Tristan put his foot on my chair.

'Scratch my chigger bites.'

I went violently red. Chiggers were the larval stage of mites that are parasitic on warm-blooded animals, including humans. The mites lay their eggs on wet grass or vegetation, and when the larvae hatch, they cling on to passing people. They attach themselves near a hair follicle or a skin pore. They vomit digestive juices that make the skin cells rupture, then eat the fluid that comes from the ruptured skin cells. It's the chigger vomit that makes the skin red and swollen. I hadn't experienced them, but I could see them on everyone else; the red bumps filled with clear pus, and the scabs that lasted for weeks.

I stared at Tristan, trying to figure out if it was a trick question. Was he flirting with me? Then it occurred to me, he was demanding grooming. Just like that alpha male monkey I saw in the forest, laid back, legs spread, while the low-ranking female pulled lice from his crotch.

'Umm,' I said, stalling for time. 'No.'

Tristan put his foot down and shrugged.

'Worth a try.'

The corner of his lips twitched in what could have been a smile.

chapter 4

Moth

†ristan was leaving in four days and it was the second last Vacas day that we would have together. I was at the dining room table, trying not to look like I was waiting for him to come downstairs. I wandered around the house for a while then sat down to do some speed tests which were tapes that Diane recorded to prepare us for hectic typing on the PSION.

'This is a focal follow of Calamity. Murder is in five and Assassin is in ten. Carnage approaches to ten, Murder threatens at Carnage, Carnage sex squeaks at Murder, Murder screams at Carnage, Carnage sex mounts Murder, the focal looks at them, Mayhem approaches to one of the focal, play pounces on the focal, the focal play hits Mayhem, oh! Assassin approaches to ten then five of Carnage and Murder, and then Assassin and Murder do an overlord against Carnage, the focal ignores them, Carnage threatens Murder and Assassin, Mayhem pulls the focal's tail . . .'

And so it went on. Were these real follows? I thought. Was this really ten minutes of a monkey's life? Freaks.

It was after lunch before Tristan came downstairs.

'Hey.'

'Hey.'

'Sleeping?'

'Packing. You can come up and keep me company if you want.'

I had never been upstairs. Charles was in a tiny room to the left, and Manuel, Angelina and Linda were in the larger room to the right. Tristan was in the middle. The top level was constructed of hard timber that swelled with the heat. The sun beat down on the corrugated iron roof, and the early morning dew condensed on the underside, turning the whole floor into a sauna. The fan in Tristan's room blew hot air around. I sat on the bed, feeling sweat prickle between my thighs.

'So,' I said in an attempt to start up a conversation. 'What are you going to do when you go back?'

'I don't know. Probably go back to lifeguarding.'

'Lifeguarding? What about your PhD?'

'What PhD?'

'I thought you were going back to do a PhD on monkeys.'

He laughed without humour.

'I graduated in Economics.'

I paused, digesting the information. Lifeguarding. It sort of made sense, he had the perfect chest for *Baywatch*.

'But I don't get it. If you've never studied monkeys before, how are you so good with them?'

He shrugged.

'I don't know. You stay here for a year, you work hard, you pick things up.'

'I don't think I will.'

'Sure you will. It's the house that gets you down.'

'How do you mean?'

'I mean these walls aren't big enough to contain some of the personalities in here. You're going to have problems with people, so just focus on the monkeys.'

It didn't make sense to me. Focus on the monkeys. How did that help anything? I picked little bits of foam out of the mattress. He interrupted my thoughts.

'What do you want to do? Afterwards.' He said 'afterwards' like it was a hard word.

'What do you mean? I'm stuck here until I get fired because I can't recognise monkeys.'

He smirked.

'You won't get fired. No one has ever been fired. Why don't you do a PhD?'

Cute, I thought, he's repeating my questions back to me. Maybe he loves me but just can't articulate it. I answered honestly.

'I don't think I could. I was never really good at science.'

'Then what are you doing here?'

'I guess I was running away.'

He kept folding his clothes.

'I'll probably go back to television,' I said. 'Get a mortgage and have kids.'

'Kids? You?'

'Yeah me. What's wrong with that?'

'You just seem too restless.'

I shrugged.

'Well, of course if I had a retarded baby, I'd drown it in a bucket.'

The air went cold. I was idly looking at the wall when I said it. I quickly looked at his face. It was frozen in disbelief. I wanted to say, No wait, I was just joking, I didn't mean it! But his face shut down, and the words inside me curdled.

'I need to pack,' he said quietly, in a voice that told me to get out.

I slunk down the stairs, shame burning my cheeks like fire.

I went over it a thousand times in my head. What had possessed me to say something so random and politically incorrect? Couldn't he tell I wasn't serious? That I would never actually drown a baby in a bucket? Apparently not. Then it came to me. I was never going to fit in here. I had nothing in common with any of these people.

When the car pulled in and the group piled out, I looked through the window and saw Tristan whisper something to Charles. Charles glanced in my direction, and they both went for a walk. When they came back, Charles did not look at me. Isolation curled around my feet. I bore the mark of Cain. No one would touch me now.

I do not know how it filtered through the group that I was cursed. Regardless of how it got around, everyone stopped speaking to me. If I asked a direct question, they answered but after the necessary communication was over, they gently presented me with their shoulders, like emperor penguins keeping out the cold.

To make things worse, I was making no progress with the monkeys. There were a few monkeys I could recognise. Havoc was hit by a car when he was younger and lost most of his tail, but sometimes I confused him with Squalor, who only had a bit of her tail missing. I could tell a male from a female when they were next to each other; males were larger, had longer canine teeth and were generally uglier, but if a monkey was by itself, I wasn't sure. There's a first time for everything and I was sure the first fired person of the monkey project would be me.

It was early evening when I took my washing out to the back porch. As I pushed my laundry through the back door, I saw a moth trapped between two layers of flyscreen. It was dead, its wings folded as though it was resting. It must have crawled through the fly screen as a caterpillar, then spun its cocoon between the two layers, thinking it would be safe from predators. I imagined the silken wet body crawling from the cocoon, its wings like crumpled paper. The blood would have pumped through the infinite veins, its wings slowly opening until they were big enough to fly. I heard the useless fluttering, the wordless shriek of a soul born trapped, the metal rasping against the fragile scales on the wings, unable to extend even once in flight, while the moon outside called mercilessly.

I carried my laundry to the washing machine and the door banged shut, jolting the moth a little further down the fly screen. I piled my dirty clothes on the washing machine lid then, burying my face in their crumpled stench, I began to cry.

The next day, I had the enthusiasm of a drug addict forced into rehab. I wandered listlessly behind Diane and Sarah. They were doing a follow of juveniles who were a blur of swinging, pouncing, hitting, hyperactive monkeys. All of them had to be identified. I was so despondent, I broke the golden rule and sat down while Diane and Sarah were still working.

A monkey sprang through the branches and glowered at me. It bared its teeth and lunged in a menacing manner. I saw its eyes, a dark outline making them as almond shaped as Cleopatra's. Then it ran away.

'You're such a bitch, Murder,' I muttered under my breath. I stood up. How did I know the monkey was Murder? I'd only seen it for a second. I ran after the monkey. It turned and saw me following and ran even faster. I scrambled through brambles, the thorns catching on my shirt and snagging my hair. When I came out the other side, I thought the monkey had gone. But there it was, picking up an insect from a leaf. There were the kohl-outlined eyes. I stood on my tiptoes to see its mouth, but the insect was in the way. The monkey licked its lips. And I saw it. A perfect, crescent-shaped scar running through the right corner of the mouth. Murder.

For the rest of the day, I was unstoppable. I stared at each monkey, like a psychic reading Tarot cards, until their identity materialised in front of me. Calamity had a bald forehead and looked worried all the time. Sorrow had eyes set wide apart and slanted so he looked like a Down syndrome baby. Every few minutes I would call out, 'Is this Scandal/Squalor/Mayhem?'

And either Diane or Sarah would come and see. You had to identify a monkey correctly five times before you had 'passed' that monkey. That day, I passed Murder, Hector, Havoc and Squalor. Only 30 monkeys to go.

When my alarm went off at 3:30 the next morning, for the first time I woke up looking forward to the day. The monkeys were high in the mango trees. I stamped my feet impatiently for an hour until they came down.

It was true. A flash of Murder's black eyes, and I knew her before I saw the scar on her lips. When Calamity looked up from picking at his tail, I saw his forehead as bald as a banker's.

Diane came up behind me while I was looking at a young female who was absent-mindedly chewing on a stick.

'Do you know who this is?'

I looked at the fluffy cheeks, the pristine white fur and the slanted almond-shaped eyes, so like her mother's.

'Mayhem.'

Diane smiled.

Tristan was still not talking to me and Charles could not look me in the eye, but it mattered less now. I was assigned to Manuel and Andreas in the field. Andreas didn't talk much, so I asked Manuel to teach me some Spanish. The first words he taught me were *los hijos de la puta monos*, which roughly translated to 'those son of a whore monkeys'. Gradually, I learnt other nouns such as heat, rain, mosquitoes, snakes, vines, wasps, cliffs and killer bees. It became a game to see how many things I could call 'son of a whore' in one day, and soon I had nearly every object in the forest in my vocabulary. Then we moved on to more complex conjugations such as 'the bastard river that rises so we cannot cross' and 'the sun that makes me sweat down to my crotch'.

It was a bitch of a day. Before dawn the monkeys ran to the top of Snuffle, a crumbling mountain ridge above the low-lying clouds. They scampered through the orange twist fruit trees, the red berries falling as tiny monkey feet shook the branches. Before I had caught my breath from the climb, they plunged back down the gravelly slope to the snake-infested Cascabel Valley. They spent the rest of the day in the Anus, so named because it was full of crappy vegetation. I had my first encounter with burn vine, a thin reddish plant covered with fine hair. If you touch the hair with your fingertips, it is sticky but harmless. If you run through it at full speed chasing a monkey, it leaves an angry welt that feels like you have just pressed your skin to a stove element. My arms were covered in slashes and I had a particularly nasty one on my forehead just above my eye.

After lunch, on my shoulder I saw a cute green bug that looked like an alien spaceship with eye stalks. When I gently brushed it off, careful not to hurt it, it spat a vile smelling substance onto my neck. When my neck began to burn, I showed Diane who said it was an acid bug and the pain would stop after a few hours, but the yellow stain would last for months.

By the end of the day, Diane and I had 23 sets of data. A good effort. I knew she was pleased with me. We walked down the path from the Gravel Pit, an old quarry overgrown with grass. The full moon rose above the pink clouds, and Volcano Arenal smoked in the distance. I wondered why I did not feel as bad as I looked. In my old life, I traded adventure for comfort, and discovered complacency was dangerous. Now my world was a savage infinite land, and I crawled exhausted over every inch, somehow feeling safe.

Diane and I collapsed at the Gravel Pit to wait for the car. Mars shone closer to Earth than it had in a hundred years. I breathed in deeply. I stank. My head ached from brambles that knotted my hair into rats' nests. The night air settled a stinging dew into my cuts. But as the headlights cut through the darkness like two blinding eyes, I thought maybe I had found what I was looking for.

Tristan brought the rains when he arrived. Now the rains were returning, it was time for him to leave. He had been with the project for twelve months, one orbit of the earth around the sun. I watched him from the corner of my eye, trying to figure out how he felt. It was impossible to tell. He wore the same scowl as always.

The night before Tristan left, we threw a party. I was not sure how you could have a party with only nine people (Diane was not coming and Sarah had gone to San Jose early for vacation) but there was enough alcohol to give it a good shot.

At five o'clock a car pulled up. The field manager and her boyfriend had returned from their four-month trip to Europe. My stomach sank. If Princess wasn't prettier than me, she was definitely close. Her hair was an extraordinary combination of natural oils and proteins that made it shimmer like the golden thread woven through my mother's wedding dress. As a brunette, I would have paid a lot of money for that hair, but even if I had it, it would have clashed with the yellow undertones in my skin.

I knew my reaction to Princess was vain and petty. Ever since I was young, I've cared too much about my looks. When my father left my mother, my sister and I used to spend the weekends with him. Every weekend there was a new woman, prettier and sexier than the last. I started to view pretty women as competition for my father's attention, and somewhere along the line I started to believe being prettier than everyone else would win me affection and love.

Unfortunately I was an exceedingly ugly child. This wasn't helped by the Chinese habit of giving children of both sexes bowl cuts and dressing them in horrid clothes from the Red Light sales at K-Mart. There is also a Chinese ritual that occurs every time you visit friends, family and neighbours.

'Oh how beautiful your daughter is,' says the friend/relative/neighbour politely.

'Oh no, she is ugly, very ugly,' my mother replies. 'Also she is not so bright at school.'

Several years of therapy helped me put a leash on my vanity but every now and then it leapt out, mostly when I was feeling insecure.

Princess wasn't too taken with me either. She flicked her flint-blue eyes over me, tossed her glorious hair as though she were pissing on a lamp post, and walked past without saying hello. She then broke into a dazzling smile before throwing her arms around Tristan.

'My God I missed you. I can't believe you're really leaving.'

I couldn't tear myself away. Tristan's face had strangely softened as he stroked Princess's hair and murmured in her ear while her boyfriend, Carlos, hung in the background, shaking hands with Charles and Billy.

Excuse me, I thought, is anyone aware that an extraterrestrial has taken over Tristan and he is about to have sex with the field manager in front of everyone? Billy saw me watching and pulled me inside to get a drink and give me the lowdown.

There had always been something between Tristan and Princess, Billy told me, but you can't exactly have an affair when you work, live and sleep with your boyfriend. Despite Tristan and Princess's best attempts not to flirt with each other, Carlos noticed and became jealous. In retaliation Carlos began flirting with a cute blonde on the project. Princess had done her best to keep them apart, but she couldn't keep an eye on them enough to satisfy her suspicion. Meanwhile, Carlos had forbidden Princess to go upstairs at any time because that was where Tristan slept. To escape the knife-edge tension in the house and to try to save their relationship, Princess had taken

Carlos to Europe, only returning when Tristan was safely leaving.

We all sat on the front porch except Ada and Andreas who were still in their room. On the way home in the car, Ada rested her head on Andreas's shoulder. It was the first gesture of intimacy I had seen between them. Although they moved like two strands of seaweed in the same current, they did not kiss or touch each other in public. It was as if public displays of affection were forbidden. I wondered if they stayed in their room so they could spend their last precious moments away from the eyes of the group. Tristan sat across from me, moodily staring at the floor, ignoring the conversation around him. Suddenly I was pretty sure it was him they were hiding from.

Faintly, above the music, I heard Ada crying.

As the night wore on, alcohol lubricated what would have otherwise been an awkward situation. For Tristan's going-away present, we were making a tape using the very expensive recording equipment used to record monkey vocalisations. The Seinhauser microphones were worth at least a thousand dollars each but no one seemed the least bit intimidated. By the time Tristan's tape was half done, the tape deck was being waved around precariously near people's drinks, and one of the cats was on the table licking beer froth off the microphone. The coherence of the messages was deteriorating rapidly until Charles grabbed the microphone and spoke to me for the first time in days.

'I dedicate this poem to Vanessa, the sexiest guitarist on this project.'

'You motherfucker,' said Tristan. 'You ain't seen me play guitar, and that's my tape, you can't dedicate it to her.'

'Shut up Tristan.'

Charles took a deep breath, but we were spared the poetry when he collapsed on the floor.

'Oh my god,' I said rushing forward and putting an arm under him. 'Is he still breathing?'

Tristan looked at me ruefully. 'He does this at every party. Help me get him to bed.'

We each took an arm. Through the throbbing haze of the vodka, I registered it was strange Tristan had just spoken to me.

Dragging Charles's dead weight up the stairs was a major operation. When we reached Charles's room, Tristan kicked open the door. The door broke off one of its hinges.

'Shit.'

We walked over the door and laid Charles on the bed. Tristan picked up the half-broken door, leaned it into place against the doorway, then stumbled back to the bed and collapsed beside Charles.

'Tristan, man, I just wanted to say I love you.'

Tristan smiled dreamily.

'I know.'

'No man you don't know, you can't possibly know how much it is that I love you.'

I was swaying on my feet.

'And when I get out of here, we're doing that bike trip across Alabama. Just you, me and the engines between our thighs.'

I thought I should leave them to their moment, but the thought of negotiating the stairs made me tired. I sat down on the end of the bed. We were all very drunk. Charles looked at me.

'Vanessa,' he began, 'I . . .' and trailed off into silence. We all drifted off, and when I came into consciousness, I had my head resting on Tristan's thigh and Charles's fingers were in my hair. I looked at the bulge in Tristan's jeans while Charles's fingers moved sensuously down my neck. My body began to swell and respond. I pressed my face into Tristan's groin. He groaned. At the same time, Charles's other hand lifted my top to expose the curve of my back.

I had a vague moment of sanity.

'No.' I pushed Charles's hand away. 'Charles. You have a girlfriend. Remember Lisa?'

I was about to think up a reason why my mouth should not be so near Tristan's cock when Charles exploded.

'Get her out of my room!' His face was red and ugly. 'Man, get her out of here. Take her to bed since that's obviously what she wants, but not here, not in front of me.'

I scrambled to my feet and would have slapped him, except the blood rushing to my head made me dizzy and I lost orientation. I probably would have fallen except for Tristan's firm hand at my elbow.

'Come on,' he said. 'Don't take any notice. He's schizophrenic when he's drunk.'

Tristan supported me as we went back downstairs. I made it unsteadily into the kitchen. It must have been late because everyone else had gone to bed.

He poured himself another drink.

'Do you want one?'

'No.'

Something in the abandon with which he threw back his drink made me sad. I realised despite his beauty and mystical connections with monkeys, he was lonely. I felt a faint but tangible connection. It didn't last long.

'You should be nice to Charles,' he said, out of nowhere.

'What?'

'You should be nice to him.'

'What are you talking about? He's been a total asshole to me for days. Ever since you stopped speaking to me, actually.'

'How could you say you would drown a baby in a bucket?'
I exploded.

'I can't believe you even took that even remotely seriously.
It was a joke.'

'It wasn't funny.'

'No shit. But you could have just thrown a tomato instead
of shooting me in the head.'

He shook his head.

'That attitude is going to get you in trouble here. Especially
with Princess.'

I didn't believe what I was hearing.

'What's she got to do with anything?'

Tristan smiled mysteriously.

'I don't think you two are going to get along.'

I felt jealousy snake its way through my brain and settle
behind my eyes. It was the first time I had seen him smile
and it was for her. I narrowed my eyes and heard myself hissing.

'Listen to me, Tristan, I do not give a shit who likes me
around here. I am not going to change to please people.'

He came closer. He put his drink down on the bench
behind me. He was so close I felt electricity thread the hair
on our arms together. I calculated how many monkey faces
I knew and where this put me on the hierarchy. I took a chance.

'Are you going to kiss me?' I said.

He regarded me evenly.

'Are you trying to make me fuck you?'

I went cold. I felt the puncture wound as the insult sank
in slowly, like a stone falling to the bottom of the ocean.
Humiliation knocked the breath from my body and pricked
the corners of my eyes. My voice was a strangled whisper.
'Why are you such a fucking asshole Tristan?'

I made to walk quickly to the door, before my vision
blurred with tears. He grabbed me as I passed him. My arm

hung in his hand like a dead thing. For the first time since I had known him, he looked lost.

'I'm just trying to understand you. I can't . . . God,' he said letting me go then exploding suddenly. 'Do you know what it's like, being surrounded by people who don't give a fuck about monkeys? None of it means anything to them. When I heard about you, I thought you'd be different. Because you were in Africa. Because you came here. I thought you were someone I could talk to. But when I try, it's like you don't give a shit either. Why?'

The kitchen light caught his eyes like fireflies in the dark.

'You can go fuck yourself.'

And I went into my room and shut the door.

I lay in bed, looking at the folds of my bright pink mosquito net. I kicked at the sheets. Soon he would be gone. Slipped out of the monkey house like a mailed letter, destination unknown, taking his monkey psychic powers with him. I closed my eyes and tried to look forward to the silence.

My door clicked open. I felt footsteps pad towards my bed. I opened my mouth to express words of anger, surprise, indignation. But before any of them could escape, his mouth swallowed them. He slipped on top of me, his hard curves pressing me into the mattress, the pressure between my thighs causing a snail-like slipperiness that covered his insistent fingers.

Then, we spoke the only language we mutually understood. To my surprise, he laced his fingers through mine and buried his face in my neck, shaking as he came, as though he were crying.

I slept through his departure. When I woke it was evening. The first thing I saw when I opened my eyes were the steel strings of my guitar, glinting in the muddy darkness. I got out of bed, picked up my guitar, and opened the door of my room.

Everyone was in the living room. Princess was sitting at the computer, Carlos and Manuel were fiddling with a broken fan, Charles was reading and Billy was writing a letter. I could tell by the way they were all not looking at me that they knew I had had sex with Tristan. I could not tell whether they cared.

Mating with the alpha male had in some way tied me to the group. I was one of them now, though none of us were friends.

I was sorry Tristan was gone, but I was glad at the same time. I wanted to believe we could become friends as well as lovers, but that was never the nature of our relationship. Too much fire, my mother would have said. We would both end up a pile of ashes.

I went outside to the porch. The moon shone through the mango leaves and geckos crawled up the walls, snapping at moths.

I waited for a moment, listening for something. A sign like a ripple in the night air, a voice like mine crying in an alien world, a shriek from the moonlight, telling me my wings were wet, broken, that I was trapped and would never reach the luminous orb pulsating like a forbidden promise in the sky.

There was no sign. Only the cicadas singing and the high-pitched hum of the mosquitoes. So, with Strider's head in my lap, I began to play.

chapter 5

Snake
follow

Vanity was sitting on a branch, kneading his tail. It wasn't a pretty tail to start with; chunks were missing and tufts of fur sprouted unevenly like rogue plants. Picking and pulling at it didn't help.

Vanity was part of the old generation of monkeys. I didn't know much about them, except that according to everyone, they were so much cooler than the current monkeys.

'Vanity and Sloth,' Manuel would say, shaking his head like they were the much-loved black sheep of the family. 'Those guys were loco.'

I felt cheated. As though as soon as I arrived, the glory days were over and I was left with the monkey dregs.

Everyone studied two out of the three monkey groups that lived in different parts of the forest; Sin, Snow White and Nirvana. My next group was Snow White and, frankly, I couldn't wait. Everyone who worked in Snow White had tales of monkeys jumping on their heads and touching their faces curiously. Andreas said that once the monkeys spent all afternoon playing with Sarah's hair as she was taking a nap on a rock.

Diane disapproved of the monkeys in Snow White interacting with us. She was afraid villagers would kill them. Whatever the monkeys meant to scientific endeavour, to the farmers they were like a plague of locusts. They ravaged entire crops and generally made a nuisance of themselves by thumping over roofs and taunting the dogs.

Diane was thinking of spraying the monkeys with water pistols every time they got too close, but I could tell none of the assistants would do it. They loved the monkeys touching them. After a day with Snow White, people came out of the forest glowing. I couldn't wait to have a monkey play with my hair, instead of flashing me its bottom as it ran away. I still wasn't convinced the monkeys in Sin could tell us apart. I kept looking for a spark of recognition in their eyes. Something that said 'Hey, I remember you—you were here yesterday. And the day before that. And the day before that.' But there was nothing. Maybe the monkeys in Snow White would remember who I was, making me feel I wasn't just part of the foliage.

Vanity definitely didn't recognise me, since it was the first time I had seen him. Diane was ecstatic Vanity was still alive. She said I should learn to recognise him since it could be a long time before I had another chance.

So there I was, staring at yet another monkey, trying to pick out discerning features. He didn't really have any besides his ratty tail. He just looked like a criminal that had been on the run too long.

All of a sudden there was a rustle in the trees.

'Oh,' said Diane, her voice trembling with anticipation. 'It's another monkey.'

Billy went off to look.

'It's Sloth!' he called out.

'Sloth!' Diane was beside herself. She turned to me. 'These are the lost males.'

Lost? How did a monkey get lost?

'You stay with Vanity,' she called over her shoulder as she ran after Billy and the other monkey.

'So,' I said conversationally. 'How would you describe yourself? Rugged male with sexy scars in secret places?'

Vanity chattered his teeth, like he was cold. Then he jumped up and paced on his branch, turning abruptly every few seconds. He smacked his lips together as if he had a bad taste in his mouth. I couldn't figure out what had gotten into him. Then it dawned on me.

'Oh shit. Another monkey.'

There was a rustling in the branches behind me, and another monkey appeared. I had never seen him before. Proud and regal, he stared down at Vanity who was now kneading his tail again. Vanity took one look at the intruder, and fled.

I stood for a moment, unsure of what to do. Did I follow Vanity, or did I stay with the new monkey? I decided to follow instructions and ran after Vanity who was just a blur of shaking branches ahead of me. I nearly crashed into Billy.

'I'm losing Vanity.'

'No worries, I'll go this way and try to catch him up ahead.'

Suddenly I was blocked by a wall of brambles that rose higher than my head. I found what looked like the thinnest part and began to hack my way through with my machete. I felt like the prince in 'Sleeping Beauty'. A log had fallen across the thicket. I stepped on it thinking I might be able to see Vanity over the brambles and radio his location to Billy.

The log collapsed under my feet and exploded in a buzzing that swarmed around my head. The first sting penetrated the soft skin behind my ear, sending pain receptors crackling to my brain. Panicking, I ran further into the thicket while stings jabbed my face, my neck, my hands. I dropped my machete and clawed my way out. A sting on my eyelid made me scream and blinded my left eye. I fell, and the buzzing closed in around me, stinging every few seconds. Half blind, I picked myself up and ran and ran and ran.

Vines wrapped around my wrists, the earth shuddered and tripped my feet, trees sprang up in my path. I fell onto rattan cane, landing on all fours, thorns piercing my hands like tiny swords. I waited for a vicious stinging battalion to descend upon me but, in a miraculous deliverance, it had stopped. Slowly I realised the buzzing in my ears came from a single creature threaded through my hair.

Billy found me beating my head.

'Vanessa, are you okay?'

I thought it was obvious that I was far from okay.

'It's in my hair!'

Diane arrived, alerted by my screaming.

'What is it? What's wrong?'

'She's got something in her hair.'

'Well, get it out!'

'She won't stay still.'

I was scrunching and pulling at my hair like a lunatic.

'It's still in there!'

'Oh, I see it,' Billy said and hit my head a few times with his hat.

The creature, more dazed than furious, buzzed erratically like it was being electrocuted. Billy plunged his hand into my hair and pulled out a wriggling black body. Diane jumped back as if it were the spawn of Satan.

'Oh my god,' she said. 'Killer bees. I'm allergic to them. I have to go; Billy, take care of Vanessa.'

Billy dropped the bee and, reflexively, I caught it. The bee stung the palm of my hand. The stinger camouflaged itself among a scattered field of black spines. Without the stinger, the abdomen of the bee wriggled away and left its head near the base of my index finger. The furry head and large compound eyes looked strangely peaceful in death. The poison pulsed through my blood vessels. I located the stinger and pulled it out, sitting down, exhausted. Billy sat beside me, holding his head in his hands.

'I got stung too,' he said. 'On my head.'

'Did you pull it out?'

'Not yet.'

I combed through his hair until I found the tiny black dagger, nestled snugly in his white scalp. As I pulled it out, a tiny drop of blood welled on the bump.

We sat together, our stings throbbing in unison. I felt panicked. It was June and I hadn't even started filming yet. The five Disney segments I was supposed to deliver by November loomed over me like the room of straw the girl in 'Rumpelstiltskin' was supposed to weave into gold. I missed sitting on the beach in Australia. I wanted to go home.

'She hates me.' Billy interrupted my thoughts.

'Who does?'

'Diane.'

'No she doesn't.'

'She does. You haven't seen her with me.'

'She can't hate you. You know all the monkeys.'

'She doesn't think I do.'

Every day I'd had with Diane was tiring but satisfying. She had endless patience when it came to explaining the monkeys, how they behaved, the language they used. She was enthusiastic about my filming because there were monkey behaviours that had never been captured on film, like lethal aggression where the monkeys fought to the death like gladiators. She also wanted me to make a short film to show Costa Rican schoolchildren.

'I've never let anyone film the monkeys,' she told Princess. 'But if anyone's going to do it, I'd rather Vanessa than some film crew I don't know.'

According to Diane, every documentary company in the world had tried to film her capuchins, from the Discovery Channel to National Geographic to the BBC. Diane had rejected all of them because she didn't want six people and masses of equipment interrupting her data collection. I was getting exclusive footage of world-famous monkeys that no one had filmed before. And how many filmmakers followed their subject fourteen hours a day, every day for a year? I was in a unique position and grateful to Diane for giving me the opportunity.

I looked at Billy. He didn't seem as mischievous or as lighthearted as when I first met him. Suddenly I realised someone besides me might be having problems.

'Ever since you came,' Billy went on, 'she started being mean to me. She loves you. She says no one's ever learnt the monkeys faster than you except Tristan, and he did them in two weeks.'

Despite Billy's predicament and the throbbing pain in my hand, my head and my eye, I felt a warm glow of pride. Good with the monkeys—me?

'And she always goes on about how you're always practising your speed tests.'

'Only because I thought I was going to get fired.'

'I'm the one that's going to get fired.'

'That's ridiculous. Besides,' I said, remembering what Tristan had told me, 'no one's ever been fired from the monkey project.'

'Not yet.' He looked really depressed. 'Diane said Sarah and I have to do speed tests, like you, even though I've been here for five months and Sarah's been here for four.'

'Don't worry, Billy, I'll help you. We can do speed tests together.'

As soon as I said it, I wanted to bite my tongue off. I was afraid he would think I was pushing him out of the way as I clambered up the hierarchy, offering my help when he was so much more senior. But Billy apparently wasn't aware of hierarchy rules.

'Thanks,' he said.

By the time the car pulled up, I was feeling sorry for myself again. My eye had swollen shut, I lost my glasses when I was running from the bees, I couldn't get any of the spines out of my hands, and I discovered a hundred more stuck in my knees. The back door of the car opened. Charles was the first face I saw.

'Hey,' he said as I climbed in beside him. 'How was your day?'

I put my head on his shoulder, not saying anything.

'She got stung by killer bees,' said Billy.

'Goddamn. Honey are you okay?'

I shook my head. Since Tristan left, Charles and I had developed a tentative friendship. Neither of us mentioned his strange outburst at Tristan's party. It was easier to pretend the sex never happened either.

'Just hang on till we get home, I have something you can put on the stings.'

'And I lost my glasses,' I said. 'And I got spines in my hands and I can't get them out.'

'Shi-et. You sure did have a bad one. Well we can get you new glasses. And we can fix your hands too.'

Someone feeling sorry for me was already making me feel better. I smiled.

In the new month, Sarah, Charles and I had the same Vacas day. I decided that though these were not technically a day off, we had to make time for fun. After pancake breakfast, a few hours were spent doing chores like mopping the floor and cleaning the kitchen. I dutifully did my speed tests, while Charles cleaned his data. Then, in the afternoon, Charles and I took the dogs swimming.

We passed the old tyre factory that signposted the turn-off into Vacas. We walked down the highway, hidden by the long grass, past the road that led to the volcano, past the orchards and the bar on the outskirts of town. Finally, we crossed the second bridge and the sound of running water gurgled over trucks flying past at 100 kilometres an hour. As we approached, Jesus lizards ran across the water, their splayed toes balancing on the surface tension, as the dogs tore down the bank after them.

We talked about everything and nothing on those lazy afternoons, our lives back home, what our plans were afterwards, who we dated in high school, ten items we'd take to a desert island. In a way, that's where we were, an isolated patch of ground surrounded by a forest full of monkeys. When the sun started to lose its brilliance, we had one last dunk then put on our wet clothes, knowing they would be crisp and dry by the time we got home. We were home in time to have dinner on the table, pack lunch and our bags, before going to bed at 8:30 p.m., ready for work seven hours later.

Hanging out with Charles made me feel like I fit in. He was smart and playful and we had fun together. He made the weirdness of the monkey world seem more normal, as though we were two mates doing something crazy for a laugh. I even liked the monkeys more when I was with him. It was hard to remember how ugly and psychotic they were when he spoke to them like they were old friends.

On the three-day rotation, for the first field day, Charles and I were out together. I liked following his strong, sure footsteps on trails he knew better than the streets of Atlanta where he was born. Charles always seemed to know where the monkeys were heading, so instead of running after them, we could take a short cut and head them off. While Diane started identifying monkeys in the dark, Charles would shrug his shoulders and say, 'I can't see them, can you?'

When the monkeys calmed down, we did as many follows as we could, but I noticed Charles took care not to make me run into brambles or up cliffs, and aborted whenever things got too difficult.

My favourite time was the afternoon when the monkeys headed for the river. If we had enough follows, we could stroll behind them in the mango orchard next to Quebrada Acacia, a long river lined with tall acacia trees. There was no undergrowth here, and there were endless places carpeted thickly with mango leaves where we could sit down and talk. With Charles I was finally confident enough to start filming and he stood behind me, chuckling when I cursed and muttered at the monkeys running in and out of my shot.

If the monkeys were still by the river in the late afternoon, we would strip down to our underwear and swim in the pristine water that had come all the way down from the mountains, gathering volume and momentum in the early rains.

Billy, however, was not having such a good time. As the month went on, he showed signs of stress. There were dark circles under his eyes. He stopped doing impersonations of cartoon characters at dinner.

'Ask him what's wrong,' I told Charles.

'It's Diane,' Charles said. 'He thinks she's out to get him.'

'Is she?'

'It's hard to say. Billy's my best buddy here but he's so damn lazy. He says Diane's really mean to him, but none of us have ever seen that side of her. We just know when you're out with Diane, you have to work harder than you do on other days. Once Billy actually fell asleep while she was talking to him.'

'Is he going to get fired?'

'No one's ever been fired. He just has to try a little harder and lie low until Diane leaves at the end of the month. I think everything will work out.'

Diane was definitely keeping Billy close. She rostered him with her on Vacas days, which meant he was in the field with her for days one and two. On the second field day, I was with them.

The first time I noticed things were not going well was the day of the snake follow. The forest was full of snakes. Cascabels, coral snakes and boa constrictors all slithered through the undergrowth. I once saw a constrictor that was three times longer than me with a body as thick as my thigh.

When monkeys see a snake, they make a cough like a cry of surprise. We were supposed to record the snake alarms and which monkeys made them. This was the cue for the assistants to drop whatever they were doing and run to the snake to record the monkey vocalisations. Diane was studying how baby monkeys learnt which snakes were dangerous and which ones were harmless. For the dangerous snakes, all the monkeys gather around and alarm hysterically, sometimes for as long as an hour.

We were just below the Gravel Pit when we heard snake alarms from SQS valley, a dry river bed choked with thickets. Diane scampered towards them. I followed her. By the time Billy arrived, she was waiting impatiently.

The snake was hidden beneath a log, its head resting lazily on its coils. The ringed rattle poked out like a finger. Diane said cascabels no longer rattled because whenever Costa Rican farmers heard them, they hunted down the snake and chopped off its head. All the snakes that rattled loudly were eliminated from the gene pool until only the quieter ones were left to breed.

Billy dropped his bag to take out the recording equipment. He fumbled with cords and the microphone, plugging in connections and putting on the headphones. An eternity later, he was ready.

'Okay,' he said. He switched on the microphone and Diane started calling out the names of the monkeys as they alarmed at the snake.

'Murder. Mayhem. Sorrow. Calamity. Sorrow. Sorrow.'

'Wait,' he said, 'I can't hear you.'

Diane's eyes widened as though she could not believe his incompetence.

'Billy, we're losing valuable data. Didn't you check the equipment this morning?'

Diane took the recorder from him and flicked a switch.

'It's out of batteries.'

Billy stared hard at the leaf litter. 'I don't have any spares.'

Diane took off her backpack and went through various plastic bags. 'Here.'

By now, Billy was shaking so badly, he could not dismantle the battery compartment. Eventually Diane snatched the recorder from him and changed the batteries herself. She started to speak into the microphone.

'The date is 3 June 2003, time 11:07:23, DP with BG and VW and we're about to start a snake follow of Sin at SQS.'

There was a click as the tape ended.

Silence.

Billy looked into her fish-like eyes, large and watery behind her glasses.

'Do you have another tape?'

Sweat dripped from his hair onto his nose. He shook his head.

We sat together in silence and watched the last of the monkeys shake a branch at the snake and run off into the trees. The snake laid its head on its gold patterned coils and flickered its tongue at us. Its eyes were unwavering.

Besides Billy's work ethic, there was another problem—Billy's Costa Rican girlfriend, Bianca. He met her a few months previously at Soda Limon, the one and only nightclub in Vacas. She was a plump, pretty girl with a four-year-old son. Billy was besotted with her. Being of old-fashioned English stock, he believed any difficulty in life could be conquered as long as he had a wife. To his delight, Bianca seemed more open to this proposition than his previous girlfriends, and he wanted to fly her to England at the end of the year to meet his parents.

However, Diane was visibly uncomfortable with the relationship. Princess had a Costa Rican boyfriend, but Diane had known Carlos for years. To make matters worse, over the past thirteen years Diane had been robbed several times. Occasionally by good friends. As a result, Diane was paranoid about the thousands of dollars of equipment. She insisted laptops were put away and locked up if there was no one in the room (even if you went into the kitchen to make a cup of tea), the back and front doors were locked at all times (even in the stifling heat), and the gates were padlocked. Even with these precautions, hiking boots, backpacks, and rain ponchos continued to disappear until Diane could not help but view all Vacas with suspicion. Especially Ticos (Costa Ricans) she didn't know.

One afternoon, Diane had heart palpitations when she found Billy entertaining Bianca, Diego and Daniel on the front porch. Diego was reasonably safe, being the cousin of Jesus, a Tico who worked as a field assistant, but Daniel was a well-known male prostitute who trafficked in illegal narcotics. Diane went straight to Princess and told her that Billy was not to invite anyone to the house.

Princess had been with the project for four years. When she arrived, she was one of two field assistants and lived with Diane in a tiny house next to the grocery store.

Princess didn't stay on the monkey project to further her career. She wasn't on any of the papers Diane published and had no research of her own. The only job she was qualified for after the monkey project was running another field station.

Everyone presumed she stayed because America would not let a poor, illiterate Costa Rican like Carlos into the country. Princess was from an upper-class family in Vermont, and her parents were none too thrilled about their golden daughter living in a dilapidated house with a Costa Rican who had never been to school and could not speak English. Unable to get Carlos into America, Princess was effectively trapped. The only way Carlos could get a visa was if they got married, and Princess seemed unwilling to part with this last vestige of her freedom. So she endured the monkey house, whether through genuine love for Carlos, rebellion, a lack of anything better to do, or a combination of everything.

Princess tried tactfully to explain to Billy why Costa Ricans were not allowed in the house.

'You have to understand, Billy, she's been robbed by people they've trusted before.'

'But not everyone's going to rob her.'

'There's so much valuable stuff here, she can't afford to take that risk.'

'That's stupid! You can't live in a country for thirteen years and not mix with the community. That's imperialism, and she's not even British!'

'She's not asking you to avoid the locals, she just doesn't want you to bring them back to the house. It's not that she thinks your friends will steal anything, but you know what this town is like. All your friends have to do is mention to someone that we have a few laptops and in minutes the whole town will think we have some undercover computer retail operation going on, and there will be those who want to rip it off. We have a set budget for this project. We can't afford to replace equipment if it gets stolen.'

'What about Bianca then, is she not allowed in the house?'

Princess sighed.

'At this stage, no.'

Billy exploded.

'This is bloody ridiculous! My own girlfriend not allowed in the house. What am I supposed to tell her? Whites only?'

'Billy, please don't stir up any trouble.'

'What about Carlos?'

Princess's eyes sharpened to pinpricks, daring him to go one inch further.

'Carlos is different.'

Billy had the sense to stop in his tracks. Princess softened.

'At least wait until Diane leaves, then we can talk about it.'

But Diane leaving was taking longer than expected. There was another three weeks before vacation. That was fourteen days of fourteen hours of Diane and Billy days, as well as Diane checking on him on Vacas days. He was unofficially under house arrest. No one said explicitly he couldn't watch a movie in Liberia or meet Bianca in Santa Cruz, but if he went, Diane would grumble under her breath and someone would tell Billy about it later. He woke up in the morning full of dread, and went to sleep knowing the next day would be worse.

It was around this time that his sleepwalking became out of control. When Billy started talking about hunting a ginger-haired monkey in the middle of the night, everyone thought it was hilarious. It was a recurring dream, and he would pace the house, searching. Sarah occasionally woke up and saw him shining a torch into her dirty laundry.

I saw him once. I heard a noise outside and I got out of bed to look. The porch light was on and Billy was staring into the garden. His face was slack and his jaw hung gaping but his eyes were wide open, as though he were blind.

'Billy?' I whispered. He didn't answer, only stared ahead, as though waiting for his ginger-haired monkey to appear. I can't image what that twilight world was like, that restless limbo between wakefulness and sleep. I quietly went back inside, leaving him blind with monkey dreams.

The long days and restless nights were taking their toll. He was exhausted. Under Diane's watchful eyes he stumbled through the forest, bleary-eyed and breathing deeply. As soon as he sat down, his head swayed and his eyelids crept over his eyes. Diane frowned.

I wanted to tell her it wasn't his fault, that he hadn't been sleeping. But, like everyone else, I was afraid. We all liked Billy, but none of us were prepared to protect him. If we had banded together in his defence, things might have turned out differently. But when a monkey is thrown down the hierarchy by the alpha, the others just watch. If the alpha isn't around, they may groom it surreptitiously or allow it to touch them, but when the alpha is watching, they behave as if it isn't there. It was no different with us.

Billy became an isolated figure. All the laughter went out of him. At the time I didn't realise I was part of the conspiracy that brought him down. That in not doing my part to defend him, I was equal to every two-faced cowardly monkey that clawed its survival from the defeat of another.

I can see it now, in retrospect. Because later on, it would happen to me.

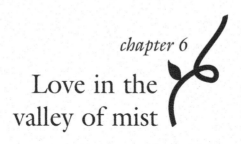

chapter 6

Love in the valley of mist

mid-month, we had two new arrivals: Kermit and Brad. In the monkey house, new people were a major event. A new person was either a new friend or a new enemy. We were speculating about Kermit and Brad a month before they arrived. What would they look like? What kind of people were they? Apparently, before I arrived Billy had said I would either look like Kramer from *Seinfeld* or Pamela Anderson. I wasn't sure if this made me a friend or an enemy.

One evening Princess passed two passport photos around the dinner table. The first one was Brad.

'He's gorgeous,' said Sarah.

'He looks like Tristan,' said Princess.

My stomach lurched. 'I don't think he looks anything like Tristan.'

'He looks like one moody sonofabitch,' said Charles.

No one said anything but we were all nervous Brad would be another terrible brilliance, a supernova of restlessness and dissent. Then the photo of Kermit was passed around. His name wasn't really Kermit, it was Ken. 'Kermit' was the name given to him by his fraternity brothers, an assertion he made in his CV under 'preferred name'. Everyone was silent as they looked at the photo. I waited until I couldn't stand it any longer.

'He's fat.'

'Vanessa!' Charles was shocked. I could always count on him for outrage at my political incorrectness.

'Fat person fat,' I said stubbornly.

Princess sighed.

'Diane's worried he might not fit under the fences.'

It was a valid concern. We crawled under dozens of fences as we trekked through the forest, and the lowest strand of barbed wire was definitely not high enough for Kermit's girth. He looked like he had never done a day of exercise in his life. How was he going to run up a cliff after monkeys?

'I wonder what made him apply?' Andreas mused.

'Maybe he thinks we're fat camp.'

Charles shook his head. 'Vanessa, someone's got to teach you some manners.'

The arrival of Kermit and Brad meant something special to me. I was no longer the newest assistant. The arrival of two new people meant I was automatically two rungs up on the hierarchy. I looked forward to their arrival with a kind of malicious glee. They were on the bottom now.

The day they were supposed to arrive, Princess stayed home to cook a feast. I was slowly learning that in our primitive, impoverished group house, Princess provided a human touch. While Diane thought we needed only monkeys to breathe easy, Princess understood how much we missed home comforts. She bought breakfast bars, ice cream and barbequed chicken. She got us an extra day off every now and then, tried to bring us home early from the field.

However, Princess and I weren't exactly getting along. I thought she was stuck up and vain. I had a feeling she thought I was arrogant and vulgar. Even though Tristan had gone, his last secret smile for her still rankled. Princess and I circled each other warily, pretending to ignore the other's existence but all the time watching very carefully, especially how we interacted with the males in the house. I surreptitiously sharpened my claws whenever she flirted with Charles, and her eyes narrowed to slits if I went anywhere near Carlos.

For Kermit and Brad's welcome dinner she prepared Napolitana and carbonara pasta, paellas, tortillas and guacamole. The table was laid out fit for a king. When their bus was due to arrive, Princess went to the station to pick them up. She came back alone.

'They weren't on it.'

It was Charles's and my Vacas day. We looked at each other. Three more buses came and went. Each time, Princess drove to the bus station and returned alone.

Finally, the phone rang. I answered it. 'Hello?'

'Hey,' called a cheerful male voice. 'Is Princess there?'

Princess took the phone.

'Where are you? Oh. Yes. Okay. Well, I guess.'

She hung up the phone. Charles and I looked at her expectantly.

'They're not coming.'

'What?'

'They met up with a girl last night, and they're going to Tamarindo. They said they'll be here tomorrow.'

We were dumbfounded. Tamarindo was a coastal party town. Tourists went there to get drunk and have sex with Costa Ricans.

I made a tentative move towards a truce.

'Princess, that's awful. You've made such an effort.'

She shrugged.

'Oh well, I guess we have to eat all this food.'

The next day, the two new arrivals were greeted with no food and no welcome except Diane standing on the porch like an avenging angel. They were as their photos suggested, although somewhat hungover after their night in Tamarindo. We heard snippets of a lecture on responsibility, obligation and how close they were to being fired. Afterwards, they slunk inside like naughty children, grinning sheepishly but wincing at the same time, as if their bottoms had been spanked hard.

After a bumpy start, Princess spread her wings over them like they were her own hatchlings. It was fascinating to watch her transformation. Her cool reserve had fallen in folds around her and she was suddenly a brilliant beating guide through the perilous forest. She took them to Liberia to show them where to shop, she brought them out into the field and taught them the monkeys. She marked their tests and pouted when she thought they were not trying hard enough to please her.

The new boys fell for it completely. They watched her shimmer her hair, push her breasts through gauzy shirts and sway her hips under short skirts. They followed her around like gambolling puppies, waiting for the next soft look or a flirtatious touch.

'She never did that for me,' I said to Charles, impressed and nauseous at the same time.

'You're not male.'

'That wasn't Calamity, it was Mayhem!' Billy cried out. 'Carlos got it wrong.'

Diane had banished Billy from spotting and was working with Carlos, who was obviously a favourite. Billy was supposed to be training me but every now and then he ran away and corrected one of Carlos's identifications.

'I'm sure he would have figured that out on his own,' Diane said. 'Anyway, I can see them too. Why don't you help Vanessa with her identifications? She's nearly passed everyone.'

Billy was in a precarious position. If the new field researchers learnt at the same pace as I did, he was going to tumble down the hierarchy and end up as the omega. In monkey world, the alpha was the leader, the beta was the back-up and the omega was totally screwed. Omegas were stressed, depressed and died sooner than other monkeys. The omega of Sin was Debacle. She reminded me of a bag lady; drab, old and senile. Whenever the other monkeys had a bad day, they took it out on her. As a result, Debacle slunk around the outside of the group, and when a fight broke out she made sure she was nowhere in sight.

For a while I thought I was the omega, but really I wasn't even close. It was a long crumbling fall to omega status but there was one sure way to get there. Diane declared you one.

Late one night, Billy broke a window pane. He didn't even know he had done it until he woke up holding the two halves of glass in his hands. Brad was Billy's new room-mate and Billy's late-night habits were freaking him out.

'It's really weird. I wake up and there's a shadow wandering the room, muttering. Now, he's smashing window panes. I could get hurt,' Brad said.

'What do you think is going to happen?' I whispered to Charles.

'I don't know. Nothing good.'

* * *

Charles was stirring a pot of lentil soup he had made for dinner, and I was trying to convince him to add some chicken. We looked up as Billy walked into the kitchen, ashen faced.

'Hey Billy, what's up?'

'I think I'm going to get fired.'

Charles put down the metal spoon. Billy leant against the kitchen bench as though he could not hold himself up. The words poured out of him in a miserable torrent.

'I had the worst day ever with Diane. It was hideous. She started giving me pretend data to see how fast I could type it in. You should have heard it, it was ridiculous. Triadic interaction after triadic interaction, stuff that would never happen unless all the monkeys were on crack. When I couldn't keep up, she said I was obviously missing important interactions in the field and she couldn't use my data.'

'Not use your data?'

'She said she couldn't be sure that the data I was taking was unbiased.'

'What's she going to do with it?'

'Chuck it. The last five months, all useless.'

Charles told me later this would not be a huge loss. Billy was not the world's most avid data taker. There would be days when Charles would return with a thousand lines, and Billy would have only a couple of lost calls.

'There's something else. Someone told her about the broken window.'

Charles whistled through his teeth.

'And other times I sleepwalked. She said she's worried about the safety of the group. Like I'll get up one night and murder you all in your beds.'

'Diane gets a bit freaked by abnormal behaviour.'

'That's not the point. Who's been telling her?'

'I don't know, anyone. It's not exactly a secret.'

'But she knows about other stuff too. Like how I fell asleep that one time under the Sloanea tree. And how it was me that broke the microphone. And how I was the one that dropped my dictaphone in the river.'

'But everyone does that stuff.'

'Exactly, but she only finds out about me. Someone here is telling her every time I mess up. I think they're trying to get me fired.'

'Billy, that's ridiculous.'

'It's not, I swear to god. Diane wants me off the project and someone's helping her do it.'

A week later, Sarah and I were on the way to Liberia to see a movie. I liked Sarah, she was a great gossip. At more than six feet tall, she was the kind of girl who was everyone's friend in high school but no one's best friend. She wasn't smart or pretty. She wasn't athletic or particularly good with the monkeys. People liked her because she was a good listener and she was nice to everyone. It made her an easy person to tell secrets to. In fact, there was nothing Sarah liked more than secrets. She collected them like some women collect shoes.

Before the monkey project she worked in Ohio as a lab rat for a pharmaceutical company. At 32, she owned barely anything besides stocks in various biomedical companies she liked to gamble with over the internet. There was a boyfriend in the picture, but she told me she secretly thought he was a loser. She had no idea what she was going to do after the monkey project, but she thought she might like working with whales in an aquarium.

Before Ada left, Sarah had been her friend. Although Sarah had been on the project for four months, she was still near the bottom of the hierarchy, which made her a perfect match for me. As the only girls on the project besides Princess, we became friends. Aware of Sarah's secret-collecting habit, I even told her about my plans to leave the project after ten months instead of twelve so I could film the rest of the Disney segments in Africa before my plane ticket expired.

On the way to Liberia, she took a document out of her bag.

'Did you see the new field guide? Princess gave it to me this morning.'

I quickly skimmed through it. It was the same one we received when we started the project. It had the monkey codes, vocalisations, what to bring and what life was like at Cielo Forest. Then I saw a new section.

Field Assistant Code of Conduct
Relationships

We urge you to consider very carefully before entering into intimate relationships while you are here, either with your co-workers or with Ticos. You are not working in isolation and your personal conduct has consequences to this project. Unfortunately the men have the machismo typical of Central/South American men, so even innocent associations will be exaggerated out of all proportions.

We do not presume to tell you who you can and can not date (though many projects do), but we do ask you to consider these matters carefully and weigh whether they are worth the risk.

'Shit,' I said. 'Billy's going to spew.'

'What do you think he'll do?' Sarah asked.

The truth was, at that moment, I didn't really care. I had problems of my own. The night before, when Charles came home, he didn't say hello. He just stood at the door, talking to Carlos. Then he hung out on the porch for ages. I went outside.

'Hi,' I said.

He couldn't look me in the eye. 'Hi,' he finally replied.

'How was your day?'

Normally he said stuff like 'Those bitches, I cannot even tell you, Vanessa, how much I want to tie a goddamn rope around their necks and put them in the backyard. All the follows would be so easy. Calamity pulls on rope. Calamity pulls on rope.'

But this time he looked up quickly, then down.

'Fine.'

Everyone knows fine doesn't really mean fine.

'What's wrong?'

'Nothing.'

And there it was. A fracture no wider than a strand of hair that ran the whole length of our friendship.

It was easy to explain away. He had a bad day. I was being paranoid. But from the way it hurt every time I watched his eyes slinking away from me, I knew. He wanted to fuck me.

I spent the years from kindergarten until my senior year at high school painfully growing from an ugly child into a not so ugly young woman. During this time, I experienced confusing relationships with men, where the boys who were my friends became angry with me. They stopped talking to me. They couldn't look at me. It took me until university to figure out if you had sex with them, the problem went away. And if I asked them why they became angry in the first place, they answered in their emotionally repressed way, that yes, sex was what they wanted all along. And yes, they were angry because they couldn't have it.

Of course, this wasn't always the case, but over the years I'd become pretty good at discerning when it was.

For the first few days I was frantic. I didn't want to sleep with Charles but I didn't want to lose him either. I was like a cowering monkey, my head bowed low, sniffing the ground around him for a sign he had relented. The most I got was an occasional guilty smile before he turned away.

On the third day, I was angry. I was in my room, reading a letter from my best friend, Heather. It was full of warmth, love and encouragement. I was sick of the monkey house people. Charles was an adult. He should either get over it or not have any female friends.

There was a knock on my door. It was Charles.

'Hey,' he said, like nothing had happened. 'Can I come in?'

I stared at him in shock before I stepped back and closed the door. I saw panic cross his face as he jammed his foot in the doorway before it could shut.

'Hey, what's up?'

I should have played along. Pretended nothing had happened and hoped it didn't happen again. But I was too angry.

'Fuck off Charles, I'm not playing.'

'What are you talking about?'

'Fine,' I snapped, losing my temper. 'You pretend you haven't been an absolute asshole for the last three days. I don't know what the fuck your problem is. All I know is that you started ignoring me once before Tristan left, and you're doing it again now. I don't have to put up with this bullshit. You're either someone's friend or you're not, and you're being a goddamn schizophrenic. I've had enough of dealing with mental cases, so get the hell out of my room.'

Before he could say anything, I propelled him backwards and shut the door in his face. I heard him stand there for a moment before he walked away.

The next morning, we lost the monkeys.

Charles and I were no longer alone. Princess, Sarah and Kermit were with us and the monkeys were not where they were supposed to be.

A few weird things happen to you on the monkey project. One of them is that monkeys come to represent your self-worth. At the end of the day, you crawl into the car with everyone looking wet and exhausted. There is the round of 'Where are yours sleeping?'

If you can say, with the smugness of a guardian angel reporting to God, 'Orange Twist' or 'Fence above Tinamu', then no matter how awful the day has been, you feel a warm glow inside you. The monkeys are safe, you have put them to bed and another day is well done. But if you have to say in an ashamed mutter, 'We lost them', no one looks you in the eye and there is an uncomfortable silence. Diane or Princess say softly, 'So what happened?', and you are aware that you have grievously failed.

Since I was already angry at Charles, it didn't take much to make me angrier at the whole project. I was angry that fourteen hours a day was not enough. Angry at the mind-numbing boredom. Angry at the invisible pressure to keep hold of the monkeys even though they never let you rest. It was ridiculous. We worked harder than sweat-shop labourers and were paid less. Most of the time we were unsupervised, so there was no reason for us to drive ourselves the way we did. But as I stepped back and looked through uncharitable eyes, I began to see that the project had ways to make you perform.

Instead of constructing a totalitarian regime, which we would have rebelled against, Diane and Princess handed us whips, and watched us flagellate ourselves. They silently cultivated the feeling of competition between the monkey groups. If Snow White had twenty follows for the day, it was a disgrace for Sin to have only ten. The follows for the day were written up on a chart on the wall, ostensibly to see which monkeys had fewer follows so the next day we could concentrate on catching up, but really it was so everyone could see which group was 'winning'. You also had to type the number of follows into the computer, so you could see whether you were doing better or worse than everyone else. If you took no dictaphone data, collected no vocalisations and shot no video, then you had to type into the computer that you didn't and therefore remind yourself that you were not coming up to scratch. If you had done these things, you could smugly tick the box and reaffirm your sense of self-worth.

When we didn't find the monkeys we split up. I took Kermit. I had largely been ignoring Kermit-and-Brad, as they were collectively known. Since their disgraceful arrival, there was something of the tainted about them and I didn't want it to rub off on me. Also, Princess was spending so much time with them, I didn't want to trespass on her territory.

Brad looked like a sportswear model; dark and rugged, with so much testosterone that stubble pushed through his clean-shaven face by afternoon. At the same time, he was softly spoken and his mahogany eyes were intelligent and gentle. A deadly combination. I was determined not to fall for it.

Kermit was a beer-drinking frat boy from Virginia who referred to his fraternity mates as his 'brothers' and swung his machete around with vigour. He was crazy in love with the monkeys. I mean, we had some monkey nutters on the project, but Kermit was in a league of his own. Not even a dead baby monkey falling on his head on his first day could dampen his enthusiasm. He could only recognise two monkeys, the ones with their tails cut off, and he would stand under their branches cooing, 'Hey there, little Havoc, how'r y' doin' there little buddy?'

'That's Squalor,' I'd point out.

'Oh Squalor, sorry about that little girl, aren't you just the prettiest thang?'

It made me queasy. So I was silent as I led him through the dew-soaked fields of Buena Vista, a trail above Snuffle that led to one of the most beautiful views in Cielo Forest. The grass grew taller than our heads and by the time the sun rose we were drenched.

We met Charles, Sarah and Princess at the Gravel Pit. There we lay panting, sweat matting tendrils of hair to our faces. Even our eyelashes were beaded with sweat. Charles had a reddish mark across his forehead where he had walked through burn vine. He kept putting his hand to it to wipe away the lymph and blood.

Collapsed at the Gravel Pit, with no monkeys and no idea where to find them, I saw Charles's fingers just within reach of mine. I turned my head away. If we had been alone, I might have said something, tried to patch things up. But now, with the addition of Kermit-and-Brad, Charles and I were never alone. I closed my eyes. The inside of my head spun around like a galaxy.

Soon we would get up and resume the search. Guard ourselves as best we could while we ran through our vine-strangled Eden, trying to find what we were looking for before the deluge of afternoon rain.

If my fundamentalist Christian uncle had seen the fences that fragmented the forest, he would have said God put them there to keep us humble. The monkey project was conducted with the goodwill of the local landowners and town councils. Part of the forest was a reserve, but the monkey's range spilled over land owned by farmers who bred cattle and planted mango trees.

The forest had been cleared and burned in large areas to graze cattle, so it was not uncommon to be battling through a thicket of vines and brambles then suddenly burst into daylight, face to face with 30 cows.

The fences that bordered the farms and property were no more than cut-up tree stumps and thick sticks that had been hammered into the ground. Rolls of barbed wire were pounded into the sticks and these rickety contraptions ran throughout the forest in a complicated and illogical network. There were no gates or openings and because we could not afford to upset the farmers by damaging the fences, the only way to get past one was to go under it. There were four lines of barbed wire and the lowest one was about a foot off the ground. To get under it, you had to kneel and put your palms flat on the ground. Then you put your face so close to the earth that your lips lightly brushed the soil, and crawled like a worm under the wire.

If you did not supplicate yourself sufficiently, the barbed wire caught on your clothes, and you went nowhere. If you were too proud to kneel, and tried to climb between the two rows of barbed wire at waist level, you came out looking like you'd been through a shredder.

On the day Charles and I were officially at war, we crossed 63 fences. The rain from the day before turned the earth to mud, so every time I knelt, a new layer of dirt and cow shit soaked into my knees, slowly spreading to my thighs. Each gesture of humility made me angrier, and anger made me careless. By the afternoon I had torn a hole in my backpack, ripped my pants from the back of my knee to my thigh, and lost an entire sleeve. I knew I looked ridiculous and that made me even angrier. Kermit and I were alone again when I saw the flash of a black tail heading for Cemetery Trail.

Not many of the path names made sense to me, but Cemetery Trail did. It was a field full of sensitive plants, whose feathery leaves shut tight when you touched them to reveal stems covered in thorns. You couldn't cut them, because they were curled and sinewy, so that when your machete cut down, they only uncoiled enough to break the tension, slicing along your hands and arms and burrowing into your skin. Once you were in, you couldn't go back, because once you had bent the mat of thorns forward, the thorns were all pointed towards you. If you tried to retrace your steps, there were a million little blades, aimed straight at your heart.

There was no choice but to go further, following the black shadows that skipped light-heartedly through the sparse trees. The sun scorched the thorns to even sharper points, and made us delirious with dehydration.

It took two hours to get across the field, by which time the monkeys were gone, and we were hopelessly lost. Our faces, arms and hands were covered in tiny slashes. Princess radioed that she and Charles had the monkeys at the top of Buena Vista. Charles was laughing in the background.

With an instinct that bordered on mystical, Princess had started flirting with Charles as soon as I stopped speaking to him. The whole day they had been acting like the best of friends. Obviously, she was going for a complete takeover, adding Charles to the list of boys who couldn't take their eyes off her. As far as I was concerned, this was violating the ceasefire. Just because Charles and I weren't speaking didn't mean he was fair game.

Even worse, while they were flirting, I started to realise how handsome Charles was. What I mistook for gangliness was actually his height; he had a way of looking down at you that made you feel cherished and protected. As he was talking to Princess, I noticed how sexy his smile was, how his eyes crinkled attractively at the corners.

If I had seen either of them at that moment, I would have torn them to pieces with my teeth.

When we arrived, Charles, Princess and Sarah were strolling after the monkeys as if they'd had them all afternoon. Everyone was joking around and laughing. I tried to join in, but my heart sank into my stomach. I fell behind.

There was a loud scream. Sarah smiled and typed it in.

'Do we care who did it?'

Princess put on her backpack.

'I'll go see.'

I stood up, anxious to get away.

'I'll come.'

We walked into the middle of a huge fight. The monkeys were fuzzy balls of fury dashing around the trees. One took off.

'I'll follow that one.'

I took out my video camera. This kind of violence was exactly what Diane wanted on tape. The monkey ran along the path. He climbed onto a low branch and looked back at me. He had a large chunk torn out of his lip and it was bleeding into his mouth. I could see his canine tooth shining behind the blood. I had no idea who he was. I took out my radio.

'Princess, who have you got? I have a male I don't recognise.'

'Hold on, I'm coming.'

The monkey in front of me was ferocious. I had never seen anything like him. He was built up around the shoulders and had a small waist like a bodyguard. He had two white spots on the black part of his head.

'Oh my god,' said Princess when she arrived. 'It's Sneezy!'

Sneezy was from the other monkey group, Snow White, who we hadn't seen since last vacation. He started to run. Determined not to lose him, we ran through the forest, skipping over logs and ducking under branches. I thought I was going to pass out when I saw another monkey.

'I wonder if it's from Snow White.'

I looked at the monkey. It was Murder. Sneezy twittered and sex squeaked at her. She duck faced and turned. I couldn't believe it. The alpha bitch of Sin was flirting with the beefcake intruder. It looked like they might even have sex.

'What the hell's going on?' I said to Princess. 'Why is Sneezy here and not back in Snow White?'

'I guess Sneezy is the new alpha male of Sin.'

It was to be a short-lived and tyrannous reign.

It began as an ordinary morning at Sin. The monkeys woke up below the Gravel Pit to the sound of Celeste puking, Carnage had sex with Assassin, while Murder screamed at them. Then, there was a far-off war cry, and Snow White ran in, ready for a coup.

Snow White was like the mob. They were aggressive, violent and looked like they were on steroids. Doc had been the alpha male as long as anyone could remember. A kind of Godfather gone senile, Doc was the father of most of the juveniles. His two henchmen, Happy and Bashful, flanked him at all times. His consort, Sleepy, was a crone at the height of her powers. She was a dark-eyed, cranky witch like Murder, but unlike Murder, who was the alpha of a dysfunctional, tormented group, Sleepy was the favourite concubine of one of the most powerful monkeys in Cielo Forest. It did nothing to sweeten her temperament.

In the old days when Hector was the alpha male, Sin could put up a decent fight. But with the group in turmoil, Sin had no solid leader that the group could fall behind.

The situation was further complicated because the new alpha male of Sin was Sneezy, who used to be a middle-ranking male in Snow White. Sneezy had left Snow White because, along with many of the young males, he was growing up. Like any teenage gangster, Sneezy wanted to have sex with females and terrorise a gang of his own. At the time Sneezy left Snow White, Sin was so weakened by the infighting between Carnage and Loss, the time had been ripe for Sneezy to take over.

When Snow White attacked, Sneezy looked from side to side, as if unsure of what to do. He ran to the front, piloerect like a hairy puffer fish, until he came face to face with Happy and Bashful. They all stopped and looked at each other. A few weeks ago they had all been wrestling and playing together. Now they were on opposite sides of a battlefield. Sneezy wheezed and sex grunted, in a pacification attempt. Happy and Bashful looked at each other, like two dumb bodyguards who had been ordered to kill an old member of the gang.

Suddenly Dopey approached. With slack-jawed imbecility and furtive eyes, Dopey was a coward. Back in Snow White, he had been Sneezy's best friend. Seeing Sneezy in charge of a new group with a cohort of fertile females gave Dopey an idea. He ran over to Sneezy, headflagging, and started threatening Happy and Bashful. Happy and Bashful looked at each other as if to say, 'What the hell does this punk think

he's doing?'

Sneezy also looked at Dopey, making up his mind. He could either accept the help and allow Dopey into Sin, or he could keep Sin and all the females to himself. He hesitated. Then his lips curled back to show his long incisor teeth and he lunged at Dopey. Dopey screamed and ran.

Like an idiot, I followed him.

Dopey kept running all the way down SQS, then straight up a steep mountain made of shale and mud. Dopey was scampering so fast from one tree to another, I had no time to look down. I slipped and slid on a slope that was almost vertical while he made like a vampire and vanished from one tree only to pop up in another tree ten metres ahead.

He was in a pathetic state by the time I got to him. I collapsed panting under the tree he was in, while he kneaded his tail like an old woman wringing her hands. Sneezy had just made the biggest mistake in his short career as an alpha male. By turning against Dopey, Sneezy had alienated an ally, one he would need later to maintain his position. But at the time, it wasn't much consolation to Dopey. He looked over the valley in the direction of Sneezy, his eyes limpid and tragic, trying to comprehend the betrayal of a friendship.

I felt much the same way. Charles and I had not spoken for a week, and I was starting to think maybe I should have sex with him just so things could go back to normal. Strangely, this idea was more appealing to me than before.

No one else noticed that Charles and I weren't speaking to each other. Sarah still asked Charles to help me with vocalisations and Billy asked us both out to the bar. The monkey house could smell two people sleeping together like sharks smell blood in water, but when a friendship dissolved, no one saw or cared. It was like friendship didn't matter. Only sex. Just like Sneezy was Dopey's best friend until he had a group full of females he wanted to screw. I sighed. The monkeys and I had more in common than I thought.

When Dopey finally disappeared, I was on the top of a ridge so high I could see where the forest turned into pasture. Sweaty and exhausted, I checked my watch. It was 7:03 a.m. Diane called me on the radio. She had lost Sin, and Charles and Sarah had followed Snow White.

'We have to find the monkeys,' she said.

Losing the monkeys was easy. You could lose monkeys in the briefest spatter of rain, during an interesting conversation or by leaving them ten minutes before dark.

Every time I stood on the edge of the forest on my own, I had what can only be called a crisis of faith. I stared down into a thick, tangled forest that plunged into darkness. Vines wrapped around tree trunks that disappeared into an underworld that would swallow me whole if I stepped inside. I felt like collapsing before I had even begun. There was no way I could find thirty tiny black bodies nestled among the infinity of leaves and shadows.

Gradually, I learnt that tracking monkeys is a religion. To find monkeys, you have to achieve a state of prayer. Even the beating of your heart must be hushed. You have to find silence between the deafening cries of the howler monkeys, the cacophony of birds, humming clouds of mosquitoes, coatis that squealed like pigs, and vultures that barked like dogs. You have to ignore a symphony of movement; dancing leaves, an occasional flash of a puma, the dumb-eyed canter of an agouti. Among more madness than a lunatic asylum, you must close your eyes and find subtle sounds of monkeys.

The best chance you have of finding monkeys is a lost call, which is a low mournful cry that monkeys make when they are separated from the group. It is the only monkey vocalisation that carries over long distances. If the monkey stays lost for long enough, you can track it down, then follow it back to the others. Of course the lost monkey could stay lost indefinitely, or it could be part of a different group, or it could simply disappear.

Then there are alarms. Monkeys alarm at anything that is a threat—birds of prey, snakes and terrestrial predators. These are short, sharp bursts, like cries of surprise. Monkeys can alarm for up to an hour, so if you hear them, you have a pretty good chance of finding them. The problem is, after alarming, the monkeys tend to vanish. So if you don't get there in time, you've probably lost them for good.

If you are close enough to the group, there is always a dependable amount of squabbling, bitching and backstabbing which manifests as an assorted range of screams, yelps and intense vocal threats.

The most common monkey vocalisation, but the hardest to depend on, is the twitter. A twitter is a friendly gesture or a signal to move on. Finding the monkeys on a twitter requires transcendental meditation. Almost every bird in the forest can sound like a monkey twittering and for this reason, you hardly ever find monkeys on a twitter unless they are right on top of your head.

But sometimes the monkeys are silent. Then it is like trying to find your way in the darkest night. You must listen for the particular shake of branches as the monkeys jump from tree to tree. There is a particular sound to it. A density you can hear, localised to a specific part of the tree. You become conditioned to it, like soldiers to gunfire. Your head snaps up, your eyes pull focus and scan the shivering leaves, searching for scampering limbs or a serpentine tail.

Of course if the wind blows so the branches shake across the whole forest, or if the rain falls so that everything sounds like a jumping monkey, or a hundred other variables, then, as my father used to say, you have a snowball's chance in hell.

But when at last you looked to the heavens and saw the flash of a black tail, or dark eyes peering at you through the leaves in idle contempt, it was like a prayer being answered. You could almost believe your own inner eye was winking impishly back at you.

I found Whisper on a lost call. A low-ranking female in the hierarchy, Whisper was constantly lost because no one in Sin really cared if she kept up. She had one surviving son, Wicked, who was a hyperactive ADHD juvenile with ears so big he looked like the monkey version of Dumbo the flying elephant. Wicked, however, was nowhere in sight and Whisper scampered through the low canopy, stopping every now and then to lost call and look pathetic.

I was proud I had found a monkey, and called Diane on the radio.

'I have the rest of the group down here at the bromeliads,' she said. 'Sarah is still with Snow White and Charles is on his way.'

A little bummed to have been out-monkeyed, I wandered to where Diane was waiting.

Bromeliads are spiky, cactus-like plants. In December they grow stalks with clusters of bulbous fruit that are bright yellow and orange and taste like unripe pineapple. But at the moment the plants were barren, the thick serrated leaves criss-crossed like swords, forbidding entry. The monkeys were lounging in a tree overhanging the bromeliads, tired after running from Snow White all morning. It was impossible to collect data.

'So,' Diane said conversationally, when I arrived. 'What happened at immigration?'

While Americans only had to leave the country every three months, Australians had to leave every month. Princess told me this before I arrived, so I had phoned the Costa Rican consulate in Sydney, then wrote back to Princess in a panic asking *her* to provide me with the documentation I needed to apply for a working visa from Australia. Princess told me not to worry, we would sort it out when I arrived.

Before I turned up at immigration in Liberia, the nearest large town, I had found the Costa Ricans to be warm and friendly. As soon as I walked into the hot, dusty immigration office that had chickens running around outside, it was as though the only bad-tempered, bitter people in the country were squashed into that little room.

'*Sí?*' said the dour-faced woman behind the counter after I had been dehydrating for an hour and a half.

I couldn't find anyone who could speak English and my abysmal Spanish did nothing to help the mood of the woman on whom my visa depended. After a game of charades, I was made to understand that if I did not want to leave the country every month, I had to apply for a working visa for a year. The paperwork was in Spanish, I needed a copy of my contract with the monkey project, certification from the Costa Rican Social Security Institution, the monkey project's legal constitution and registration documents, a copy of my degree which had to be translated into Spanish and authenticated by a Costa Rican Consul and the Ministry of Foreign Affairs, and a US$100 deposit. I also had to be fingerprinted in San Jose.

I told Diane about my immigration debacle. She laughed and said, 'Well, it's a pain, but you may just have to go to Nicaragua every month.'

I felt panic crawl up the back of my neck.

'I can't. I have to film.'

Diane's face hardened.

'Your filming isn't really a priority for us. We didn't know about it before you got here.'

'Neither did I! I only found out about the Disney contract three days before I left.'

'Well, it's still not our problem.'

Until now, Diane had been relaxed about my filming. Then again, I had not expected anything else. I did not think my filming was incompatible with being a field assistant. I was committed to the Disney segments but I planned to film most of them in the vacations. If I had to go Nicaragua every month, I would not have time to film anything. While I was prepared to give fourteen hours a day for 25 days a month, I was not prepared to sacrifice my filming career, which was what cancelling the Disney segments would have amounted to.

I looked at Diane, who was staring pointedly at the monkeys. Then I made a big mistake. I tackled the situation the way I would have while I was working in television. I put on my professional voice and started to negotiate.

'Diane, before I came here I asked Princess to provide documentation that would allow me to stay for a year without leaving, and she told me not to worry about it. Her decision should not have a detrimental impact on my leave. Or on my ability to conduct contract work outside my normal working hours. Can I have two extra days a month that I can use to cross the border of Nicaragua? Also, will the monkey project provide me with the costs of travel and immigration?'

Diane looked at me like I had just taken off all my clothes and run around singing 'Old MacDonald had a farm'.

'No,' she said slowly, 'I don't think that would be appropriate.'

We were silent. After a while she said, 'What do you want to film in Costa Rica that you need to go away for?'

'Volcano Arenal.'

'Well, Rincon de la Vieja is a volcano next to Vacas, on one of your days off you could go there.'

Rincon was a mass of bubbling mud pools. Disney wanted exploding pyroclastic lava, which could only be found at Arenal. And it still did not solve the problem of the other four segments.

'Diane, I really need to go away to film.'

'Well, that's not our problem,' she said again, an edge to her voice.

I saw Charles walking towards us. I felt besieged on all sides. I couldn't tackle them both at once. I had to make peace with someone. At that moment Diane's incredulity at my nerve was less intimidating than Charles's stony countenance. I thought quickly and said, 'What if Princess rostered my day off next to the vacation so I could leave the country every month?'

Diane nodded slowly. I could tell she was not trying to be difficult. She just wasn't accustomed to anyone having another agenda besides the monkeys. Besides, she had her hands full with Billy and did not want another problem assistant on her hands.

'That would be acceptable,' she said.

The monkeys left the bromeliad patch and went down SQS valley. Diane left to catch the monkeys on the other side, leaving Charles and I alone. We sat in silence. It began to drizzle.

Everything changes in the rain. The forest becomes a dream world, threatening and unfamiliar. You lose your sight. The monkeys' faces blur as the water falls in your eyes, and a gentle mist rolls over everything. The animals and birds become silent, and there is only the slight patter of rain on the leaves, which rises to a crescendo as the downpour sweeps over the canopy. The poncho you put on as protection restricts your movement and makes talking impossible. But your sense of smell is heightened, and as the rain soaks into the earth, the rich aroma of humus and damp wood rises. You become aware of your fingers as the drop in temperature makes them cold and stiff. After hundreds of scratches, lashes and bruises, the light touch of rain on your skin is as welcome as a caress.

As Charles and I took out our rain gear, I was glad we had an excuse to be silent. Covered in my bright blue poncho I sat on a branch, feeling like a poisonous mushroom. Charles was cloaked in a more appropriate green camouflage and he stared into the valley like a druid divining the future. I looked at him the way Dopey looked at Sneezy that morning. I wanted to tell him we were being stupid. I wanted to rip off his clothes and get it over with. I wanted to push him over the edge and watch his body go bouncing down the cliff with the crumbling rocks.

But he was untouchable. The rain ran over his face like it was marble and his eyes were pale as a statue's. Like an unforgiving curse, he stood there scanning the distance for the twisting black bodies of monkeys in the rain. And it was then, while the valley filled with mist, that I realised I loved him.

It was not a comfortable realisation. When I gave the feeling a name, I dug my nails into the branch. 'Don't be a bloody idiot,' I muttered. I closed my eyes, and felt hot moisture rim my eyes and fall with the rain onto my poncho. But the more it hurt, the more I realised it was true. I'd been so afraid and confused about what he felt, I'd never confronted my own feelings.

'Vanessa.' I kept my eyes closed, and waited for the tears to clear. I may be in love with the bastard, but I'd be damned if I'd let him see me cry.

'Vanessa!' His voice was like a slap. He obviously thought I had fallen asleep.

'What?' I was angry now.

'We've lost the monkeys.'

Like I give a shit, I thought. I stood up.

'Where do you want me to go?'

'You stay here, take Luehea [a brown, brittle fruit] and go to the Gravel Pit. I'll go down and take Orange Twist.'

I watched him run down the cliff, stones tumbling in the mud. He did not stop until the whole valley of mist was between us.

A week passed and nothing changed. The house thought Charles and I were friends. Charles thought we hated each other. I was in love with him. It was a mess.

If we were somewhere normal like an office, we would sit in our respective cubicles buffered by the hum of computers and the traffic of people in the corridor. The only time we would have to enter each other's keinosphere would be by the coffee machine. It would be a little awkward, but people cope with these situations all the time. Unrequited drunken

Christmas party confessions. Guilty averted eyes across the boardroom. But no matter how much you humiliated yourself, you could bow your head low over your computer, and at the end of the day, you got to go home.

In the monkey house, it was different. It was like being in a compression chamber. There was no escape. In the morning, Charles was one of the shadowy figures lurking in the kitchen. His hand plunged into the same snack bin I needed to get to. His tall frame obstructed the sink where I had to fill up my water. At each physical proximity I felt a wave of nausea, excitement and disgust. We were like two fish in a tank. No matter how much I wanted to, I couldn't hide forever in the little plastic log. Every morning we piled like sardines into the monkey mobile, barely a breath's space between us. Sometimes we accidentally sat next to each other and I had to feel the whole length of his warm body as we went hurtling down the highway. And when the working day was done, we went home to each other. Sat on the same porch unlacing our shoes. Ate at the same table. Then after dinner, there we were, back in the microcosmos of the kitchen.

There was no one I could talk to. I could not talk to Billy, since he was Charles's friend. Sarah was Charles's main field partner, so I could not really talk to her either. Andreas hardly existed without Ada and we had nothing in common. I was ignoring Kermit-and-Brad and they thought I was a bitch.

The truth was, besides Charles, everyone was a shadow. I knew their names and where they were from, but I didn't know the name of their best friend, the person that bullied them in high school, or the million other details that turn an acquaintance into a friend.

I started to realise why the last group were so damn good with the monkeys. They did not speak to each other. As I ran out of idle chit-chat with my human field partners, the only option to save me from going insane with boredom was to watch the monkeys. Really watch them. Watch them the way bored unhappy housewives watch soap operas. In the last five weeks I had learnt their faces. Now I learnt who they were. I became obsessive about every gesture, every nuance. As I looked beyond their scars and blood-red birthmarks, I saw signs of a dark and troubled group.

Like a Machiavellian drama, Hector, the benign king, had been overthrown by Carnage and Loss, who may have been his sons. Unable to agree on who was the new ruler, Carnage and Loss had nearly torn each other to pieces, so when Sneezy stormed in like a psychotic powder puff, there was no one strong enough to resist him.

Like all alpha males, Sneezy wanted to mate with all the females so they would provide him with offspring. The problem was, all the females were pregnant or had small babies. The first baby killed was Trouble, Torment's baby that he ripped from her back and tore in half on Kermit's first day. For the next month, Torment slunk around the outside of the group, her fur matted and lustreless. She had a gaunt look about her, like she was starving. Every now and then, she would lie down and close her eyes, as though she were too tired to go on.

The rest of the group were in shock over Trouble's death. Murder, the dark-eyed queen with a perfect crescent scar through her lips, was not used to living in fear. She was also heavily pregnant and knew the survival of her baby depended on keeping Sneezy at a distance. She rallied her closest ally, Assassin, also pregnant, and together they fought, screamed and threatened Sneezy in a desperate attempt to protect their unborn babies.

Sneezy had reason to be wary. The former alpha female of Sin, Pride, and her best friend, Lust, had overturned the alpha male, Greed. Greed was found alone with an inch-long slash on his left foot and one double the size on his left shoulder and puncture wounds inside his left arm. He moved by dragging himself up trees by his arms. No one saw exactly what happened but in the preceding weeks, Pride and Lust had stopped grooming Greed and started grooming Wrath. Not only that, they attacked Greed at every opportunity. After he was found injured, he was chased out of the group. When Greed tried to re-enter, he was chased off by the females and the new alpha male they had chosen, Wrath.

Only time would tell if Murder and Assassin could do the same thing.

The strong female bonds in Sin made me miss my own friends. I missed being around people who knew who I was. I was tired of seeing myself through new eyes. As I spent more time obsessing about the monkeys, I noticed I was becoming like the people in the old group: introverted and unhappy.

'This isn't me,' I wanted to tell Kermit-and-Brad, who were nervously avoiding me. 'I'm usually bright and bubbly.' I wanted to tell them about the flamingo-pink party dress I wore for Sydney's New Year's Eve party in 2001 when we danced till 7 a.m. and stripped down to our underwear and swam at Manly Beach. But they would not believe me capable of such light-hearted, flamboyant behaviour, anymore than I would have believed it of Tristan.

Being in love was making me miserable. I started to make overtures of peace to Charles. I tried to catch his eye several times a day. I asked him to pass me the salt at dinner. But nothing broke the blank stare he looked at me with.

Usually in this situation I would wait for a Saturday night, put on a lot of make-up, wear something tight and try to seduce him. But in the monkey house I couldn't exactly turn up to dinner in red lipstick and black leather. Even if I did, I wasn't sure Charles would fall for it.

It made me wonder if I had been mistaken all along. Maybe he never wanted me. Maybe, in my sweat drenched field clothes with insects crawling in my hair, he didn't find me the least bit attractive.

I stopped looking in the mirror with satisfaction and started scrutinising my face. If sex wasn't the issue, what would it take to make him like me again?

Maybe being pretty wasn't enough. Maybe, and I cringed at the thought, maybe I wasn't good enough for him. It occurred to me that I hadn't fallen in love with Charles for his looks. I had fallen for his warmth, his intelligence, his laughter. Maybe if you took my looks out of the picture, there wasn't enough of me left to fall in love with.

These were all sobering thoughts. Worse, I couldn't run away from them. There was no way to forget about Charles and move on to someone else who would give me the kind of validation I was looking for.

I stopped looking in the mirror altogether. Nothing I saw there gave me any comfort.

Eventually I decided I'd had enough. The moment came while I was watching Assassin and Murder. Murder was sprawled on her back, her head in Assassin's lap, eyes closed blissfully while Assassin carefully groomed behind her ears. I felt so lonely. I felt like dropping my head into Assassin's lap and asking her to groom me too.

Charles and I had not spoken for eleven days. I tried to remember what we were supposed to be fighting about. Something that started with him ignoring me, then me becoming furious because he wasn't paying attention to me, then me thinking he wanted to have sex with me but really he was just sick of my egocentricity.

I realised I had a choice. Charles was not in love with me. It was unclear whether he ever found me attractive. But he liked me once. He had to be feeling unhappy as well. I had to make the first move to talk to him.

Murder lifted up her arm and hung it around Assassin's neck. Assassin obligingly combed the hair in Murder's armpit with her deft fingers. Murder sighed.

I was excited and nervous on the way home. I decided to talk to Charles after dinner. I would go up to his room when everyone was getting ready for the next day and ask him to walk the dogs with me.

I waited, becoming more nervous by the second through dinner. Charles seemed relaxed, cheerful even. I began to doubt whether our stand-off was affecting him at all. Before everyone had finished, Charles and Billy stood up. Princess asked the question for me.

'Where are you going?'

'Out.'

They didn't ask anyone else to come. I felt a stab of disappointment, but our Vacas day was tomorrow. I'd just talk to him in the morning.

I couldn't sleep. I rehearsed my speech over and over. I would be contrite, but not grovelling. I would be sincere, but not desperate. The problem was choosing the time. I wanted to go up to his room at eight in the morning, before everyone else was up. He would be sleepy, so his defences would be down and he should be more receptive to an apology. Although it could go the other way. He could roll over and tell me to fuck off. I decided to chance it. The truth was, the suspense was killing me. I could not wait a minute longer than absolutely necessary.

When I finally nodded off, I did not sleep well. I heard the front door open at around 3:30 a.m. I considered jumping up and going to talk to him then, but Billy was with him and from the sloppy footsteps, I knew they were drunk.

The hours ticked by until, finally, 7 a.m. arrived. I had a knot in the pit of my stomach telling me it was suicide to wake up a hungover male, but I ignored it. I brought him a glass of water and some Berocca as a peace offering.

His door was closed. My heart beat so hard it was making me dizzy. I stood outside his room. Once I saw Whisper, the low-ranking female, looking at Sneezy from behind a tree branch. He was lying down and couldn't see her, and she stared at him, looking guilty and afraid. She wanted to approach him, but she didn't know what he would do. He might let her groom him, or he might scream and hit her. She froze for a long time, then she poked her head around the branch. Sneezy lifted up his head and stared at her. She moved forward a little, and he did nothing, only fixed her with his eyes and didn't move. After a few minutes, she turned and walked away.

I knew I should do the same thing. Turn around and walk quietly down the stairs. But then I grew angry at myself. I had to stop comparing myself to monkeys. I pushed open the door. It creaked a little. Before I went in, I peered around the door and saw Charles's ice-blue eyes open at the noise.

And then I saw a fan of long black hair on the pillow. The smooth curve of a shoulder, the swell of a breast. I stood at the door for a whole second that thumped out every microbeat of its existence against my collapsing heart. I stepped back, and closed the door.

There was an unwritten code of conduct that if you had to indulge in vices that were forbidden in the monkey house (drugs, gambling, sex), you took them far away from the white iron gates that kept out all evil, preferably to Nicaragua. Having sex was bad enough, having sex with outsiders was outrageous. The part of me that wasn't writhing in humiliation was tingling with a sense of sacrilege that Charles had actually brought someone back to the monkey house.

I went downstairs and stood in the middle of the kitchen. I had to do something. I could not go back to bed. Sleep was impossible. I wanted to sit on the kitchen floor and stare at the wall, while my brain processed what I had just seen. Instead I took out my laptop and set it up on the dining room table as a facade.

There were footsteps on the stairs. I started typing frantically. I heard the back door open, and a murmur of voices. The wet click of a kiss. Then Charles's footsteps back up the stairs.

I sat at my computer for two hours, staring at my screen saver. Damage control. What must he think? It must look so bad, me turning up to his room at an ungodly hour of the morning. He probably thought I was about to proposition him. My stomach turned over. Would he have said yes?

I took out my Spanish grammar book and started typing out various Spanish tenses of the verb 'to have'. There were fourteen different tenses, from did have, to should have, to would have, to could have. I conjugated various sentences. 'I *should not have* gone to his room. I *could have* avoided this. I *would have* thought twice if I were not such an idiot.'

An eternity later, Charles came downstairs. He looked hungover, exhausted and guilty. I remembered he had a girlfriend who was waiting for him in the States. Who had been waiting for a year. It couldn't feel good. I prepared to give him a reassuring smile but he walked straight past me without looking and went outside.

I looked at my computer, hurt at the rejection. But, I thought, enough is enough. I am going to sort this out today. I walked out after him purposefully. He was lying in the hammock, reading James Joyce's *Ulysses*. Or rather, he was just staring at the page. His eyes were not moving. He glanced up as I came outside and raised his eyebrows, giving me a look as if to say 'If you give me even a morsel of shit for what you saw up there, I will slam you into that there brick wall'.

I sat down on the little stool next to the hammock.

'I'm sorry,' I said.

His face froze. Then it crumbled. 'Oh my god, I'm sorry too.'

'You have been such an asshole.'

He laughed. 'You've been a total bitch.'

I fell into his arms and hugged him.

'It has been the most awful two weeks,' he said.

'Eleven days.'

Then I pulled back.

'What the FUCK was that girl up there?'

'Shit Vanessa, I don't know. I am in so much goddamn trouble.'

'I can't believe you brought a prostitute back to the monkey house.'

'She was not a hooker!'

'She looked like one.'

'She wasn't. Her family comes from here, but she lives in Pullman, in the States.'

The name rang a bell.

'Wait. Pullman—isn't that where Lisa lives?'

Charles was sheepish.

'She goes to the same university.'

I sat back on my haunches, dumbfounded.

'Wait. Let me get this straight. You slept with a girl who goes to the same university as your girlfriend . . . You IDIOT!'

'I know, I'm so dumb.'

'Charles, that's not just dumb—that's catatonically stupid. I can't believe you! I mean if you had to do it, if you REALLY had to do it, you could have shagged any one of the village girls, strippers, hookers or girls over fifteen in this village. But you have to pick the one who goes to the same university as your girlfriend. What were you? Homesick?'

He smiled at me.

'I've missed you.'

I hit him.

'I don't speak to you for eleven days, and look what happens.'

'I know. Don't ever do it again.'

I considered confessing that I loved him and that finding him in bed with another woman made me insanely jealous. I also wanted to ask why he stopped speaking to me in the first place. But I was so relieved we were talking again, I didn't want to risk damaging the fragile peace between us. So I said nothing, and put off the confession for another time.

Charles was leaving in three weeks, and I was glad we were friends. We hung out at Soda La Fuente, ate ice cream the colour of nuclear waste, and he told me the gossip of the last group. Apparently, Princess had left for Europe not only because of Tristan, but also because the rest of the house was on the verge of a mutiny. Everyone was angry with her because she would take days off to do accounts and other housekeeping.

'But she's been on this project for four years,' I said. 'Maybe she needed the time off.'

Charles shrugged.

'We didn't see it that way. We all worked so hard. And then she would roster Carlos off with her so he could do "home chores". It made us resentful.'

Charles told me the only person who defended her was Tristan. The rest of the group felt betrayed he was taking her side. Then came Andreas's relationship with Ada that split the house. Then Billy's laziness annoyed a few people, and Sarah just floated desperately around the edges.

It was quite a revelation to me that all this was going on. I had thought they were all so perfect in a way I could never be. But they had given up on belonging, and the monkeys were all they had in common. I didn't want to be that way. I resolved to be nicer to Brad and Kermit, and to try to get to know the shadows I lived with.

I told Charles my new resolution and he said he'd help me. We asked everyone to Las Tehas for drinks and to Soda La Fuente for papaya batidos. We hung around the table after dinner, laughing and telling monkey tales. Slowly I started feeling like I was part of a group although Charles fit in with the new people more easily than I did.

In the meantime, I was really getting to know the monkeys. I saw what people were talking about when they called Murder a bitch. She scowled at everyone, groomed no one, and frequently hit her daughter Mayhem. I envied her friendship with Assassin; no matter how bad things got with the males, Murder and Assassin were always together, grooming each other (or rather, Murder would half-heartedly pick at Assassin's fur and then demand Assassin groom her for half an hour).

They gave birth nearly at the same time. The tradition of the monkey house was that if you found the baby, you got to name it. Diane found Murder's baby and called it Mischief. Carlos found Assassin's baby and called it Arsenic.

The new monkey babies grew up fast. Within a few weeks they were playing together, and would obviously become friends when they grew older. They were like human children, fingering leaves with wonder, slapping berries and pulling each other's noses. Relatives would come and make machine-gun vocalisations, and the babies would affectionately sniff them and gargle.

After the initial euphoria of making up, Charles and I were still a little awkward. We hung out and chatted, but there was something missing. I thought a million times about telling him how I felt, but I couldn't do it. Not with the girl in his bed unexplained. Not until he told me why he stopped talking to me. There was so much that hadn't been said, and there never seemed to be a right time to talk about it.

Charles seemed distracted. I put it down to him going home in three weeks, and not being able to focus on what was here. I let it rest. He was going back to a girlfriend in the States. We were friends. Sometimes you just have to be happy with what you have.

chapter 7
The
rock

i knew it was going to be a bad day when I woke up at 1:30 a.m. with something crawling on my arm.

'Oh fuck off!' I growled, flicking it onto my sleeping bag. It made a rustling thud, the kind made by an insect of considerable size. I waited for it to scurry away. It didn't. I wiped my sleeping bag with my hand to try to get it off. There was a sharp stab on my wrist as a tiny amount of poison was injected into my skin. The poison reacted with my pain receptors which sent a chemical message to my sleepy brain, telling it that whatever was on my bed would not fuck off without a fight.

I bolted upright, wide awake. I flicked on the light. There, on my sleeping bag, was a black scorpion. I was too shocked to scream. I had seen scorpions in my room before, but none of them had actually touched me. I was flooded with visions coupled with scorpion mythology. Me writhing in pain for the next 24 hours. Me paralysed, unable to move my arm for a week. Me dead in an unmarked grave.

I leapt out of bed, grabbed my hiking boot and slammed it down on the bed. Cushioned by my mattress, the gesture was completely ineffectual. The scorpion reared up its tail. It was really pissed off.

I dragged my sleeping bag onto the floor, and slammed my boot on the scorpion like I was hammering a very stubborn nail into the floor. You would think that after six weeks in the jungle I would be used to killing large invertebrates. I wasn't. I hate killing bugs. Especially big ones whose gooey yellow guts seep out of their exoskeleton when you squash them.

The scorpion refused to die, almost. Even when its head and pincers were disembodied, its tail was still waving around, looking for me. Eventually I kicked it outside and closed the door.

I did not sleep much before my alarm went off at 3:30 a.m. Despite everything I had heard about scorpion stings, this was not a bad one. It felt no worse than a wasp, but the thought of the scorpion's internal organs all over my sleeping bag made my skin crawl. Also, at that hour of the morning, I was afraid it would come back like a bad horror movie, with two heads and an army, looking for revenge.

To this day I suspect the spirit of the dead scorpion played some part in tripping me over a log and tangling my hand in vines at 6:35 a.m. My other hand was carrying my machete, and as I fell, my one thought was to keep the machete away from my throat. I succeeded, but the problem was I had no hands to break my fall. I fell face first onto a rock, so hard that a kaleidoscope of colours exploded in my head. I watched a black shutter close over my eyes, then I passed out. When I woke, Sarah was beside me.

'I'm fine,' I said. 'I just tripped.'

'You are not fine, miss,' Sarah said, looking worried. 'We're getting you to the doctor's.'

'No really, I'll be fine. Just let me sit here. I'll be okay in a minute.' I put my sleeve to my head, trying to apply pressure to the pain. There was a high-pitched ringing in my ears. Sarah pulled me to my feet, and half dragged, half carried me out of the forest. I realised Billy was missing.

'Where's Billy?' I asked.

'He's gone to get the car.'

'How long was I out for?'

Billy's voice came over the radio.

'Calling Charles, Charles, Charles. We need the car.'

Shit, no, I thought. Not Charles, anybody but Charles. I didn't want the man I was in love with to see me with a big bump on my head looking stoned. I started to protest. Then I looked at the sleeve I had been holding to my head. It was drenched in blood. Maybe I did need to see a doctor. Charles's voice came over the radio.

'Hey Billy, what's up?' He sounded bored.

'Vanessa's hit her head. We need the car, right now.'

Great, I thought. I sound like such a baby. I hoped the injury looked serious enough so he didn't think I was doing this to get his attention.

'Where are you?'

'Crossing Lomas.'

'We'll be there in five.'

I stood on the side of the road, my arm to my head like a fainting damsel. The sight of the dirt-caked aubergine Toyota, with its nonexistent suspension, was strangely comforting. Charles drove up in the car with Billy and Manuel.

'Come here.'

I thought he could have bothered to get out of the car, but I did as I was told. He pulled my sleeve away from my head. To my surprise he turned on Billy, furious.

'You said she bumped her head! This is a major fucking laceration! For fuck's sake, Billy!'

'I didn't know!' Billy protested. 'I didn't see it, I just ran to get you.'

'Go with Sarah and find the monkeys.'

Charles spoke more tenderly to me than he had in weeks.

'Honey, what happened?'

I felt like a dog that had been hit by a car.

'I don't know. I just fell.'

'Get her into the car. She's in shock and probably has concussion. We need to get her to hospital.'

The Liberia hospital was more like a mechanic's garage. The waiting room was a kind of cement courtyard that had a roof and only two walls. The rest was exposed to the outside. There was construction work next door and as the fine white dust blew through the waiting room, I wondered how much of it ended up in people's surgery. Over the sound of the construction, a noise came from the emergency room that sounded suspiciously like a chainsaw. The chairs were the cheap plastic kind found in primary schools. I sat down with Charles while Manuel went to find a doctor. Charles turned to me as though he had been waiting for Manuel to leave.

'My god,' the words rushed out. 'When I saw your face and all the blood I wanted to kill someone if anything ever happened to you I'd never forgive myself not with all that's happened I didn't know how much I . . .'

He stopped, but his words hung in the air like the smell of rain. A thought wriggled into my head. Maybe it was the dull pain that was starting to work its way through the shock, but I suddenly thought perhaps all this time I had been wrong. Was it possible that his anger towards me, the cold silences, the girl I had found in his bed amounted to more than sexual frustration? His clear blue eyes were wet and I felt for the first time since Edward smashed my heart like a whiskey bottle that someone might love me. I wanted to drop to my knees at his feet. Instead, I held his hand and said, 'I don't know what I would do without you either'.

I wanted him to kiss me, but it was not the right time. I had blood caked on my face and through my hair, and one eye was swollen shut. My arm was starting to ache from being held to my head for more than an hour, and the blood had dried and the sleeve was stuck. I wondered how bad I really looked.

'I have to see it.'

He looked at me warily.

'I don't think that's a good idea.'

'I want to have a look,' I said stubbornly

'You can't, your shirt's stuck over the top.'

'Stop bossing me around.'

He smiled, worried. For a moment I wanted him to go with me, so if my face was an utter wreck he could tell me that looks weren't important.

I decided I had to do it on my own. I stood up resolutely and walked to the tiny bathroom at the end of the hall. I went inside the toilet cubicle and locked the door. I tried to pull down my arm but my sleeve was stuck to the dried blood on my forehead. Standing in front of the mirror, I wriggled my arm out of my sleeve and lifted up as much of the material as I could. And nearly vomited.

The gash ran the length of my eyebrow and was so deep that the weight of my brow sagged over my right eye. The eye itself was swollen shut. Beneath the blood and cut flesh was a glistening white. It was bone. I made a sobbing sound.

My skull was probably fractured. I could have brain damage. I could go blind.

When I went back to the waiting room, Charles was talking to a middle-aged woman with a pink polka-dotted dress. She pointed with her lips at me.

'*Que paso?*'

'*Cayo en una piedra,*' Charles said. She fell on a rock.

I felt like an idiot.

The woman started talking. My Spanish was not very good but it sounded like she was waiting for her mother who had been hit by a car two weeks ago. Her mother, who was 81, had been cycling into Canas to sell oranges when a car with surfboards on top had knocked her off her bicycle into a ditch. The fall had broken her shoulder, but she had gotten back on her bicycle and pedalled home, climbed into bed and lay there, getting up every few hours to put on compresses of tea, until her daughter found her. The bone had set so badly that the doctors would have to break the bones again and reset them. She was so old, the doctors were not sure whether the pain and shock would kill her. The woman spoke like she was talking about the market price of onions.

'What happened?' I asked Charles, unsure if I had heard right. He looked at me nervously.

'Pregnancy check up,' he replied. I didn't argue.

Manuel came back and sat behind me. His arm went around my neck and hung there like a boa. I pressed my chin on it and thanked god I wasn't sitting alone. As my Spanish was improving, Manuel and Angelina were becoming two of my favourite people. Charles took my hand.

'I don't think I can see,' I whispered.

'Of course you can honey, your eye's just swollen shut.'

'No it's different. Even beneath that, it feels strange. When it opens, I don't think I will be able to see.'

From the depths of the hospital came a low moan that turned into a scream. The scream went on and on, echoing down the halls and eerily emptying into the outside. Charles's hand squeezed mine. I was not reassured.

A male orderly appeared and pointed at me.

'*Venga.*' Come.

Charles and Manuel stood up. The orderly shook his head.

'*Sola.*' The feminine noun for alone.

I followed him into the emergency room. It was empty. There was another set of doors that were just swinging shut and I caught a glimpse of a stretcher being wheeled away down a corridor. There was one bed in the room which had what looked like a desk lamp hanging over it. Two orderlies were changing bloody sheets. I did not want to lie down on that bed. The orderly pointed at it. When I refused to move, he gently shoved me towards it. I lay down on the bed. My bloody sleeve was still stuck to my forehead. The orderly tugged at it, but it would not budge. He left and came back with a large woman with enormous breasts and a clipboard. She was obviously the ward matron. She looked at me the way butchers look at slabs of meat—cold, appraising and completely uninterested.

'Is there a doctor coming?' I asked.

The matron's nostrils flared.

'The doctor is in surgery,' she said, clearly implying that I was not a genuine emergency. 'He can't come.'

'Oh.'

The matron pulled at the bloody sleeve. When it did not come off, she ripped it off in one swift movement like she was waxing a bikini line. It felt like half my face went with it. I felt the blood pool into the wound and dribble down my temple. I started to cry.

Clearly impatient with gringas who had no more courage than children, the matron barked an order and a silver tray with gleaming implements was brought forward. I nearly asked if they had been properly sterilised, but I did not want to make her angry while she was holding sharp implements. She jabbed what looked like a horse needle into a jar and drained the contents. I am terrified of needles. I stopped crying and broke out into a sweat.

I saw the needle hovering above my eye before the matron jabbed it into my forehead. The anaesthetic stung like the scorpion as it flooded the infinite capillaries under my skin. When the anaesthetic had deadened the nerve endings, the matron split open the wound and shone the desk lamp over it. She peered inside and poked and prodded as though she were looking for a small creature that would not come out. She then threaded a needle, prodded the flesh again, and started stitching up the wound, much the same way my mother sewed up a Peking duck.

On the third stitch, I asked in my poor broken Spanish, 'Will I be very ugly after this?'

I was fishing for empathy from a fellow human being.

'Maybe,' the matron replied. 'Depends how it heals.'

The whole procedure took twelve minutes. The stitches were crude and perfunctory, the black thread looked like a bad Frankenstein joke, and the flesh was swollen and angry. I paid 11 000 colones, about A$40, for the whole operation, and stumbled out of the building, swearing never to set foot in it again. It was not until much later that I wished I had.

Everyone was disappointed in the innocuous piece of Elastoplast taped to my head. In the car on the way home, Billy told them I ripped half my face off, holding up his blood-stained shirt as evidence. When they saw me, they made sympathetic noises and gathered around, wanting to see blood and torn flesh. But I was not taking off my bandage for anyone. I could almost hear millions of invisible bacteria buzzing around the wound just waiting to infect it. The others' bloodthirsty attention was making me uncomfortable, so I told Charles I wanted to look at the Green Book.

Most medical books gave perfunctory advice, like how to splint a leg or treat a snake bite, but the treatment was usually just enough to get you to the hospital. The Green Book understood that sometimes there was no hospital. It was for trips to the Amazon, into the heart of darkest Africa, to places where you were more likely to be treated with a headless chicken than antibiotics.

Charles's room was the smallest room in the house, and was always dark and warm. His scent was in the sheets, the pillows, the clothes hanging in the cupboard. I sat on the bed and Charles pulled out the Green Book. Its hardback cover was the colour of mould. The pages were yellow and spotted with age. You could probably kill someone if you hit them with it hard enough. On the front it said 'Medical encyclopaedia for remote situations'.

Charles sat beside me on the bed. The book opened onto both our laps. Now we were alone, we knew something had changed between us. It was as though a festering splinter had finally been pulled out. We turned to the section on head injury, the Green Book just an excuse for his legs touching mine on the bed.

'"Head injuries often lead to concussion",' read Charles. '"Without x-ray, it is difficult to ascertain the extent of the damage. The patient may experience dizziness and faintness. The most crucial period is twenty-four hours after the injury where the patient may fall into a coma and die. To prevent this, the patient should be woken every ninety minutes to ensure they do not lose complete consciousness."'

'Great,' I said. 'Fall into a coma and die. Sounds fabulous.'

Charles put his arm around me.

'You won't die. But we should give you those concussion alarms. You could stay here . . .'

I shivered.

'I can't. Everyone will think I faked a head injury so we could have sex.'

He laughed.

'I love the way you always think the best of people.'

'The hospital didn't give me any antibiotics. I wonder if I should get some.'

Charles frowned.

'If they didn't give you any, I'm sure you don't need them. Besides, the over-prescription of antibiotics in developing countries has led to a lot of resistance in bacterial strains. I think it's best not to encourage it.'

I didn't really understand what developing countries had to do with my head wound, but I let it rest. We had another blissful 30 seconds with his arm around my shoulder and his leg touching mine before Kermit hollered dinner was ready.

It was decided Sarah should give me concussion alarms. I felt guilty she had to wake up every 90 minutes to check I was still alive. But I didn't want to lose consciousness and die either.

I settled into bed. The pain was only a dim awareness thanks to some industrial-strength painkillers I bought over the counter in Liberia for twenty cents each. Before long, I was sleeping.

The alarm woke me at 11:30 p.m. On the other side of the room Sarah was snoring. The alarm screeched out its shrill existence, and still she slept. I lay in bed, wondering what to do. I told myself I shouldn't wake up Sarah and tell her she missed my alarm. People were so exhausted, it wasn't fair to take away what little sleep they had. I could go back to sleep and forget about it, but I was suddenly fretful. How do people with concussion feel? I lay in bed for another 30 minutes before I crept upstairs.

Charles sat up as soon as I opened the door.

'What's wrong?'

'Sarah forgot to give me my concussion alarms. I could die.'

He moved over.

'You can sleep here. I'll wake up.'

I paused on the threshold. It was like chasing the monkeys on Orange Twist trail in the rain; the slope only went one way—down and fast.

It smelled earthy and warm in his bed. He put his arm around me and I curled into him.

'I was so scared when I saw you today,' he whispered. 'I was sure it was all my fault.'

With his arm wrapped around me, and his lips pressed into my neck, we crossed into territory as beautiful and frightening as the jungle we crawled through from morning to night.

We kissed like animals, angry and afraid, until we slept.

At 4 a.m., Charles smoothed the hair from my face, kissed my forehead and got out of bed. I returned the kiss guiltily, then rolled over and went back to sleep.

I woke at 10 a.m. to a woman crying. I wrapped myself in my sarong and followed the sound down the corridor to Manuel's room.

'Hello?'

A blown nose and a hurried sniffle.

'*Si?*'

I opened the door. Angelina was sitting on the edge of the bed, her eyes red and swollen.

'*Angelina, que paso?*'

With many pauses and repetitions, I finally had the whole story. Manuel was not Linda's father. When Angelina was sixteen, she fell in love with and pregnant to a man in Vacas. He beat her. This was not considered a spectacular crime, and many expected Angelina to stay and accept the hand life dealt her. But she left him, and met Manuel, a kinder man who loved Linda like she was his own. Angelina's ex-husband still lived in Vacas but ignored both his child and his ex-wife. He didn't pay any child support and the law in Costa Rica didn't oblige him to.

Angelina worked at a factory on a production line. Manuel helped support her. Manuel had just accepted a new job in Panama where he would set up a new field site. Angelina saw the chance for a fresh start. They would have their own house on the field site, more money and hired help for the cooking and cleaning. Angelina was desperate to leave Vacas. She had lived forever in the one tiny town. Women gossiped about her and nearly everyone disapproved of her leaving her ex-husband.

But under Costa Rican law, a child must have the father's permission to leave the country. Linda's father refused to let her go.

'But why?'

'He is a bad man. He wants money.'

'How much?'

'I don't know. Too much.'

The law was on the side of the father. Angelina must either stay behind, or leave her daughter with her family. I realised how spoilt I was. I took for granted crossing and recrossing borders like they were bus stops, my Australian passport a magic key to every door I wanted to open.

In the country I came from, Angelina could have been anything she wanted. She was bright, beautiful and hardworking. She would have had child support from the government and from her ex-husband.

I gave Angelina a hug. I couldn't help but care for her. She was beautiful, with her waist-length black hair and almond-shaped eyes, but I never felt competition or distrust from her like I did with other girls. She treated me as though we were part of a sisterhood and should help each other. When I was with her I could pretend to be a better person than I was.

'Ay, Banessa,' she said sadly. *'La vida es la vida.'*

I met Manuel downstairs. Ever since the hospital he was acting like I was his little sister who couldn't keep out of trouble. He ruffled my hair in the morning and held my head between his hands so he could scrutinise my bandage. Every time I left the room he said,

'Cuidado de rocas.' Careful of rocks.

He wasn't joking now. He looked tired.

'Banessa. Como paso tu cabeza?'

'My head's fine, but Angelina's really upset.'

He shook his head.

'I know.'

'Can you talk to him?'

'I don't know. I'm going to try.'

That afternoon Manuel sat with Linda at the table. A book with a page full of angry scribbles was between them.

'I don't want to do my homework. I want to play football.'

'You can play when you've finished. You're still behind. If you don't do well in school, you will end up as nothing. Banessa,' he said seeing me, 'tell her she has to study.'

'Can I help?'

Manuel threw down the pen.

'You see if you can make her. She is stubborn.'

Linda looked at me with her huge brown eyes.

'What's the homework?'

'Learning words.'

'Well, if we do your homework, maybe later we can get some ice cream.'

She straightened her back and tilted her head like a flower towards the sun.

'Papa?'

'If you can make her work, she can have what she wants.'

An hour later, the homework was done and she was happily licking her chocolate cone.

'Come to my grandmother's and see my puppy!'

Angelina's mother lived at the edge of Vacas. A river full of tin cans and plastic bags flowed beside the broken dirt road that led to their house. Behind the house was a large grassy field and then the Pan-American Highway. The house was not painted and chickens ran around the front yard. Standing at the door was a large woman who was wiping her hands on her apron.

'Chiquita!'

Linda ran towards her.

'Abuela, where's my puppy?'

The woman smiled a great beaming smile.

'Out the back, precious. But who is this?'

'My friend. A monkey person.'

The woman took my hand and held it in her own. Her hands were warm and dry, like tissue paper.

'You must call me mama.'

Mama led me inside and gave me the seat of honour, a lounge chair wrapped in a pink cloth. The house was carefully decorated, everything arranged and polished with great pride. Angelina's father turned off the television, and Angelina's sisters, Sofia and Rosa, came inside. They were a handsome family. I wished for the millionth time I had paid more attention in Spanish lessons as we began a stilted, formal conversation. Linda ran in with one puppy under each arm.

'Mine,' she said, dumping one in my lap.

I stayed all afternoon. It was the first time since I arrived in Vacas that I had felt so welcome.

'Ah Australia! Where kangaroos are from.'

Angelina's family, like all of Vacas, had cable television and plied me with questions about kangaroos they saw on the Discovery Channel.

'How far can they jump?'

'Do you have one in your house?'

'Can you ride them like horses?'

Rosa was studying at San Jose University and the family watched proudly as she and I had a conversation in English. She wanted to work in America, but like all Costa Ricans, found it hard to get a visa. So she studied hard hoping if she could talk like an American, they would accept her as one of their own.

It was late in the afternoon when I said goodbye. Everyone gave me a hug and made me promise to visit soon. I said I would return in a few days to help Rosa with her English paper.

I thought about how much happier I'd be if I could live with Angelina's family, instead of at the monkey house. It was the kind of family I'd always wanted. A father sitting regal and bemused at the chatter of women around him. A mother who could stay at home, cooking fajitas and fussing over her family instead of working twelve hours a day and coming home just alive enough to put rice and chicken wings on the table. The giggles of sisters who had never been separated.

I loved sitting in the pink chair, smelling the black beans cooking in the kitchen. I loved listening to their gossip. How the Nicaraguans kept sneaking over the border because Costa Rica was the most prosperous country in Central America. How the Guatemalans were trafficking in babies. It was so different to the monkey house where all that mattered was hierarchy and monkeys.

For the next year, I'd visit Angelina's family whenever I could. I would never take anyone from the monkey house. For some reason I felt Angelina's family were special to me and I didn't want to share them.

In the late afternoon I took Linda to the playing field, a cleared patch of dirt where some boys were running ragged. As soon as she saw them, Linda took off, never once looking behind her. Linda ran faster than all the boys, the ball weaving between her feet and her long legs flashing fire as the sun set behind her.

It was a week until vacation. Charles and I were inseparable. We didn't talk about what had happened in his bed, and it didn't happen again. But that night wrapped itself around us like an invisibility cloak; we huddled together beneath it and shut the world out.

After weeks of ignoring our crumbling friendship, the whole house suddenly wanted to know if we were sleeping together.

'So,' Sarah asked me slyly, 'are you and Charles, like . . .'

I knew I had to nip it in the bud.

'No.'

'But it's coming, right?'

'No!'

'Then where were you the other night? I woke up to give you your concussion alarms, and after looking all over the backyard because I thought you crawled under a bush and died, I find you in Charles's room.'

'Sarah, you slept through my concussion alarms. I had to be with someone who was going to actually wake up. Nothing happened, leave it alone.'

But it was impossible. People in the monkey house were obsessed with sexual relations. We couldn't help it. We spent all day watching monkeys go up and down the hierarchy because of who they had sex with. Sleeping with a high-ranking individual raised their position in the hierarchy, and subsequently demoted someone else.

Rank in the house went according to time served. Besides Princess and the Ticos, Charles had been there the longest and was therefore one of the highest ranking. I was already protected by him through friendship, but if we were sleeping together, my position would be even more solid. Everyone was desperate to find out if this was the case.

In some ways, it would have been advantageous for me to admit it. I could have overtaken Billy, Sarah and Andreas and nestled snugly just beneath Charles. But the shadow of Lisa hovered over us. I felt sick every time I thought of her, waiting for Charles to come home. He was never really going to be mine, and everyone knew it. Also, he was leaving in three weeks, and once he was gone, I would be at everyone's mercy.

So like guilty celebrities, Charles and I refused to comment. When Charles went out with Billy, Kermit and Brad, they plied him with alcohol and subjected him to a rigorous inquisition.

It was hard for Charles, especially since Billy was his best friend and Charles felt he was betraying him by lying. But if Charles told Billy, he effectively told everyone; Billy couldn't exactly keep his mouth shut.

So we drew our limbs in tightly under our cloak, holding our breaths if anyone approached and closing our eyes against their curious, ravenous stares.

Playa Hermosa was an hour's bus ride from Vacas. I had not gone into the forest since I hurt my head. The stitches were healing well, but there was a dull pain behind them, and I wanted to wait until it passed before I went crashing through the undergrowth. But the thought of another day staring at the walls made me shriek with boredom. When Charles suggested we go to the beach, I nearly smothered him with gratitude.

The sand was dirty and the water was tepid, but a beach was a beach. I tore off my clothes and ran into the water. Sandstone cliffs rose on either side of the bay, covered with long spindly trees. Before the monkey project I might have wondered if it would be pleasant to walk through the forest on top of those cliffs. Perhaps it would be cool and shady, with a light breeze fanning the leaves. But now I knew better. It was dense, sweltering and full of bugs. I splashed happily in the water, grateful to be looking at the forest from a distance instead of from within its bowels.

Charles smiled as he followed me into the water. I could almost believe we were two ordinary people, falling in love.

'Why don't monkeys like the beach?' I said dreamily.

'We could stun them with a cattle prod and haul their asses down here. They'd love it after a while. Murder tanning, in

ten metres of Assassin, sipping a margarita.'

I giggled. He put his hands under my back and held me as I floated. I was on another planet, viscous and weightless, without pain or exhaustion, just the water soothing my skin and gently pulling my hair. I wanted so much more than those few hours. But the shadows grew longer and soon it was time to go home. Back to the dirty, smelly monkey house with its layer of grime and stench of human sweat.

Charles held my hand as we walked to the bus stop, a patch of dirt marked by a white stick. A gnawing feeling started in my gut.

'Charles,' I started. He looked sombre. 'We can't, you know, keep . . .'

I didn't know how to say it. I couldn't say 'having sex', because we hadn't quite, and I didn't want to say 'making out', because it sounded so high school. I waited for him to pick up the thread. He didn't.

'We can't keep messing around like this.'

Perfect, I thought. Very eloquent. Not.

'I mean, there's still Lisa. You're going back to the States soon and moving in with her. It's not right we should be . . . I mean, getting drunk and sleeping with a hooker . . .'

'She was NOT a hooker!'

'Whatever. Sleeping with her was one thing. What we're doing is premeditated. It has to stop.'

He looked at the dirt. The bus came. The sun flitted on our faces as we rushed away from the only place we'd been happy together. I was suddenly afraid I had offended him. Then he said, 'I wonder what kind of person I would be, after a year with you.'

'Traumatised.'

He laughed.

'Probably. But with more direction, I think.'

As Vacas loomed closer, I knew I had one chance to say what had been plaguing me late at night.

'Charles,' I said in a small voice. 'Why did you stop liking me?'

He looked me straight in the eyes.

'I never stopped liking you, Vanessa.'

'You did so. You and Tristan.'

Charles snorted.

'Tristan didn't know how to handle you.'

I stared hard at him. Was that jealousy I detected?

'But you and I were friends, then all of a sudden you couldn't look at me. What did I do?'

'You didn't do anything. You're just so ... *Australian.*'

'What's that supposed to mean?'

'You don't need anyone. You turn up with your camera and your Disney contract and none of us knew what to do with you. You just expect everyone to adore you. It was easy to feel my adoration didn't matter.'

I frowned. We were standing on the bus, holding the rails above our head. Charles was facing me, and his hands were almost touching mine. I didn't get it. What did being Australian have to do with him ignoring me? The last month had been very confusing. Charles and I were friends, then we were fighting. Then I thought he wanted to have sex with me. Then he had sex with someone else. Where were we now? Did he want to have sex with me or not? I was suddenly very tired.

'Why can't I fit in here?'

He put his arm around my shoulder.

'You will.'

I put my head against his chest and felt his heart beat in time with the bumps in the road.

'My head hurts.'

'It'll get better. Everything will be fine, you'll see.'

My head only got worse. I started taking painkillers so strong that I was unconscious for most of the day. But beneath the protective shield, the pain was there, like a beast with one eye open.

Sometimes it gnawed the inside of my skull in the middle of the night, pulling me moaning from sleep. If I slept until morning, it crept on me as my eyes opened, gnashing its fangs and growling.

I became nervous, knowing that all that separated me from unbearable agony were the little white pills by my bedside. The thought of someone touching my stitches made me shrivel. So I locked myself in my room and spent most of the day in bed, the rank smell of antiseptic curling into every crevice.

The problem was the more it hurt, the better it looked. The stitches were healing well and the flesh wasn't inflamed. On the first day, a lump the size of a cherry tomato slowly moved from my forehead to my eye. My eye swelled shut for a few days, the tomato sitting on my eyelid like a bump in a cartoon. Then it dissolved, and the pain started.

I suspected a fracture. The rock I fell on had a sharp point. It was possible slivers of bone were floating around behind my eye. The hospital didn't take x-rays. My cranium could be in pieces and how would anyone know?

Vacation was in three days and my friend Sean was flying from Australia to see me. I couldn't run around Costa Rica with a cracked skull. I might have to tell him not to come, and the thought hurt worse than my head.

In desperation, I went to the pizza house next door. Diane opened the door.

'Vanessa, what's wrong?'

'I think I have brain damage,' I blurted out. 'Are there neurologists in Costa Rica?'

'Oh,' Diane looked flustered. 'You know, there's a private clinic in Liberia. The one we always go to isn't there anymore, but we have the number for another one. Let me get it for you. They're trained doctors, and at least they can recommend places in San Jose if you need them.'

St Augusta clinic was a pretty house in the side streets of Liberia. Diane asked if I wanted her to come, but I was too embarrassed at practically bursting into tears on her doorstep.

The receptionist wore a veil, like the novice nuns in *The Sound of Music*. The guard in the lobby had a gun. There was no one else in the waiting room. After half an hour, I was shown in to the doctor's office.

The doctor had twinkling eyes and a voice I trusted. Unfortunately, he spoke almost no English.

'*Que paso?*'

'*Cayo un piedra, y mi cabeza dolor,*' I said, which roughly translates to 'I fall a rock and my head to hurt'.

He nodded and came closer to examine my head. I jumped out of my chair.

'No thank you,' I said. 'Please don't touch.'

He smiled.

'I have to see why it's hurting.'

I shut my eyes and started to sweat. He pressed the flesh around the stitches. The agony was unbearable. I started whimpering. After an eternity of excruciating poking and prodding while tears leaked from my eyes, he nodded as though his worst suspicions had been confirmed.

'You have pooss,' he said.

'Pardon?'

'Pooss. Like yellow cream in your head.'

'Pus?'

'Yes, pooss. You need to lie down on the bed.'

I remembered what happened the last time I lay down on a bed, in the Liberian hospital. For a moment, we were at an impasse. Me, shaking my head emphatically, and he, sitting calmly in his chair, waiting. Eventually he won.

I lay down and gripped the sides of the bed, stiffening like a corpse. The doctor pulled out a scalpel.

'Wait, what are you doing with that?'

'*Tranquilate.* I have to cut one of your stitches.'

It was all very well him telling me to be tranquil while the scalpel was heading straight for my head. I closed my eyes. My brain was flooded with images from a film by Salvador Dali where a girl gets a scalpel slit right across her eye. I felt sick.

The doctor loomed over me. I shut my eyes, and felt the cool tip press into my forehead. I thought for a moment he was going to slice the wound open, but I felt sharp pulling, then a snap as he cut one of the threads. He cut another one.

He put down the scalpel and I breathed a little easier. He took out a syringe big enough to inject an elephant. Instead of a steel needle at the end, it had a thin plastic tube. He pushed the thin end of the syringe into my head, ignoring my screams, and pulled on the plunger for what seemed a long time.

'Look,' he said.

Stupidly, I looked. The syringe was full of yellow gelatinous pus threaded with blood.

'Ew! Get it away!'

He chuckled and squirted the syringe into a bucket. Because the hospital had not prescribed me antibiotics, he explained, the wound had become infected and formed an abscess. The pain in my head was caused by the increasing amount of pus pushing against my skull.

I was no longer frightened. I was furious. I gripped the edge of the bed tighter.

'Get it out. I want all of it out.'

He filled the syringe twice more, each time squirting the contents into the bucket. He smoothed the sweaty hair from my forehead. His swarthy hands felt dry and cool, and I had a momentary respite. Then he put his thumbs on either side of the cut. And squeezed. The pain was indescribable. The thought of a leaf brushing against my head was enough to make me cringe, and here was the doctor, squeezing so hard his hands shook. I ground my teeth and shut my eyes so tightly that white spots danced on my eyelids.

After enough torture to envelop a lifetime, the doctor wiped a cotton swab across my forehead.

'Look,' he said again.

'No way.'

He chuckled. He seemed to find the situation amusing. Maybe Costa Ricans were fascinated by the sight of a milk carton of pus coming out of someone's head, or maybe he was proud of the sheer amount he managed to extract. I felt like vomiting.

'Are we done yet?'

He threw the cotton swab into the bin. It made a smacking sound as the wet pus landed against the plastic.

'Not yet.'

He took out another syringe. But this was not a plastic one. It had a long, evil metal spike at the end.

'What's that for?'

'Antibiotics.'

I broke into my needle sweat. My eyes rolled like a panicking horse.

'Can't I just have some pills?'

'You're very infected. You need the medicine straight into your bloodstream.'

The longer I looked at it, the harder it was to let him stick it in me. I held my breath and rolled over, pulling up my skirt ungraciously. I felt every nanometre of the needle slide into the fleshy part of my bottom. The liquid hurt even more, and I clenched the bed sheets, sick and tired of all the pain.

Finally it was over.

'Be careful of rocks,' he said, patting my shoulder. 'Come back and see me if you need to.'

'Not if I can help it,' I muttered as I walked out, carrying two syringes with potent straight-to-the-blood antibiotics with me.

'Right,' I said at dinner. 'Who wants to inject my bottom?'

Everyone looked at me like I had finally gone crazy. I told them about the abscess, relishing their faces as they went pale over the details.

'The antibiotics have to be injected into my ass. But they're motherfucking long needles, so whoever does it has to know what they're doing. Who's injected before?'

Injecting a needle was like stabbing an orange. It has to be done fast and fearlessly. But these needles were so long, they would either bend or come out the other side. It was going to need a certain finesse.

'Hell,' said Kermit. 'I'll have a go.'

'Have you injected anything before?'

There was a pause.

'No.'

'I've injected marine mammals,' Sarah volunteered.

'I'm not a whale.'

'I worked at a vet clinic,' said Charles. 'I've injected dogs and cats.'

I sighed.

'Hasn't anyone injected a human?'

Silence.

'Shit. Okay, Charles, you can do it. I'm more closely related to a dog than a sea cow.'

I caught a few knowing glances across the table. Like having Charles stick a needle in my ass was a metaphor for something else. I looked at him.

'You'd better know what you're doing.'

'Don't worry, darlin'. You're in good hands.'

It turned out Charles was the worst needle injector of all time. He blunted the end by stabbing it through the metal cap of the antibiotics.

'My god you have a hot ass.'

'Can you keep your mind on the job please?'

I didn't make a sound when the blunt end of the needle stabbed into my bottom and Charles pushed the length of the needle through. Nor when he slowly pushed down the plunger and the antibiotics flooded my capillaries like liquid cement. He pulled out the needle, and wiped it in a satisfied manner on his jeans.

'There now, that didn't hurt did it?'

I sat up and started hitting him.

'You asshole! That fucking killed! This is all your fault. You're fired. Tomorrow I'm going to a professional.'

For the next two days, I was brimming with blissful happiness because there was no fracture in my head. I emailed my friend Sean and told him not to worry, my head was fine, and we could run recklessly around the whole country.

I had the doctor in Vacas take out my stitches and inject my last needle with much more skill than Charles. The wound looked good. I would have a scar, but it was nowhere near as bad as when I limped into the Liberia hospital.

Everyone else was equally happy. Diane was leaving, and we looked forward to more relaxed data collection and afternoon naps. Kermit and Brad were going to San Jose, and Andreas was going to Nicaragua. Princess and Carlos were staying in Vacas to mind the house. Billy especially was ecstatic. With Diane gone, his days from hell were over, and he would be free to take siestas and go to Santa Cruz with his girlfriend Bianca. All in all, a perfect end to the month.

On the last day before vacation, I helped Linda with her homework and went to visit her puppies at Mama's. Angelina was there. When she saw me, she jumped up and gave me a big hug.

'He's letting her go!' she said, laughing. 'Linda's father signed the papers. We're going to Panama with Manuel on Saturday.'

We squealed and jumped up and down.

'I'll miss you,' I said as we hugged. I was happy for her but I couldn't help feeling worried that two of my allies were leaving. The house wouldn't be the same without Linda tearing into my room demanding I play with her, or Angelina floating in and out like a fairy. And I would miss Manuel shaking his head at the monkeys and saying, 'Fuckers'.

'You must keep visiting Mama,' she said. 'She loves having you around.'

'I will,' I promised. 'And you have to come back and visit.'

'Claro, Banessa. *Estamos amigas, verdad?'* Of course. We're friends, right?

Sean and I missed each other at the airport and it took seven hours for us to be reunited in the dingy Hotel Alejuela in San Jose. I first met Sean two years earlier at a party in Sydney while I was dating Edward. Sean is one of those guys who are so well groomed and good looking you assume they're gay but they're not. I was wearing a glittering red dress and Sean was the only other person in the room not snorting coke off the kitchen benches. We hit it off right away and have been friends ever since.

'Hey babe!' Sean said as I stumbled through the door, panicking, tear stained and exhausted. He was chatting to the hotel desk clerk, smoking a cigarette and drinking Jim Bean.

'How's my jungle girl?'

At that moment, I was just me, shaking and crying in Sean's arms.

'Hey, sweetie, it's okay. I'm here now. I knew we'd find each other.'

I didn't tell him I wasn't exactly crying over him. I was just so relieved to find someone who was familiar, in a way no one else had been since I arrived.

I sat down in the chair next to him.

'Here you go darling,' he said. 'Have a cigarette.'

We chain-smoked the pack, drank whiskey and did not stop talking until two in the morning.

'Wow,' he said. 'I can just tell, this is going to be the best vacation ever.'

Volcano Arenal is the most active volcano in Costa Rica. Only 3000 years old, it's a young volcano, geologically speaking. Its claim to fame was the 1968 explosion which literally blew off the west side of the volcano, destroying two villages and killing 78 people.

Sean and I pulled up to the lodge late at night. Staying anywhere below four star was never an option for Sean. He might get fleas from backpackers on his Prada sweaters. I felt like trailer trash beside him, despite his assurances that I looked as pretty as ever.

I woke up at around 7 a.m. from the deepest sleep. After months of sleeping on a piece of foam on the floor, I could have rolled around in that king-sized bed for a week. But I had not forgotten my purpose. The main reason we were here was so I could film my Disney segment on volcanoes. All the postcards in the lobby showed masses of exploding lava, and I couldn't wait to get it all on camera. I leapt out of bed. But when I looked out the window, something was wrong.

'Where the fuck is the volcano?'

Sean groaned and opened his eyes.

'What?'

'The volcano. Where is it?'

Outside was a thick blanket of mist. I couldn't see beyond the balcony.

'It'll turn up. Go back to bed until the mist evaporates.'

I went back to bed and slept until 10 a.m. Still no volcano.

At breakfast I asked one of the staff, 'Excuse me, when does the volcano show up?'

He shook his head.

'Senorita, it is the wet season. The volcano is cloudy.'

'Motherfucker.'

If I had done my research, I would have known that the best time to see the volcano was during the dry season, in December. It was July. Another example of my absolute inability to think ahead.

We sat for two days in the outdoor jacuzzi, waiting for the volcano to appear. Sean was as happy as a fish in water, splashing around, cigarette in one hand, beer in the other. At night we could see the faint glow of lava rolling down the sides. But nothing bright enough for my camera to pick up. We drove all the way up to the scattered lava fields where the black rocks tumbled down on all sides. We sat and drank beer, ate peanuts, and listened to the rumblings of the massive volcano, which sounded like a plane flying overhead. It shuddered and trembled, puffs of smoke billowing from the top like a dragon's breath. It was impressive, but no Disney segment.

On the third day I called Charles.

'There's no goddamn volcano here. I'm totally screwed. We're coming to pick you up tomorrow, then we're going to the beach.'

Jaco was a dirty, seedy tourist town that looked like a run-down version of the Gold Coast. It was one long street of hotels, bars and strip joints. But guided by Sean's nose for luxury, in half an hour we were lounging by a turquoise pool in a whitewashed Mediterranean-style hotel.

That night, we went to a bar and got smashed on B-52s. I was so drunk, Sean and Charles had to carry me back to the hotel. I woke around midnight with Charles's mouth on mine and his hands undressing me.

We didn't speak. There had been so many useless words between us and they didn't mean anything in the end.

After the sex I wrapped myself around him and he put his lips to my ear and whispered over and over again, 'I love you.'

It seemed those words rolled off whitewashed waves, carrying me across the sea to safety.

Sean left and Charles had two weeks to go. I still had nine months left to spend, day in day out, with the monkeys. We started the long drive back to Vacas.

As we sat at a roadside diner eating *gallo pinto*, a mixture of chicken, black beans and rice, he said suddenly, 'You know, I don't have to go back.'

I snapped out of my reverie.

'Huh?'

'I meant what I said. I love you. I'm sure Diane would let me stay. It's cheaper than training a new person.'

'What about Lisa?'

He sighed.

'I have to go back and tell her myself. But I can be back here by August.'

I was quiet as we walked back to the car. This changed everything. A relationship in the monkey house wasn't easy. I thought of Carlos and Princess, how they never had any time together. How every angry and loving word was overheard by someone else. But I had found someone I loved, who said they loved me. It was worth taking a chance on.

'Okay,' I said. 'If you're sure.'

He stopped the car and kissed me, until the bright lights of a truck pulled up behind us and startled us into putting our clothes back on.

The monkey house gate loomed in front of us. Even in the darkness I could see the rust corroding the white metal paint, the long metal spikes threatening to impale any who tried to climb over.

Charles squeezed my hand before we went inside. We decided not to tell anyone of our plans. I breathed deeply, and hoped no one would make any snide comments about Charles and I going on vacation together.

As soon as we opened the door I had a quick glimpse of Princess before she shut herself in her room. Billy was in tears.

'Billy, what's wrong?'

'I've just been fired.'

'What?!'

We followed him into his room. On his bed was a large yellow envelope. Charles picked it up and looked through its contents, then handed it to me.

'Goddamn.'

Inside was a letter from Diane telling Billy he had not fulfilled his requirements as a field assistant and he was to leave the house by midnight.

We were dumb with shock.

'Princess just gave it to me.'

Billy's face was white and his eyes were red-rimmed from crying.

'I can't believe they made Princess do this,' Charles said.

Sarah came in.

'Hey, what's going on?'

Billy wordlessly handed her the note.

'Shit.'

'They can't be serious about the midnight part,' I said worriedly. 'Where will you go?'

Billy sniffed.

'I can stay at Theresa's.'

Theresa, one of the local Tico friends Billy had made, lived on the other side of town.

'I don't want to go,' he said, welling up. 'I love it here. I love the monkeys. I have nothing to go home to.'

'What about Princess?' I said. 'Maybe she can do something.'

Billy shook his head.

'She knew about it all along. She knew even before vacation.'

'God,' Charles burst out. 'It's such bullshit. I can't believe they fired you with such a chicken-shit note. What the hell were they playing at?'

We sat around, made powerless by the envelope that sat on the bed like black magic. Midnight approached. All Billy's worldly belongings fitted into his backpack and a garbage bag.

'I'll look like a right tramp won't I?' he said, trying to lighten the mood. 'Hauling this all the way through Vacas.'

'It's just not right, you leaving this way,' Charles said.

'I'll miss you guys.'

'Man,' said Charles. 'If I wasn't leaving in two weeks, I'd quit over this.'

Billy looked at Charles like a drowning man sighting a ship.

'Wait a minute. I bet that would work.'

'What?'

'If you all threatened to quit, Diane would have to keep me.'

It was the perfect plan. The project couldn't survive with four people gone. If we all banded together, Billy would have to stay.

None of us could look him in the eye. We all stared at the floor, shuffling uncomfortably. Sarah spoke first.

'I'd love to help you out Billy, but I need a job after this. I can't piss Diane off.'

'Yeah man,' said Charles. 'I need the return flight paid for.'

'You wouldn't have to go through with it,' Billy said. 'It's like a strike. Just to let them know what they're doing is wrong. You do think it's wrong, don't you?'

'Of course we do,' I said. 'It's just that . . .'

He looked at each of us in turn. Diane was a powerful influence in the academic world and no one was going to risk making her angry. Billy swallowed, and I could almost taste the bitterness of betrayal sliding down his throat.

'No worries then. I was only joking anyways.'

He gave everyone a hug. We felt it ricochet through each of us. Charles said goodbye to Billy at the gate. I lay awake for a long time, imagining him hunched over with his backpack and his garbage bag, wandering off into the night.

The safety net was gone. Someone had been fired from the monkey project, and we all knew he might not be the last.

The next few days were tense. Princess skirted around all of us with a 'don't any of you give me shit about this' look on her face. She was in charge now but, besides Carlos, she didn't have any allies. Sarah, despite a great outward show of respect and affection, didn't like her. Andreas was, as usual, unreadable, Charles and I were both suspicious of her role in having Billy fired, and Kermit-and-Brad were terrified they would be next.

chapter 8

Expulsion from Eden

Charles's departure approached with the speed and ferocity of a bullet train. One moment we had weeks, then suddenly he was leaving the next day. Charles and I were forgotten in the furore of the Billy drama. All anyone talked about was why Billy was fired and whether it would happen to anyone else.

Charles and I made plans in secret. Since Diane was back in the States, we had the use of the pizza house. I had one of the rooms, and Andreas and Sarah had the other two. Finally, Charles and I could go somewhere where no one was watching. We talked about moving out when he came back, getting our own little cottage far away from the monkey house. We could move near Angelina's family, have real friends, a separate life. No one would be able to keep track of us on Vacas days. No one would be listening through walls or slyly watching us from the corner of their eyes.

I could taste another, better future just around the corner and it took the sting from goodbye.

Charles's last day in the forest was with Carlos and I. Carlos seemed to know we wanted to be alone, so he took crazy routes to find the monkeys, lay down and napped for an hour, did follows with Charles, then slept some more. Charles and I spent the whole day talking about whether he would move to Australia, or whether I would move to Atlanta to bake pies and sew curtains. In between discussions he put his hand inside my shirt and we tried desperately not to have sex in the forest.

I used to think outdoor sex was romantic. Then came Costa Rica. Forget lying down on a soft bed of moss and leaves, the forest creatures all singing in harmony. There were ticks that could worm their way into your genital regions through two pairs of underwear and canvas pants, never mind a stark naked body. The ants were painful enough when they bit calloused fingers, much less soft, sensitive flesh, and mosquitoes swarmed so viciously, you could never relax enough for orgasm.

Then, what did you do with bodily fluids? We didn't carry enough water to wash. So unless you were near Julie's pozza, where the water pooled into a swimming hole and you were likely to get sprung by locals, you had to rinse off in stagnant pools or muddy streams. The only option left was to unzip, take out the relevant bits and do it quickly and furtively as if you were strangers in a public toilet.

People did have sex in the forest. Andreas and Ada had sex on Toledo trail, and Carlos and Princess did it all over the place. But one look at the forest floor crawling with every life form imaginable and I suddenly wasn't so horny.

So Charles and I had to be content with passionate kisses, and grand plans of our little cottage, where we could lie down in our king-sized bed and have sex any time we liked.

Towards the end of the day, Charles started to wilt. He kept looking around sadly, as though he was seeing everything for the first and last time.

'It's so hard to leave,' he sighed. 'I was sure after a year here, I couldn't get out fast enough, but it's not like that. You hate it with all your might but then, one day, you're leaving and you realise how much you want to stay.'

I wanted to understand, but I couldn't. I was damn sure when I left, you'd see my dust all the way to San Jose.

Charles kept talking. He was frightened of returning to a city full of niceties. Where everything was combed and groomed, but beneath it all was the same savagery we saw every day. At least you could look the jungle in the face and call it for what it was. There was no gloss to it, no pretty sheen. He wanted to remember what it was like to exist where everything was the savage truth. It was the first time he had been himself. There was no point pretending to be smarter, fitter or better looking than you were, because the jungle would find you out and punish you.

And the monkeys. Charles said it was like being a guardian angel for spoilt, ungrateful children. You knew everything about them, their friends, their enemies and those who betrayed them. You watched them be born and killed, mate and fight and scream and tear each other to pieces. In the onslaught of death that was to come, not one would happen before our eyes. Like the bogeyman, it always struck when we weren't looking. The monkeys never greeted our benevolent protection with anything but disdain. But in the end, like guardian angels, we loved them just the same.

Princess picked us up at four, two hours earlier than our monkey vigil was supposed to end. She arrived with a litre of beer in one hand and six more in a bucket of ice in the back. Drink driving was legal in Costa Rica, a significant contributor to their road toll. Charles's party was Princess's first with the new group, and she was determined to show us partying was one thing she did well.

There was barely enough time to have a shower and change before music was blasting and beer bottles were popping and fizzing. Everyone surrounded Charles, wanting to know about his last day, who was the last monkey he saw, and if any sexual acts had been committed.

The reality of his departure hit me. How did I know he was coming back? It could be the last time I saw him. I went outside and put on a load of washing. I watched the wash go around and around, the filth from my field clothes turning 40 litres of water to a muddy black.

Hands circled my waist. Charles's lips pressed into my neck. I was suddenly nervous.

'I'm coming back, you know.'

'I know,' I lied.

The screen door burst open and Kermit came out. Charles and I moved apart awkwardly.

'Hey big man. Brought cha somethin.'

Kermit handed Charles a beer.

'Man, I don't know,' Charles faltered. 'This is my third one.'

'Hey one more, then we're on to kaseke.'

Kaseke was Costa Rica's national drink. Its alcohol content was near toxic and it smelt and tasted like nail polish remover.

Charles reluctantly followed Kermit inside. It was going to be a messy night.

Everything was progressing roughly on schedule. Jungle stories were exaggerated proportionate to the number of empty kaseke bottles lined up along the kitchen bench, the shots were getting nastier, and staying vertical was becoming a challenge. In the kitchen, Charles told every memorable event of the year, stories becoming less coherent but strangely funnier by the minute. There was the time Havoc, the dwarf monkey with half a tail, had run towards him with a huge erection. Or the time Sleepy, the alpha female of Snow White, had sex squeaked at him. Soon we were laughing so hard, we had to hold ourselves up on the kitchen benches.

I hadn't drunk as much as the rest of them, and I couldn't shake off a sense of foreboding. The kitchen was becoming claustrophobic with all the hilarity, so I wandered into the dining room. Brad was sitting alone at the table. I sat down next to him and spoke to him directly for the first time since he arrived.

'You aren't drinking?'

'I don't feel like it.'

'What's your vice, then?'

'I'm gay.'

My mouth fell open. The confession slipped out nonchalantly, like he had just told me his favourite colour. But he was watching carefully, as though waiting for judgement. I leant back in my chair.

'Was that before or after you saw your options on the project?'

He laughed. He had a nice smile.

'Actually,' he said. 'My father was an alcoholic. I don't like getting drunk.'

'Mine too. Me neither. I mean, unless hypothetically I was stuck in the middle of the jungle going crazy from isolation and confinement.'

We stared at each other, surprised to find common ground.

'So where's yours?' I asked.

'Married to a bitch with plastic tits. What about yours?'

'In a Buddhist monastery in Laos.'

We smiled, the thread of recognition darting back and forth between us, intangible as spider's silk, and just as strong.

I saw trouble coming when I caught Charles watching us. He was eyeing Brad as though he was stealing something that belonged to him.

'Hey Charles,' said Princess, handing him a nasty-looking concoction of kaseke, vodka and rum with whipped cream on top. 'You have to drink this, it's called Havoc's erection spell.'

The kitchen erupted with laughter, and I saw the alcohol hit Charles's stomach like concrete hitting water. He swayed a little on his feet.

'Where's Brad?' he yelled suddenly. 'He's neglecting his drinking responsibilities.'

'Hell yeah,' said Kermit. 'Get that irresponsible bastard in here.'

With relish, Charles grabbed Brad's arm and dragged him into the kitchen. Brad looked at me helplessly as Charles threw him a little too hard against the kitchen sink.

'Hey!'

'Sorry bro. But you have to do this. It's my last night, we're all shit-faced and you're sober. You're ruining tradition.'

'Whatever,' Brad shrugged, which made Charles angry. Charles poured half a tumbler of vodka and kaseke. There was a sudden silence.

'Whoa,' said Brad. 'Isn't that a little excessive?'

I felt drunk just looking at it.

'Charles, leave him alone.'

'It's tradition,' Charles maintained stubbornly. Conflict scattered across his face as he realised he had backed himself into a corner. If Brad had to drink it, then he and everyone else had to drink it too. It was the Sicilian assassin's trick. You poured poison into your enemy's drink and yours, and hoped you were strong enough to live to see victory. Charles solemnly poured six half glasses of the mixture and handed one to everyone.

'Don't even think about it,' I snapped when he brought one to me. 'Brad, you don't have to drink that.'

Charles's eyes flashed at me. Brad shrugged.

They clinked glasses and on the count of three they all downed the concoction. Kermit let out a scream like a steam engine taking off.

'Whooooohoo! Goddamn! That's one hell of a tradition, big boy.'

'Another one?' Charles asked as steadily as he could. Brad raised an eyebrow.

'Why not?'

An hour later we were all drunker than any of us could remember being in our lives. Andreas had one lollipop in each cheek, and kept dropping to the floor in a kind of a breakdancing manoeuvre. Kermit was armwrestling anyone who came within two feet of him, and Brad was doing the Bronco to Destiny's Child's 'Bootylicious', which consisted of jumping from his feet onto his hands and back again. Princess and I were cheering and clapping wildly, when suddenly Charles threw one of the plastic chairs across the room. He stormed around, ripping posters from the wall. I didn't recognise him.

'Charles, what are you doing?'

'Brad,' he roared, full of emotion. 'Get in here.'

Brad was mid-Bronco and looked through his legs at Charles. 'What for?'

'You need another drink.'

'Fuck no, man, I've had enough.'

Charles went over to Brad, picked him up and carried him to the kitchen. I tried to follow them, but only made it to the dining table where I collapsed in a chair. I couldn't remember why Charles had to get Brad so drunk, but I knew I had to stop him.

'Charles, stop it,' I called out feebly.

Brad nearly collapsed when Charles put him down.

'Man, I feel sick.'

Charles propped him up against the sink.

'Be a man.'

Charles poured another drink. His hand was unsteady.

'I think I got the ratio wrong.'

'Fuck the ratio man, that stuff is acid,' Brad started pumping his index finger like a rapping homeboy. 'A-C-I-D. *Acid.*'

Charles gravely handed the drink to him.

'You have to drink it, bro. It's tradition.'

'Man, cutting the top of your dick off is tradition in some countries and you don't follow that.'

'You ain't seen my dick, have you bitch? I'm all over tradition. Because tradition . . .' Charles's voice was slurring into a stronger southern drawl than usual. 'Tradition is what makes us humanity goddammit.'

Charles was wagging his index finger very close to Brad's face.

'Now drink.'

Brad put his hands up.

'Okay, okay, man. All I'm saying is, the change of tradition is what makes progress.'

Brad took the drink and Charles took his drink. They tried to clink glasses but missed. And missed again. On the third time they connected and Charles tipped the contents of his glass down his throat. As he did so, from the corner of his eye he saw Brad pour his drink down the sink.

'Goddammit!'

Brad ran.

'Ahhh! Help!'

Charles stomped after him like a dinosaur. Brad dived under the table and crawled under my chair.

'Vanessa, you have to save me. I can't drink anymore.'

'Brad . . .' Charles's voice took on the sing-song quality of a pantomime. 'You have to come out of there.'

Brad curled himself tighter under my chair.

'Don't let him take me.'

'Charles, leave him alone. He's had enough.'

Charles didn't reply. Instead he stood in front of me, looked into my eyes, put one hand on either knee and gently but firmly pulled my legs apart. He could see Brad's upturned face through the slits in the plastic chair between my thighs. Lines of light fell across Brad's eyes. He was genuinely frightened. Charles puffed up like a genie.

'Brad. I love you man. I love you. But I know what you're doing. And you can't be pulling that shit.'

'What . . .' Brad pleaded.

'Brad. Brad. You can't have . . .' he stopped just in time. 'I know what you want, man, and I know what's best for you. Now get into that kitchen.'

'Vanessa, he's insane. I don't know what he's talking about. You can't let him do it to me.'

'I won't. Charles stop this shit right now. He doesn't want to.'

'Brad, you can't be hiding under pussy, man.'

I was starting to get angry.

'Charles, don't be a wanker.' I put my hand on his arm and tried to convey the mistake he was making. 'It's not what you think.'

'Honey. You have to trust me.'

I couldn't exactly stand up and scream out that Brad was gay. I grabbed Charles's arm and pulled him as hard as I could towards my room, but he was too strong for me. He pushed me into the chair and pinned my arms to my sides. His eyes were wild and his face was red. I didn't recognise him. And then I did. He looked like my father.

Charles let me go and crawled under the table, dragging Brad out, kicking and shrieking into the kitchen.

'Okay. Okay!'

Brad was nearly hysterical. 'Okay, I'll drink, just let me walk.'

Brad walked into the kitchen like a condemned man. Charles, the executioner, followed. Charles poured the drink and handed it to Brad. They stared at each other. Then, like a true Sicilian, Brad drank the poison. Ironically, as soon as Brad finished it, Charles ran outside and vomited about four litres of alcohol and stomach acid into Carlos's immaculately pruned hedges.

The party ran out of alcohol and everyone was more or less assembling themselves to go to Soda Limon. Princess was trying to convince Kermit that he needed to wear a shirt to get into the bar and Kermit was convinced this somehow impinged on his rights as an American. I was avoiding Charles when we left the house, and I ran up to Brad and took his arm as we walked up the road together. He was going to have a very bad hangover in the morning and it was all my fault. Kermit suddenly burst out of the gate.

'I don't want to wear my shirt, man. It's my civil right not to wear my shirt. They can't constrict me like that and they can't enforce the clothing police because that would be communist and communism is outlawed.'

Princess had in fact managed to get Kermit into a shirt but at the end of this tirade in the middle of the street, Kermit tore off his shirt, the buttons making little tapping sounds as they hit the gravel. It was the first time we had seen Kermit's naked chest. It was as pale as the underside of a fish, covered in black hair, with substantial man boobs. Oblivious to our shocked stares, Kermit threw his shirt down, walked haphazardly to the other side of the road and lay down on the pavement.

'Man overboard!' cried Brad. We gathered around Kermit, like soldiers around a fallen comrade. He had completely passed out. I grabbed Brad and practically threw him onto Kermit's immobile body.

'Quick, give him mouth to mouth!'

Brad shrank back into me.

'Uh-uh. That man is poison.'

I looked around. Charles was gone.

'Okay,' I said. 'This party is officially over.'

I found Charles upstairs, curled in his bed like a wounded animal.

'Hey,' he said, sweetly. 'You're here.'

I began to think I'd imagined the whole evening.

'Charles, why did you try to kill Brad?'

'Oh my god, I'm sorry. Is he dead?'

I was out of humour. I snarled something and he grabbed my hands and pulled me down to the bed and started babbling, words running like a lava explosion, pyroclastic and incoherent.

'I'm so sorry, my god I'm an ass but you don't understand I can't stand not being able to claim you I know we said we couldn't they couldn't know but I didn't know then what it would be like I couldn't get to you I wanted so badly just to be near you god I'm so in love with you I can't stand it and he was there in the way and I had no right and he . . . he . . .'

He couldn't go on. I started to laugh, desperately.

'You bloody fool. Brad is gay.'

His pupils shrank to pinpoints like he had just had a hit of smack.

'What?'

'Brad is gay. Hom-o-sex-ual. Likes to fuck men. Whatever they call it where you're from. What the fuck did you think I was trying to tell you while you were giving him alcohol poisoning?'

'Oh my god,' he moaned, crawling under the bed sheets. 'Oh my god.'

'I don't believe you. You're a goddamn schizophrenic when you're drunk.'

He pulled me towards him and pushed his hands under my shirt. I was not in the mood.

'No,' I said. 'I'm going to bed.'

'You can't go, stay.'

'I'm angry with you. We'll talk in the morning.'

My head throbbed in time to my footsteps down the stairs, so it wasn't until I was outside the pizza house that I realised he had followed me. Sarah saw us. Her face was expressionless, but for a split second her eyes locked with mine.

You lied to me.

I didn't then understand what it meant, that viperous accusation. But I would learn, sweet Jesus would I learn. What I did know was that our cover was blown. The whole house would know by morning that Charles and I were lovers. I was so frustrated, I wanted to cry.

I let him follow me into my room, then I turned on him.

'Charles, you put us in this ridiculous situation,' I hissed. 'You're the one with the girlfriend. You're the one going home. I'm the one who's going to look like a slut and a liar and I have to live here after you go.'

'I'm coming back. I'll make it all better. I can't go now, I have to stay here.'

He touched my leg. I stiffened.

'Get out.'

'No,' he murmured. 'I'm staying. You can't make me go.'

It was the same, but different. Edward's drunkenness had been cold, clear and soft. He never raised his voice, he just became vicious. Charles's was a violent, boiling rage that made the veins stand out on his forehead. The thought of him touching me made my skin shrivel. It was supposed to be our last night together and I just wanted him gone.

'Charles, if you don't get out of this room, I swear to you, I will scream. I'll get the whole house in here and leave you to explain yourself.'

It took a few seconds for the words to sink in. His body clenched like a fist. Then it relaxed.

'Fine,' he said, got up and walked past me, then shut the door.

I was sitting on his bed when he woke. Dawn streamed white and harsh through the window. Howler monkeys rustled in the mango tree outside, foraging for bitter unripe fruit. The male called. It was a mournful, broken sound that made my blood ripple.

I had hoped when I woke up in the morning that everything would be better. That I would have forgiven Charles and we could go on as we had been. But it wasn't better, it was worse. I'd been running from alcohol my whole life. I was tired, but not tired enough to give up.

Charles opened his eyes. They were soft and wet, like creatures without a shell.

'I don't think,' I said slowly, 'that this is what I want.'

He bit his lip, but still didn't speak.

'I can't be with someone who drinks, Charles. Not again.' His eyes welled.

'Vanessa, don't, please don't. I won't drink again, ever, I can give it up. I won't touch it. You mean so much more please—don't end this on something that means so little.'

If he had been the first, I would have believed him. He had broken through my loneliness and carried me away from our mosquito-infested, jungle-trodden world. When I was with him, I stopped running after the little demon gods that tore through thickening vines and endless rain. I was in love with every awkward fault, his crooked smile, the way he kicked at the dirt, his calm, sure fingers in my hair.

But he wasn't the first. And I knew, if this was what I took, then this would be all I'd ever have.

Our fingers interlaced and clenched. I could feel his pulse, or was it mine, over the fragile bone between the knuckles.

'I'm sorry,' I said. 'But you can't come back.'

He faced the wall, his body shaking as though he was cold. I walked downstairs, my face frozen in place like a mask about to shatter, dreams scattering in front of me like white rabbits.

If I was Alice in Wonderland, I would have flooded the world with my tears.

chapter 9

The golden month

i was squatting in the bushes when I felt something trickle down the back of my neck. I looked up. A monkey was squatting above my head.

'No, you didn't, tell me you didn't.'

The monkey took off.

There is not a lot you can do with dignity when your pants are around your ankles. It was enough dealing with a host of winged predators buzzing around your bottom, not to mention finding something to wipe with. We weren't allowed to leave toilet paper in the forest, so unless you wanted to carry a plastic bag full of dirty toilet paper all day, you had to use the foliage.

I was never organised enough to pick the leaves before I squatted. Once I absentmindedly reached for a benign-looking maple-shaped leaf. It never made it to my bottom because the tiny needles started pumping poison into my skin as soon as they came into contact with my fingers. I howled and clutched my hand, thinking a nest of wasps was hidden in the leaves. The plant venom buckled my flesh like cellulite.

It was a famous botanical specimen the Ticos called *malamujer*, literally 'evil woman'.

After that I learnt to pay attention. Waxy leaves only. But my focused concentration left me open to attack.

'That little asshole!' I ranted as I tramped through the bushes towards Andreas, still doing up my fly. 'A monkey just pissed on my head!'

I waited for Andreas's reaction. Disgust. Surprise. Even laughter. But his antelope eyes were blank.

'I think it was Paradise,' he said.

'I'm going to flush her down a toilet,' I stormed. 'I'm going to tie her up in a plastic bag and throw her on the highway . . . as soon as I know who she is.'

After Charles left, Diane banned me from taking my camera into the field and banished me to Nirvana.

I was sitting on the porch with Brad, planning to film him eating a caterpillar. He volunteered to eat the first one, but I was convincing him he needed to eat four or five so I could get it from different angles. Princess came outside looking nervous.

'You can't film anymore,' she said without preamble.

'What?'

'Diane doesn't want you to take your camera into the field.'

'Why?'

'I don't know. You'll have to ask her.'

'But we had a deal! How can she have changed her mind since she arrived in the States?'

Princess threw up her hands.

'Vanessa, I didn't have anything to do with this. Also, you're not in Snow White anymore. We're changing your monkey group. You're in Nirvana.'

Nirvana was like a galactic wormhole. People were sucked in first thing in the morning then spat out somewhere crazy at the end of the day. On the way home, the car was full of chatter about who was the next alpha of Sin, or how many people were jumped on in Snow White. Nirvana people were silent. No one knew what happened in their group, and no one cared. I didn't even know where Nirvana was, only that it was far and I never wanted to go there.

On my first day, Andreas and I walked for 35 minutes through the forest, crossed two rivers (one of which I fell into) and battled through a field of bamboo. We stumbled onto the highway which we followed until we came to an ugly quarry called Quebrador. Machines were halted mid-motion like great beasts eating away at the mountain. Piles of gravel glinted in the moonlight. A polluted stream circled the site, carrying out the effluent.

Andreas threw down his backpack.

'Are you serious?' I said. 'Nirvana lives above a construction site? Are they deaf or just crazy?'

He shrugged.

The sky paled and the branches above the Quebrador began to shake, as though spirits trapped within were struggling to break out.

All morning we chased Nirvana along the cliffs of Quebrador. Occasionally I caught a glimpse of what looked like a troll; a protruding tooth, a scowling brow. But I never managed more than a glimpse before they bolted.

'They aren't as habituated,' Andreas said. 'They don't like it when you look at them.'

'How am I supposed to learn them if I can't look at them?'

'Try not to be so obvious about it.'

I finally stole a peek from behind a tree. I was shocked. They were trolls. The males of Nirvana had bald foreheads and ogreish teeth that protruded from their lips. The females had eyebrows that stuck out from their heads as though they'd been electrocuted. Apart from distinguishing the sexes, I couldn't tell one from the other. When I asked Andreas, he had helpful advice like 'Ecstasy's the one hitting her baby' and 'Tranquillity's always chasing trucks down the highway'.

There was no way around it. To recognise these monkeys you had to be intimately acquainted. I knew from the start, this was the last thing I wanted.

Also, they liked going to the toilet on you. At first I thought inbreeding had given them weak bladders. But after the fifth or sixth time I realised they were doing it on purpose. They seemed to get an especial kick out of pissing on you when you had your pants down. Then, if they defecated on you, oh boy, that was the jackpot. It was hard to believe such tiny animals could shoot such vast quantities of foul black poop from their bottoms. Their aim was flawless. They were like little Robin Hoods.

'I hate these monkeys!' I said for the fiftieth time that day. 'I hate them and my filming career is over.'

'I knew Diane would freak out,' Andreas said sagely. 'I can't believe she said yes in the first place.'

'But why? Diane wants us to film monkeys to verify the data. Why doesn't she want me to do it properly?'

He shrugged. 'I think documentaries make her nervous.'

'Is that why I'm in Nirvana?'

'Probably. I know she didn't want you to film how much contact we really have with Snow White.'

We stared at the monkeys in silence. I was out with Andreas a lot these days, since he was the only one that could recognise them. I knew Andreas was 24, with a Mexican mother and a gringo father. Though we'd been living in the house for three months, we still had nothing to talk about. We tried music, but he had uber cool, reactionary taste and I had never heard of anyone he'liked. He didn't read books and wasn't interested in filming. So we spent most of the day with me running around calling out monkey IDs and him shaking his head as though I'd never get it right.

Towards the afternoon the clouds darkened and it began to rain. It had been drizzling since I arrived, but now the sky was flexing its muscles and getting serious. After an hour the rain was so thick I couldn't see my hand stretched in front of me. Most monkeys stopped moving in the rain. Nirvana ran like motherfuckers.

We lost them across the river. I started to cross it, but Andreas grabbed my arm and shook his head. We watched as the river came tumbling down the hill, gathering speed and ferocity as it whipped branches from the sides of the banks and pulled rocks into the rapids. Its gurgling cries were the only sounds we could hear above the rain. Slowly, it crept to our feet. We moved to higher ground.

I stared moodily into its hypnotic surge of destruction. The rain slithered under my shirt and down my breasts. Charles said I was as wretched as a cat in the rain. I missed him. A hundred times a day I thought of something to tell him, only to realise he wasn't here. He called a few times, the sound of his disembodied voice strange without his smell or touch. He never asked to come back, but we still talked as though we were lovers. He said he missed me, I said I wished he was here. The thought that he could jump on a plane and be in Costa Rica in four hours was even more painful than if he was on the other side of the world. After those phone calls, I crept into my room and curled up on my bed, sure I had never been so alone in my life. Four phone calls later, I couldn't cope. I told him I loved him but he couldn't call me again. He didn't.

The days I had left stretched out, too many to count, and each night I closed my eyes, dreaming of an escape from the little trolls that dwelt above the moonlit quarry.

The reign of Sneezy was over. He and the Snow White boys were no match for the menacing new rule that slunk into Sin. Nirvana had arrived. And they hadn't come for a tousle in the locker room. They were hard and sleek, and they aimed to kill.

There aren't many species that kill each other deliberately. Humans are one, chimpanzees are another. No other non-human primates did it, except for this group of capuchin monkeys.

I wonder, as Sneezy was chased out of his troubled kingdom, if he thought of the day he betrayed Dopey. Would it have been a consolation to have Dopey by his side? Would it have made a difference?

In Sneezy's short rule, he killed two babies of low-ranking females—Torment's baby and Debacle's baby. Killing infants, or infanticide, was the strategy of new alpha males to pass on their genes. Females couldn't fall pregnant while they were nursing, but if the male killed the baby, the female would come into oestrus sooner and could have another baby.

Murder and Assassin knew, sooner or later, Sneezy would come for their babies. So they watched from a distance with hard eyes as Sneezy was overturned. They could only hope the next ruler would be easily intimidated, or easy to avoid.

The new alpha was Angel. It would have come as a surprise to the other monkeys in Nirvana that Angel had triumphed and secured a group of his own. The males of Nirvana reviled him and the females wouldn't touch him. He spent most of his time slouching maliciously around the outside of the group, disappearing for days and returning torn up as an alley cat.

He was without doubt the ugliest monkey I have ever seen. The skin stretched over his face had the liver spots of an old man. His top lip didn't quite cover his mouth, leaving a sinister slit, as though his very breath brought darkness and death. A thickset brow ridge made caverns for psychopathic eyes. When he looked at you, you could tell that this was a serial rapist, a murderer of infants.

And so he was.

When Angel took over Sin, Diane told us to drop Nirvana. I was back in my old group. When I saw Murder, I felt a surprising rush of fondness. After the hoary-eyebrowed witches in Nirvana, her dark beauty was a welcome change.

The females in Sin were looking haggard. I felt for them, these victims of war. Four females had babies—Murder, Assassin, Whisper and Scandal. All they wanted was a strong male who would take care of them, and provide their children with safety. Those who had lost babies were still mourning. They were shadows with hollow eyes flitting around the outside of the group, avoided by the others like a curse.

Angel was sprawled on his back while Whisper picked and nibbled between his legs. Her son Whimper slept on her back.

She was trying to establish a bond with the new alpha in the hope he would spare her infant. Angel lay back, closing his eyes in hideous rapture.

Brad approached me.

'Is that Angel and Whisper?'

I yawned.

'It's a gangster getting a blow job.'

Brad made a choking sound and screwed up his face. Oh shit, I thought, goddamn my filthy mouth. I've offended another American.

But he was laughing. He dropped his backpack and leant against a tree. His laughter rang out so loudly, Whisper stopped her grooming and Angel gave us a dirty look. I started laughing too. Soon I was laughing at him laughing and he was laughing at me laughing and we couldn't stop even if we wanted to.

Andreas came to see what all the fuss was about.

'What's up?'

'She . . .' Brad gasped. 'She just said Angel was a gangster getting a blow job.'

Andreas was deadpan. What's funny about that? his perplexed eyes were saying.

'Wait, Vanessa,' said Brad. 'Angel thinks you're hot. He's checking you out.'

Angel looked from side to side, sex grunted twice, slapped a branch in my face, then ran away.

We collapsed on the ground.

'Oh my god,' said Brad in between breaths. 'He sex grunted at you. He totally wants to have sex with you.'

Brad and I had been less like enemies since Charles's leaving party, but suddenly, with nothing more eventful than that, we were the best of friends.

The monkey project was about to get crowded. Four new people were arriving in the next four months and the hierarchy was in for a shuffle. Brad and I were sitting on top of Buena Vista, watching the monkeys feast on orange twist. It looked like a Japanese painting, the monkeys perched on a tree high above the valley, the little red berries falling like rain.

'Annie arrives today,' said Brad thoughtfully, chewing on a stick. 'I wonder what she'll be like.'

I hated her on sight. There's no use pretending I ever gave her a chance. Something about the way she stood on the porch like a little dog begging for acceptance made me want to kick her. She reminded me of myself during my awkward, ugly adolescence and I couldn't get far enough away from her.

'Hi!' she shrieked, before we even got out of the car.

I had fallen in the river that day, while Brad cackled on the other side. All I wanted was a shower. But the intruder would not move away from the door, insisting we shake her flaccid hand and talk for twenty minutes.

She was wearing a hippie rainbow-coloured skirt with a khaki top. She could have been beautiful, if she stood up straight and kept her mouth shut. Instead her hunched shoulders pushed her chin into her neck, while her nasal voice twanged like an off-key banjo.

Though I never could have liked her, it was a mistake not to hide it. As a monkey, I could have scratched and clawed at her to my heart's content, and drawn everyone else into the fight. But we are the species of lies. Our extraordinary talent for deception is one of the keys to our success, but when it came to hiding what I felt about people, I was hopeless.

'Look down!' my Chinese aunt would screech, brandishing a slipper above her head. She tried everything to instil the silk screen impassiveness of a good Chinese girl. How was I going to control my husband if I couldn't even control my face? She threatened to poke out my eyes. Burn off my tongue. But even though I believed she would, I couldn't stop my emotions lighting up my face like neon signs.

So I looked down as I mumbled something to Annie and went in through the back door.

Princess didn't like Annie either, judging from the way she didn't say a word to her, but then she had an excuse. She was leaving for Boston for a short holiday. As she prepared, she lost all regard for propriety. She rostered herself to stay home and 'administrate'. Carlos was also kept home, 'fixing' things around the house, although we suspected this was so they could have lots of sex before she left. Attitudes cooled towards her. Her management style was an insecure mix of friendly overtures and manipulative control, and even her cheerleader prettiness couldn't save her from becoming resented.

Everyone breathed a sigh of relief when she left. Except Carlos. He stayed in their room and didn't come out. I wondered if he was afraid Princess would decide America, with all its wasteful bounty, was more appealing than a tiny village with a jungle full of monkeys. What could he give her that she couldn't find in that land of plenty? All he could do was hope his love would bring her back.

The rest of us were ecstatic. With both Diane and Princess gone, we looked at each other sideways, like a bunch of kids about to get into a lot of trouble.

'Okay everyone, line up. Kermit in front, Sarah in the middle and Brad at the end. Now walk towards me in a straight line.'

I sent a barrage of whining, pathetic emails begging Diane to let me take my camera out again. The Disney segments were due in November, two months away, and I was panicking I wouldn't get them finished. She finally relented. Unsure how long the hiatus would last for, I was determined to finish the filming as soon as I could. The plotline of the first segment was the life of intrepid monkey researchers, battling the dangers of the Costa Rican jungle.

'Vanessa, what's my motivation?' called out Brad.

'Can you please take this seriously?' I yelled back. 'This is for national television.'

I filmed them storming up cliffs and down valleys. I made Kermit swing his machete through thickets he never would have attempted in real life. In the afternoon, the monkeys came down from the trees and tumbled on the ground in front of Brad and Sarah. I was floating with relief. It was going to be alright.

When the monkeys were asleep in the guanacaste tree above Tinamu trail, Kermit and Brad walked ahead with film-star swaggers to the car. Alone with Sarah, I seized my chance. I'd been too wrapped up in Charles to get much closer to Sarah, but now he was gone I wanted to try. I'd always liked her, and I thought we could be friends.

'Sarah, I'm sorry I lied to you. About Charles.'

'Oh,' she said, not looking at me. 'Don't worry about it.'

I didn't believe her. I decided to confide in her, since she liked secrets. 'I was having problems coping. It was hard to talk about.'

'It's okay, I understand. I wouldn't want to either. Have you two figured out what you're going to do?'

I sighed, frustration escaping like a hiss of steam.

'I just want someone who loves me enough to make it work. I can't be the one in control anymore. Why do I have to be the one making the effort all the time?'

Sarah looked conflicted between staying mad at me for lying to her and gaining a new ally and possibly a friend. She sighed.

'Is there anyone for us out there?'

We had a moment of female bonding. Then came a cry from one of the only men we had available.

'Vanessa!' crooned Brad. 'I'm ready for my close-up!'

Sarah and I looked at each other and laughed. It was an uneasy truce but neither of us wanted more enemies.

Brad and I stood at the Transect Fence that divided Sin's territory from Nirvana's. The fence ran all the way from Buena Vista to the river near the highway and was the only mechanically cleared path in the whole forest. We were dropping in on Nirvana to see if any earth-shattering developments had taken place. We needn't have bothered. Nirvana decided to spend all day on the wrong side of the highway. The area had been logged so the majestic trees that once stood there were nothing but stumps, and the thickets grew like pubic hair. We stood along the fence looking down at the monkeys. There was no point going in. We had been tracking them for three hours with no data collection. Annie was with us, but we were ignoring her, so she sat next to the new member of the group, Jesus.

Jesus was a Tico who had worked for Diane before. Since he didn't move into the monkey house, we didn't really notice him arrive, and most of the time he just slipped under the radar. Unlike Carlos, who chattered loudly and liked slashing through the undergrowth without his shirt, Jesus didn't even carry a machete. He could silently pick his way through the densest thicket and you would never know he had passed. Every tree, flower and fruit the monkeys sat in or ate from merited his careful attention. If he found one he didn't know, he would pocket it and look it up in an ancient botanical book when he got home.

There was no excess to Jesus. Not an extra word, not an extra gram of fat or muscle other than what he needed. He had a way of looking off into the distance, as though there was a secret in the cluster of dense vegetation he was trying to understand. Sometimes I'd ask him what he was thinking about.

'Ay Banessa,' he'd say. *'Solo pienso.'* Just thinking.

It was pleasant to lean against the fence in the sun. Nirvana was staying close to the edge and snacking on dates in scrappy palm trees.

'So,' Brad said for the hundredth time. 'Did you start *Harry Potter*?'

'I'm not reading it,' I lied. 'I think JK Rowling is crap.'

'Stop being so counter culture,' Brad snapped. 'What have you been doing then, going to bed so early?'

'Wanking.'

Brad snorted.

The truth was, I was addicted.

'Besides,' I said. 'She totally lifted that bit about the magic mirror from Lewis Carroll.'

'You have been reading it!' Brad crowed triumphantly. 'And you like it, go on, say it. You LOVE *Harry Potter*.'

I was spared the confession because suddenly Brad started slapping his head.

'What are you . . .'

'Run!' he screamed. 'Ruuuuuuuuuuuuuuuun!'

Then I felt it. Sharp jabbing stabs into my skull, my ear, my neck.

We took off down the road. Brad ripped his shirt off and twirled it around his head. I pulled the elastic out of my hair and shook my head like a lunatic. In the background, I could hear Jesus laughing.

The swarm of bees chased us down the road. I started to see the funny side.

'Stop laughing,' Brad panted. 'You stupid bitch, I can't run if I'm laughing.'

Eventually our legs gave out and we collapsed on the ground. Tears streaked with dirt ran down our cheeks. If the bees had made it that far, they could have feasted on our scalps, but luckily they had given up.

'You looked like such an idiot,' I howled. 'Twirling your shirt like a stripper.'

We screamed and rolled around on the ground. I actually peed my pants. Brad started to drool. It was a long time before we regained control of ourselves. Brad put his shirt back on, I tied up my hair, and we tried to walk with dignity back to Jesus, who was still killing himself with laughter, and Annie who was looking like she didn't see the joke in two bona fide lunatics hunted down by a swarm of killer bees.

But that was what I learnt in the forest. The only way to survive while it was stabbing you full of venom was to laugh and laugh, until it forgave you every sin and welcomed you back into its arms.

We called it the golden month, after the crystalline mornings that glittered after a night of heavy rain. As the sun rose, spears of light pierced the leaves and turned the forest into an Emerald City. Raindrops clung in diamonds to spider webs, while the spiders sat like red and yellow jewels in the centre.

The whips were gone. There was no Princess when we came home to transmit all our failings through a magic cable straight to Diane. We were free to shift focus from the monkeys and take every drop of beauty that shook from leaves arched like swans' necks towards the ground.

The rain had a strange effect on us. Usually we followed the monkeys like penitents, careful not to make a noise or movement that would disturb them. But when the rain fell in great sheets from the skies, it was as if we were released from a long enchantment. We hooted and shrieked like banshees, danced wildly, and belted out Broadway musicals. We climbed trees, and lay on the branches like monkeys, with our stomachs pressed to the branch and our limbs hanging over the sides. We dreamed of dry clothes and talked about warm food like castaways stuck on a desert island.

If the monkeys ran, we let them go, laughing at the last disappearing tail.

At the end of the day, we dried our clothes lovingly in front of a fan all day and all night, and when we put them on they felt like the finest silk against our skin. We showed each other our toes that looked like wrinkled white grubs. Monkey food.

'No video, no vocalisations and hell no I don't know where they're sleeping tonight,' Brad would sing cheerfully as he filled out the worksheet. 'Those monkeys ran like motherfuckers.'

During dinner, we told stories of rain and monkeys and shit, of pissing on our feet to keep the fungus away, of people nearly getting swept down the river, and we laughed until we were louder than the rain, and even Andreas put his head in his arms to hide his mirth.

Then, exhausted but restless, we went out into Vacas. I saw Angelina's sisters, Sophia and Rosa, and Theresa, who told us Billy had returned to England, taking Bianca with him. We did the Bagaces version of a pub crawl; dancing at Miravailles, and whooping and cheering at Shakira video clips on the enormous screen at Las Tehas.

I think each one of us believed that it could always be like this, that finally, we could all be friends. Then, two things happened that made it the last time of happiness we would all have together.

Princess came back, and Angel started killing the babies.

chapter 10

Valley of Death

'We aren't getting enough data.'

Princess stood at the dinner table, something she did when she wanted to be authoritative. It was clear from the way she said 'we' that she meant 'you'.

'It's been raining,' said Brad patronisingly. 'We lose monkeys in the rain.'

But Princess was ready.

'I have an email from Diane. This time last year, Tristan's group was getting twice as many follows.'

'Bunch of suckers,' Kermit muttered under his breath. We looked at our dirty plates. We had not felt the whip of competition for a month. Princess let our skin prickle in anticipation before she tried the camp-counsellor approach.

'What seems to be the problem?'

We were silent.

'Well,' she said slowly. 'Maybe it's not such a good idea to go to the bar the night before you work.'

Kermit tightened his fists. Brad looked at me and rolled his eyes. Annie rolled her eyes at Brad which made me want to punch her. Sarah looked at the table, her bottom lip hanging slack as it always did when she was upset. Andreas had his Andreas expression, but he raised his eyebrows as though Princess had just said the dumbest thing he'd ever heard.

'Okay,' said Princess brightly. 'What time tomorrow?'

Brad shot a meaningful look at me before disappearing into his room. I followed him. He was lying on the bed naked, his legs spread wide in front of the fan. He held his scrotum up with one hand while the fan blew into the deep recesses of his bum crack. It was his nightly ritual to dry out the day's fungus that had accumulated in his crotch. Since I was Brad's 'bitch', as he liked to call me, I had the same privileges as Cleopatra's eunuchs.

'I want Andreas,' he whispered conspiratorially.

'Okay,' I said, standing up to get him.

'No you idiot. I want him want him.'

'Oh.'

We had joked about having sex with Andreas, but I only did it because there was no one left. Jesus was too philosophical and Kermit was too fat. Brad, on the other hand, was taking things more seriously.

'He has a faint smell. I have to be really close to him to catch it, but it makes me really horny.'

Suddenly I wondered if Andreas, with his slender limbs and long eyelashes, was gay. Or at least bisexual. Perhaps Brad had a chance.

'There's something else,' he said. 'That wretch Annie has started to flirt with him.'

'But Annie's in love with you!'

Annie's attraction to Brad had been the source of many hours of amusement for us. She clung to Brad like lint. She smiled coyly at him through her eyelashes, two deep dimples plunging through her cheeks. Completely unaware of the devastating pitch of her voice, it became louder when Brad was around, sailing through the air like a scud missile.

Finally, it was too embarrassing to let it go on any longer. We had to gently break Brad's homosexuality to her. The three of us sat in Nirvana because, by some travesty of scheduling, Annie seemed to be intruding on us all the time. The conversation went something like this.

'So Brad, tell me what it's like to get fucked up the ass.'

'Well Vanessa, the important thing is lubrication. Lubrication and getting your bowels clean, if you get my drift. Let me tell you about a very messy accident my butt boy once had in the bathtub . . .'

After half an hour, Annie looked like she was going to throw up, whether from nausea or disappointment wasn't clear.

She recovered the next day, apparently decided that if Brad couldn't be her lover, he would be her best friend. Which of course sent me into paroxysms of territorial aggression. If he had been a fire hydrant, I would have peed on him. I don't know what made her think she had a chance. I was higher up, more aggressive, and had been ready to run a skewer through her from the second I laid eyes on her. Only a thin veneer of civilisation kept me from sinking my fangs into her neck. Brad found it all very amusing, until she started to touch him.

'Why is it,' Brad said through clenched teeth, 'women think because you're gay, they have the right to paw you?'

Annie started touching Brad more than it was decent to touch anyone. She took his arm when they were walking. If she was standing behind him in the dinner line, she'd tickle his waist. She gave him impulsive little hugs and whenever she could, stood so close to him the hair on their arms were touching.

'I can't stand her pudgy little fingers,' Brad said. 'They're always disarranging something. She pulls my shirt out. She ruffles my hair.'

'It's your own fault. Why were you so nice to her when she arrived? You should always start off nasty, then people are grateful when you start being nice.'

'Well you should know. You were an absolute bitch to me for months after I arrived.'

'I had Charles, and you weren't worthy.'

'Oh please. Anyway, you owe me. You have to stop her from touching me.'

'So now I'm your guard dog.'

'Well, you do like to pee on my leg.'

It was like keeping a puppy outside. I kicked her, and she ran away whining. Then, when I wasn't around, she sidled up to Brad and begged for affection. Finally, after a lot of kicking and no affection from Brad, she got the message.

We hadn't heard much from her in a while. The new development with Andreas was a surprise.

'When did she start liking Andreas?' I asked, puzzled.

'I think it was that day Nirvana was in the fig tree for six hours. Remember, we were talking about how hot Andreas was? The next day she was out with Andreas and me. All of a sudden she starts flirting with him. It was repulsive.'

'I don't think you have to worry. She'll start molesting him and he'll tell her to fuck off.'

'No, that's just it. I think he *likes* it. Even worse, she's correcting me. Of course she's as useless as a beached whale at identifications, but when I'm spotting, she'll call out "you missed a handle leaf" or "that was a berry the focal just ate, not an insect". I'm about to kill her.'

Just then, Kermit knocked.

'Wait a minute!' Brad scrambled for a towel to drape over his privates. 'Come in.'

'Hey man, hey darlin', we're going to the bar.'

'But Princess said we weren't supposed to.'

Kermit's face wrinkled in disgust.

'That's bullshit man, they can't tell us that. Come on, we're all going. Summer's just arrived, what kind of a welcome is that?'

Summer was the bright-eyed new recruit Princess brought back from Boston. Summer's parents were hippies at Woodstock, hence her name. She even looked like summer, blond haired and blue eyed and as tanned as if she'd just walked off a beach. My new technique was to ignore everyone until I was sure they weren't annoying prats, but Brad liked her.

'Okay we'll come,' said Brad. 'The month hasn't even started and I need a drink already.'

The rain grew steadily worse. Each morning we woke to the sound of thunder. Lightning flashed blue against our tight-shut eyelids. Nothing was dry. Our clothes, damp and cold from the day before, left slimy streaks on our skin as we pulled them on. No fastened belt or masking tape around socks could keep out the chiggers that bred under our skin. Our legs were as pockmarked and cratered as the surface of the moon. We wrinkled our noses and squeezed our feet into stinking wet socks. The skin between our toes was white and flaking with fungus, deep fissures cracking the skin almost to blood. On the way to the car, we threw on our ponchos, knowing if it wasn't raining at that moment, it would be soon.

In the forest, the monkeys peeped and twittered, shaking their sodden fur. We waited beneath them, knowing we were damned if they vanished. Every time we looked up, water covered us as if we were thirsty flowers, running all the way down our stems to our soaking boots.

The rain washed away insect repellent, leaving us defenceless. Mosquitoes gathered under the hood of our ponchos, made invisible by dark clouds and soundless by rain. Free to gorge their skinny black bodies, they didn't stop until they were swollen and red with blood. Once I killed 55, and left their corpses floating in a puddle of water in my lap.

We waited for five hours to pass. Five long, interminable hours in the rain, watching the leaves go drip, drip, drip. Breaking the minutes into seconds and the seconds into microseconds. After five hours, if it was still raining we could go home. There was no point collecting data on those huddled black bundles, waiting, like us, for the rain to stop.

At home, we had a warm meal and sat in heaven because the water pounding on the roof was not seeping through our skin. Then, when the setting sun was turning the clouds black, if the rain had stopped we went to find our little demon gods, shivering in their hell now devoid of fire.

Carlos brought Sorrow home in a ziplock bag. His eyes were full of maggots. When Princess did a brief autopsy, she found a depression in the side of his head and several wounds covering his body.

'Villagers,' she said. 'They stoned him to death.'

In Nirvana, Elysium was electrocuted by a power line. A long line of naked flesh ran from his shoulder to his flank. His matted fur fell out in tufts. The skin on his stomach was smeared with blood.

In Sin, Whimper clung to his mother's shoulders, his tiny eyes squeezed shut. Whisper's forehead creased in concentration as she leapt from one branch to another, not resting for a moment in case Angel found her again. Across Whimper's tiny back was a gash so deep you could see his fragile white spine.

A stray kitten I brought home from the bins outside the supermarket went to sleep under the hood of the car. When Carlos started the engine, the kitten was caught in the fan belt and mangled beyond recognition. It was still meowing. Carlos cut off its head with a machete.

We called that September the Valley of Death.

'It was just a monkey,' I kept telling myself.

When I retraced the events that ended with me limping from Costa Rica to a psychologist's office in Sydney, they always began with Sorrow's death.

His body looked so pitiful against the harsh white of the plastic table top. Stiff with rigor mortis, he could have been a specimen stuffed for a museum exhibit. The stench of rotting flesh drifted from him like a thin coil of smoke. He had been dead for more than a week, and already the skin stretched over his cranium was brittle and peeling.

I used to watch Sorrow when I felt like being alone. He didn't play with the other monkeys. If you wandered a little way from Sin, you would sometimes come across him taking a sip from the river, or peering closely at the underside of a leaf. He was a meditation monkey; watching him made you feel calm and relaxed.

I couldn't stop wondering how it happened. Whether a group of kids laughingly pelted him with rocks, each hit making him flinch until the last death blow to his skull. Perhaps it was a farmer, who gathered some pebbles from the river in his hand and flung one after the other. Was it a quick death? Or did he crawl for most of the day, his brain haemorrhaging slowly in the heat? Who picked out his eyes, and was he alive or dead when they did it? In the back of my mind, I heard his feeble bird alarms as raptors circled above.

Angel was closing in for the kill. Whisper ran as fast as she could with the tiny bundle on her back. She tried to be soft footed, but every time she landed on a branch, Whimper screwed up his face in pain and clenched his tiny fingers. Every few minutes, Whisper stopped and looked at Angel, who began to resemble a ghoulish panther. He lay low as he crept forward, never taking his eyes off the tear he'd made in Whimper's back with one swipe of his sharp fingernails.

'Run, Whisper, run,' panted Brad, as we chased them like earth-bound angels.

As we ran, I left behind the callous shrug with which I greeted the deaths of other babies. Of course, I'd felt sorry for the mothers, but the actual babies I thought of as cartoons: cute but two dimensional. For some reason, Whimper mattered. My heart tightened each time he winced.

Brad and I decided Angel wouldn't murder Whimper if we stayed close. For five hours we stayed beneath her, hoping our eyes would keep her safe. I wanted to beat Angel away with a stick. I wanted to tell Whisper we would stand guard while she rested, and give some relief to the tired lump on her back, who had not nursed all morning. But that was forbidden and would be looked upon with the gravest displeasure by higher powers crunching our data in the laboratory. Princess made it clear that witnessing infanticide was a priority. We were to record every detail on dictaphone and take video if we could. Diane desperately wanted us to film Angel actually killing a baby. It was important for science. It would make a good paper.

It was hard to believe anything was good or important about Whimper's broken flesh or Whisper's harrowed eyes. But that was the monkey house for you. Through the looking glass and into the jaws of the Jabberwocky.

We lost them in the afternoon drizzle. Exhausted, we sat under a tree calculating how long its thick canopy would keep us dry. I figured about fifteen minutes. Brad sat with his head on his knees, totally depressed. I rubbed his back.

'Honey, don't worry, Whimper is going to be fine. We'll find them later and throw a couple of rocks at Angel. We'll say villagers did it.'

'It's not Whimper. It's Andreas. I'm obsessed. Why doesn't he like me?'

I was surprised Brad's infatuation had survived the week.

'Andreas doesn't like anyone. He has no facial expressions and no conversation. You're trying to seduce a mute.'

'You don't understand. We have long, meaningful discussions. He opens up to me. Then an hour later, he ignores me. It's totally screwing with my head.'

'Maybe if you hang out together, you know, create a comfortable space.'

'I can't! Annie is always there. When it's just her and I in the field, she follows me around like a manic depressive, not even trying to identify anyone. But if we're out with Andreas, she perks up like a pair of tits. She actually pushes me out of the way to stand next to him. And she corrects me all fucking day.'

'I can't believe Andreas's taking her seriously. He's going to Germany to be with Ada in a month. He's probably just putting up with it.'

'He *loves* it. He thinks she's *hilarious*. He actually said to me the other day, "Annie, she's funny". I could smash her face in.'

Just then we heard a lost call from Whisper. We jumped up and ran after her until nightfall, when we were forced to abandon her to the darkness.

Brad wasn't the only unhappy camper. Kermit was derailing like a freight train. He refused to stop going to the bar and partied all night with a new-found pack of Tico friends.

'They're just using him for his money,' Princess said spitefully. 'He's free beer as far as they're concerned.'

It didn't stop him. He started to reek of alcohol in the mornings. I occasionally suspected he was still drunk. When the car got a flat tyre at 4:23 a.m., Kermit jumped out to change it. Unfortunately, only Carlos knew where the crowbar was, and he talked rapidly in Spanish to Jesus who jacked up the car. Kermit tried to contribute but kept getting in the way. When it was really obvious he was being a nuisance, he backed off and started doing push-ups on the road.

'Uh, Kermit?' I said. 'What are you doing?'

'Had a Red Bull this morning,' he panted. 'I'm fired up and ready to go.'

He did ten more push-ups, leapt up, clapped his hands, added a 'whoop' and jumped in the car.

I told Brad of Kermit's disturbing behaviour, and we both agreed Kermit was suffering from frat withdrawal. For the last four years of college, he'd lived with the same group of jocks who were always ready to get drunk and do something stupid. In the monkey house, Kermit regarded Brad and I as his best friends, but we weren't really drinkers. As a result, Kermit was feeling left out.

A sense of isolation drove his testosterone levels through the roof. He convinced himself he was now the jungle-crashing Indiana Jones of Costa Rica. His most annoying habit was some kind of ninja routine with his machete, which he twirled around under his arms and over his head.

'You're going to cut yourself,' said Princess. 'Or someone else.'

'I've got control of it,' he retorted.

Right on cue, he sliced open his head. It was only a skin wound, but it bled profusely down his neck and into his shirt. Infuriated, he threw a tantrum. He stomped around, kicking the ground and swearing. Princess raised her eyebrows and turned away. When he got home, Brad told him to put some disinfectant on it. He refused.

'Kermit, don't be a jerk. You cut open your own head with a rusty machete. It'll get infected.'

'Yeah,' I chimed in. 'You remember what happened to my head!'

'I'll even do it for you,' said Brad.

'Leave me alone,' growled Kermit, sulking at the table.

'Fine,' snapped Brad. 'I hope you get blood poisoning and die.'

A week into the Valley of Death, Kermit shut out everyone. When Brad and Summer went to the bar and saw Kermit with his Tico friends, Kermit didn't even acknowledge them. This could have been because Kermit hated Summer who had been bossing everyone around since she'd arrived. Being 30, she decided independently that the hierarchy should go by age and put in her two bits whenever she felt like it. This disturbed the hierarchy greatly, but everyone was too preoccupied to put her in her place. For some reason, she was especially bossy towards Kermit, and it drove him crazy.

Sarah was also struggling. We were still friends, but she was so unhappy it was hard to talk to her. We went to the movies every week and she would perk up a little over a batido, but as soon as we got back to the monkey house she sank into herself. When we were out together in Sin, she confided that Princess was criticising her every night through the monkey notes. Each night, Princess gave the monkey notes where she imparted any news from Diane, mistakes she'd noticed in the worksheets, and anything else we were doing wrong. It struck me later that not once were we told we were doing a good job. Monkey notes were strictly for criticism and Sarah was convinced most of it was aimed at her. One night, Sarah refused to eat at the table, and took dinner into her room. She did the same thing every night afterwards, sending a message loud and clear to Princess.

Go fuck yourself.

I wouldn't have known what Annie was going through and I wouldn't have cared, except for the week that we were in Nirvana together.

'Great,' I groaned, looking at the schedule. Brad gave my arm a little squeeze.

'Have fun.'

Never in my life have I seen such a spectacle of extravagant misery. On the first morning, we lay on our bags on the highway outside the Quebrador. We couldn't see each other, but I could feel desolation leech from her like toxic waste. It surrounded her like an aurora, glowing green and yellow in the darkness.

For four hours we didn't speak. She followed me silently, and I felt the force of her suffering press the air at my back. It was like someone was dragging her over a bed of knives. Eventually, I couldn't stand it anymore.

'Annie, are you okay?'

'I hate these monkeys,' she whispered.

Despite my previous feelings towards Nirvana, I was offended.

'I know they're ugly,' I said. 'But it's like they're so ugly, they're fascinating. Like Michael Jackson after plastic surgery. They have *personality*. Just look at Ecstasy. It's kind of cool how she's the worst bitch that ever lived.'

'I don't think she's the worst,' said Annie, looking directly at me. I was surprised. Of course, I had been mean to her, but not as mean as I could have been.

I thought the look she gave me was unjust. The strange thing was, I couldn't be angry. She was just too miserable to hate. No nasty thing I could say would punish her more than she was punishing herself, and it took all the satisfaction out of it. Then, after nine hours of silence, I recognised Annie's bed of knives—she was in love.

No wonder she looked as though someone was throwing her a gut punch every minute. I was on familiar terms with those heavy limbs, the way you had to choke down the thought of your rival, innocently combing her hair on the other side of the ocean.

Sure enough, as soon as we got home, Annie jumped out to find Andreas. She giggled as she pulled the waist of her pants down to show him where an acacia ant had left a hot, red swelling on her thigh.

Princess barely went into the forest that month. She had a bladder infection, followed by a cold, followed by some absolutely urgent matter she had to attend to at home.

You would think she had learnt her lesson from doing the same thing to the last group, and probably the group before that. Everyone thought she was faking her illnesses but I had no doubt they were real. She would rather be pissing blood than go out with the monkeys, and her body was obliging her.

But however safe she was from the jungle, she couldn't escape the glares of accusation and resentment that followed her everywhere she went.

In the middle of the Valley of Death, Rachel arrived. She had thick glasses that magnified her eyes like a snorkel mask. The glasses looped around her neck with a chain of plastic links that middle-aged women wore in the 1980s, and she completed the effect by wearing her hair in a braid. Within minutes she declared loudly through her bucked teeth that she was a lesbian Jew. She paused with her head cocked, waiting for prejudices to be flung at her so she could martyr herself on them. Brad and I looked at each other sideways, and like everyone else, tried to pretend she wasn't there.

As for me, I looked in the mirror one night and saw the beginning of the end. A wrinkle. It started at the bottom of my right eye, balancing on the ridge bone of my socket. It ran all the way to the corner, meeting, to my horror, a whole delta of fine lines spreading from my eye's point to the sea of my temple. I scrubbed my skin, hoping it was mud streaks. No luck. I clutched wildly at the hope it was an exhaustion wrinkle, and would be smoothed away with a good night's sleep. But I knew it wasn't true. Exhaustion causes dark circles, red sclera and puffy eyelids, but not wrinkles.

It wasn't pure vanity that was making me panic. I even felt I was making progress since I hardly ever looked in the mirror anymore and cared less about my appearance. No, the wrinkle symbolised more than the deterioration of my looks as I pushed past optimum fertility into my late twenties. It raised an important question: What the fuck was I doing here? It was excusable to be running around jungles when you were 22, but at my age? I was supposed to be working on my career. The Disney segments were a thin veneer of productivity, but I could have made them in a few months then gone on to something else. At the end of Costa Rica I would have a tiny amount of filming experience and expertise in monkey vocalisations. How the hell was I going to get a job?

Then there was the question of mate potential. By the time I walked out of the jungle, I would be nearly 27. I wanted a baby by 32 to ensure my ovaries weren't shrivelled as a bunch of raisins. That left five years to find the love of my life, trick him into marrying me and having the child. It didn't feel like enough time. And deep down, I wasn't sure he was out there. Which meant I would have to follow Madonna's lead and have an illegitimate child with my personal trainer. Which meant I would have to support it on my own. Which meant I would have to have a successful career. And back I was at the beginning of my wrinkle dilemma.

'You can't even see it, darling,' said Brad when I threw myself on his bed, weeping. But he was 24 and had the smooth arrogant skin of youth. He sat blank and uncomprehending while I lay like a cracked porcelain vase, leaching water onto his coverlet.

One afternoon Brad burst into the house like a madman and ran straight to his room. Obviously, he wanted to be alone.

I barged into his room without knocking.

'Darling, what's wrong?'

His face was bloodless.

'Smoke fell on my head.'

'What?!'

'It was Angel. We heard a scream and found Scandal with Smoke clinging to her back. His neck was bleeding. When Smoke couldn't hold on anymore, he fell on my head.'

Brad's voice broke.

'He was still alive. Still moving. Then he died on the ground right in front of me. It was horrible, horrible!'

I touched his shoulder. It seemed an ineffectual gesture.

'The worst was at the end of the day. Annie jumped in the car and kept digging her elbows into my ribs, laughing. I totally ripped her head off. I said, "It's been a VERY bad day."'

I hardly thought this was ripping her head off, but Brad wasn't often assertive to anyone except me.

'You can't go out tomorrow. Stay home and rest.'

'You've got to be joking,' he said bitterly. 'Stay home just because a baby monkey fell on my head and died right in front of me? What kind of an excuse is that?'

'You're clearly traumatised. You can't go out tomorrow.'

'It's beneath me as a scientist. We're supposed to be objective about these things.'

I stayed with him until dinner and listened as he choked up pieces of Smoke's death, like broken bits of glass.

Two weeks before Andreas left, I finally appreciated him. We sat in Nirvana together, eating our lunch. The silence was peaceful. Since the Smoke episode, Brad had been withdrawn and distant. When he did talk, it was to obsessively bitch about everyone, and much as I wanted to join in, his fervour exhausted even me.

Between bites I stole looks at Andreas, trying to figure out what Annie and Brad were fussing over. I could see how his soft lips and luminous eyes could be devastating if you were, hypothetically, stuck in the middle of the jungle with no other options.

I wondered if he had ever considered me, and if not, why not. He looked up and caught me staring. Embarrassed, I tried to appear as if I had been looking behind him.

'Seraph's over there,' I said. 'Do you want to follow her?'

I might as well have hurled myself off a cliff, it was such a stupid thing to say. Seraph, like all the young monkeys in Nirvana, and unlike the older ones, was exceptionally beautiful. It had taken me a while to notice them because the juveniles hid from new observers, but when they finally came out it was like woodland nymphs emerging from a cavern of goblins.

Seraph was the loveliest of them all. She had a heart-shaped face with fur so white it glimmered. Her large eyes shone like obsidian and her ebony cap came to a perfect widow's peak in the centre of her forehead. Her button nose perched elegantly above her lips which had just the right amount of pinkness.

However, like any top model, she was difficult. It was harder to get Seraph follows than any other monkey, because as soon as she caught you looking, she would flee like Kate Moss from the paparazzi.

Andreas raised his eyebrows. I wasn't in the habit of proposing difficult follows, especially when it was my turn to run. He shrugged and stood up.

'Sure.'

When we began, Seraph was daintily chewing on a stick. I fervently hoped she had found a large bug that would keep her going for at least five minutes. However, as soon at the stop watch beeped, she started to run.

'Abort?' Andreas called.

'No!' I yelled over my shoulder as Seraph skipped over the brambles. I swung around to the left and cut her off at the other side. She looked surprised I had caught up. In front of her was a rocky escarpment.

'I've got you now, my pretty.'

She looked up.

'Oh no,' I said, catching on. 'Don't be a shit.'

I could have sworn she smiled as she ran up.

'Abort?' called Andreas.

I should have, but Seraph was thirteen follows behind on the monthly worksheet and I didn't want to be beaten. There were two minutes left of the follow. I stepped on a rock that jutted out of the cliff and pulled myself up by tree roots that looped between the cracks.

I almost made it. I could see over the edge to an enchanted garden covered in moss. Tall trees stood like wizards, their wrinkled trunks uncluttered by brambles and undergrowth.

My eyes were level with the moss when a rock came loose under my left foot. I managed to grab a thick root above me and swung in midair while my feet scrambled for a footing. I felt a spasm beneath my shoulder blade, like someone tying a knot in my muscles. I hauled myself over the edge and looked up. Seraph was gone.

'Fuck.'

It wasn't until I tried to get up that I realised something was wrong. I walked a little way, and a sharp pain hit the middle of my spine.

I was born with a slight curve in my spine, a maladaptation from our ancestors standing upright so suddenly. My back muscles are constantly clenching and compensating for the curve of my vertebrae to the left. I frequently experience sharp pains in my shoulder blades, but these can be managed with exercises I do every morning. But every now and then, something goes wrong. My muscles lock and every tiny movement sends spasms of agony shooting in all directions.

I lay down, my back flat against the earth so I looked up at the sky. Andreas sat down beside me. He took out a biscuit and ate it, shaking his head at my Seraph folly. When he finished, he crumpled up the plastic and put it in the top pocket of his bag. He got up to go. Finally I said it.

'I can't move.'

He frowned, as though I'd made a joke he didn't find funny.

'I can't get up. It's my back.'

He looked from side to side, not understanding.

'What happened?'

'I don't know. When I was coming up the cliff, I hurt something. Now I can't get up.'

Tears crept into my voice at the same pace as the panic speeding up my heartbeat.

Andreas looked alarmed. 'The car isn't here. I don't have the keys, do you?'

A major flaw in the occupational health and safety practices of the monkey project was that there were only two sets of car keys. Carlos always carried one and another group carried the other. This meant one group didn't have them. Today, that was us. There were at least two valleys between us and the other groups. The keys might as well have been flung far into the forest for all the chance we had of finding them.

'I have to find the keys to the car. Do you need to go to hospital?'

I had flashbacks of the matron with the clipboard who stitched up my forehead.

'No hospital. Just take me home.'

'I'll find the keys, then I'll bring the car. I don't know how long I'll be. But we have to get you to the pasture. I can't drive the car in here. Do you think you can get there?'

'You'll have to help me stand.'

Stooped like a hunchback and gritting my teeth in pain, I shuffled an inch at a time to the pasture. Getting through the barbed wire fence nearly finished me. Andreas held me up, a strength in his thin limbs I never imagined, and laid me gently down beneath a fig tree. He knelt above me. His eyes, usually so blank and uncomprehending, were troubled. Suddenly, I realised what Brad and Annie were so fascinated with. Andreas's impassivity was only a mask for a swirling mass of emotions that never made it to the surface.

'I'll be back as fast as I can,' he promised. 'Wait for me. Stay here.'

I smiled weakly.

'I'm not going anywhere.'

I watched the clouds sail across the cobalt blue like ships on their way to exotic lands to trade for silks and spices. I plotted their journeys. The wispy cirrus bound for Zanzibar. The nimbus to Persia. I arched my head and saw a fleet of cumulus pressing onward from the horizon. A cool wind raced along the ground. I felt my back stiffen as the cold seeped from the earth into my flesh. Muscles clenched around my spine like a fist. I took four painkillers I had bought over the counter in Nairobi, no doubt a potent fusion of illegal substances. Strange shapes danced in and out of the rain drops, then numbness raced through my bloodstream and I sank gratefully into oblivion.

I woke just in time to see the cumulus cover the sun like great sweeping sails. A few fat drops fell on my feet. The fig tree kept me dry for a while. I listened to the increase in intensity of drops hitting the leaves. They filtered down the canopy, one by one, each carried a little further by the slippery wetness of the leaf before. The first drop to fall on my face made a little splash of triumph. The tree, like a sponge, had reached saturation point. Now for every drop that fell from the clouds, another fell from the tree to the ground.

The soil turned to mud. The dirt beneath me that I had managed to warm with my body became cold. I started to shiver. As the sky bled into the leaves, raindrops fell in my eyes. Rivulets of water ran around my head, and the floating dirt clung to my hair like survivors of a shipwreck.

That is how they found me. Shivering and covered in mud. Andreas jumped out of the car like a white knight, Sarah and Annie scampering behind.

'It's alright honey,' said Annie as they lifted me into the car, and I thought I must be dying if she was already using endearments.

The ride home was torture. Every rock the car went over jolted me unbearably. As we hurtled down the highway I could barely breathe from the pain.

'Oh my god,' said Princess when she saw me, no doubt envisaging the first death of a field assistant.

'I'm fine,' I said, teeth chattering. 'I just need to get into bed.'

I looked at them all. For just a moment I had no enemies. Seeing me suffer upset them. I felt a surge of affection and gratitude. But I was still covered in mud.

'Sarah,' I said in a small voice. 'Will you help me take a shower?'

So Sarah undressed me and washed the dirt out of my hair, as carefully as a lover might. Afterwards, she helped me lie down in my bed, the crisp sheets sliding over me like a cocoon. The world spun behind my closed eyes, and I let my back lock into place. All movement leeched from me like rain disappearing into parched fields. It was ten days before I could walk again.

chapter 11

Dr Club Med's fingers

'**M**ischka,' Brad said, waggling his bottom into my room. 'You look awful.'

Mischka was Brad's new pet name for me. It came from some obscure Russian playwright I had never heard of.

'I thought I was getting better.'

With the help of my Nairobi painkillers and Tylenol Bedtime, for three days I did my best to remain unconscious so I could ignore the feeling someone was knocking a chisel into my spine. But there was no way to avoid what became the most dreaded part of my day—going to the toilet.

I couldn't turn my neck, so to get up I had to roll myself onto my side very slowly as pain shot down my collarbone. Then I rolled a little further until I had both palms on the mattress. The weight of my head was too heavy for the tendons in my neck so I leant forward until my forehead rested on my pillow. Slowly, very slowly, I pulled my knees beneath me, and used the extra height to lift my torso. Keeping my back perfectly straight, I took little steps out of my bedroom like a Chinese princess with bound feet. Each time my foot hit the floor an electric shock pulsed through the holes in my vertebrae like a thread through the eye of a needle. I kept my head as high as a debutant's, and walked two rooms to the toilet. When I had finished, I waved my right hand around until it hit the toilet paper, then wiped with as little disturbance to my neck, spine and buttocks as possible. I tottered back to my room and lowered myself onto the bed, reversing the steps of getting up.

To minimise the number of times I had to go through this ordeal, I sipped at the cup of water by my bedside, ignoring the aching desert in my throat. Of course, in the heat, this kind of behaviour was a one-way ticket to dehydration and added a piercing headache to the back pain.

After the third day, I decided to cut down on the Tylenol, which led to the kind of boredom usually reserved for prisoners and toll-booth operators. I counted holes in my mosquito net. I traced cracks in the wall with my fingers and imagined them as rivers of the world. I read five volumes of *Harry Potter* then re-read them.

Every night Brad brought me my dinner and sat on my bed, recounting the day's adventures. He seemed to recover from the Smoke ordeal, but though his gestures were as flamboyant as ever, there was an apathy behind them, like an actor in an empty playhouse.

'You are so lucky you're not out there.'

'Please, tell me stories of misery. I'm so fucking bored I could start knitting.'

'Well you can hear the rain, it never stops. Princess is still getting shit from Diane about our data, so the five-hour rule is over. We have to stay out there, full stop. No coming home to see you for lunch, Mischka.'

The rain had been so hard lately, Brad was almost always home by noon and stayed with me until 3 p.m. 'Angel is stalking the babies Jack the Ripper style. Did you hear he bit off Arsenic's foot?'

'Oh my god, he's moving up the hierarchy. After Whimper, Arsenic and Mischief are the only ones left.'

'The foot is hanging by a thread. The stump is all deformed and swollen, it's disgusting. Princess told us in monkey notes that Diane said we have to take the video to Sin every day, try and get the massacre on film.'

'Shit. How's Whimper?'

'Better, we think he might make it. He doesn't look like he's in so much pain now. Princess says monkeys have recovered from worse. Me, however, I'm dying out there and no one cares. I have fungus everywhere. No matter how much I blow-dry my genitals, it just keeps coming. And my feet are disgusting. I've never been in such a state.'

There was a knock at my door. It was Andreas.

'Hey,' I said. 'My knight in shining armour.'

He smirked, which was an indication he found something really funny.

'How are you doing?'

'Better, thanks. I'm sure I'll be up in a few days.'

'Cool.'

As soon as the door shut, I said, 'If I walked into his room and took off all my clothes, do you think he'd have sex with me?'

'You bitch. Absolutely not. You can't walk anyway. You're a cripple.'

'I'm so tempted. Why isn't he in love with me? What does it take to get a reaction out of him? Do you think he changes his expression when he comes?'

'That is so over the line. How dare you tread on my territory.'

'Chill out, darling. I've already made two catastrophic mistakes on this project. You can have him. How's it going with you lovers anyway?'

'Annie's still rubbing her crotch on him like a bitch in heat. But I think the rain is grinding her down. You know she's clumsier than you?'

'Impossible.'

'True story. She can't balance for shit. But when she falls in Quebrada Acacia, which is every day, she doesn't even have the grace to laugh like you do. She totally loses her temper. It's ugly. UG-LY. She says "Shoot!" then storms around like the Midwestern Jersey freak she is. I'm sure Andreas will see any minute now that she's a total scrag and he should screw me instead.'

'I'm sure. You know I've been thinking, while I lie here like a paraplegic all day, I wonder if I could write a book.'

'About me?'

'No you idiot. About us, about here. Don't you think people would be interested in what we do?'

'All we do is grow fungus on our genitals.'

'Can you forget about your crotch for two seconds? I'm having a serious literary idea.'

'I think it's fabulous. Of course everyone wants to know about the stupid disgusting things other people do so they don't have to go out and do them. And besides, what else have you got to do all day?'

'Thanks.'

'And Mischka?'

'Mmm?'

'Make me dark. Dark and beautiful.'

One night Brad didn't come to my room. I waited, thinking he must be on the phone. Seven o'clock came and went. I heard Andreas packing his bag in the kitchen, which meant dinner was over. I waited until eight, then as Sarah walked past my room I called out. She stuck her head in.

'Hey miss, how are you feeling?'

'Good, but do you know where Brad is?'

'He's in the other house.'

'Oh.'

I was worried. And hungry. I waited until everyone went to bed, then I did my toilet contortions except I detoured to the kitchen and poured a bowl of cereal. I sat up until nine, just in case, but when he didn't appear, I read *Harry Potter and the Prisoner of Azkaban* for half an hour then fell asleep.

The next morning was Andreas's day off. I heard his door creak open.

'Hey Andreas?'

'Yeah?'

'Did anything happen yesterday?'

There was a pause.

'With what?'

'With anything, with people, with the monkeys.'

'Well, Whimper died.'

I struggled to a sitting position.

'Who was in Sin yesterday?'

'Summer.'

'Summer and who?'

'Um, I think it was Brad.'

The French had a torture device they called the oubliette, from the word *oublier*, to forget. It was a deep pit in the ground with no windows and no doors. The prisoner was lowered through a grate at the top, and once they were at the bottom there was no way out. There, they suffered the worst kind of torment: solitude and absolute darkness.

When Whimper died, Brad lowered himself into an oubliette and pulled down the rope. He stopped shaving and his meticulous grooming habits. He scratched his crotch uncontrollably, and I suspected he had abandoned his nightly blow-drying routine. When I spoke to him, he didn't answer and couldn't look me in the eyes. When he did speak, his voice was faint and flat. The spark was gone. He wasn't Brad anymore.

Ironically, as soon as I lost Brad, I gained a whole lot of new friends I didn't want. My room became a kind of therapy session, like the Diary Room in *Big Brother*. People came to bitch, whine, cry and confide in me because I was a captive audience, and didn't have any stories of my own to compete with their misery.

Sarah sat on the end of the bed and looked sadly out the window while she tried to think of a future when her time was up in five months. She was 32 years old, and still had no idea what she was doing with her life. Summer was 30 too, but she was a sprightly 30, the kind of 30 going on sixteen where you'd expect her to do something crazy like leave her well-paying job and run around the jungle in search of adventure. Summer was also beautiful. She'd probably be dating 22-year-olds until she died. Sarah, on the other hand, was 30 going on 40. Not only did she look old, she was one of those sensible people. You'd expect her to have married her high-school sweetheart and have two kids by now. Instead, she had no job, and was wasting a year on something that would do nothing to help her find one.

Kermit walked around my room as though he was disturbed I couldn't walk around it for myself. He picked up objects and put them down again. He kicked around my clothes that were lying on the floor. He sat on the bed and got up again. His eyes were red from drinking all night then going into the forest without enough sleep.

I heard the story of Whimper's death from Summer. It took nine hours for Whimper to die and Brad and Summer were there for all of it. He was so weak he fell off his mother's back. Whisper would nudge him onto her again, but she couldn't hold him and travel at the same time. Eventually, he fell off and didn't get up again.

'Whisper just kept lost calling,' Summer said with tears streaming from her eyes. 'Lost calling and swatting away the flies.'

A few days later the kingdom of Sin was in turmoil again. Angel had fallen, chased out by a new ruler who clawed his way to the alpha position. And who was brutal enough to overcome Angel the Tyrant, Angel the psychopath? We all gasped in shock. None other than the cowardly Dopey. Dopey who had looked longingly over his shoulder as his best friend Sneezy was groomed by a harem of females. Dopey who I chased up a shale mountain while he kneaded his tail like an old woman wringing her hands. Yes, Dopey was the new alpha of Sin, which just goes to show, the cowardly, the stupid and the inept can take over as easily as the wise and the just.

Dopey's first act as the new ruler was to murder Arsenic.

Summer and Sarah found the body, broken but still moving. At the time I was able to totter the short distance to the monkey house and do simple tasks like log the video. The monkey project had hours of video sitting in boxes like uncharted territory. I watched each tape, beginning to end, and wrote what happened against a time code. I started with the most recent, so Arsenic's death was the first.

The forest was impossibly green. Each leaf glowed with an abundance of moisture pushing chlorophyll through the delicate veins. They seemed to grow as I watched, pushing, unfurling, coiling upwards to seize the treasured position where sunlight rained, precious as gold. They pulsed and throbbed, exhaling puffs of wispy air from their stomata that turned the light emerald.

Arsenic lay amongst some saplings that surrounded him like the bars of a cage. His left foot hung by a thread of tendons. He held himself up with two arms, dragging his wasted little body behind him. So much blood had drained from the artery in his foot, his face was blue.

Assassin, his mother, was nowhere in sight; she must have given him up for dead. But he wasn't dead. He was frightened. I could see it in the prophetic eyes that looked straight down the lens to me. If I had been there, I would have scooped him up in my hands and run all the way out of that jungle to a place where nothing could hurt him.

He was so different from the Arsenic I was used to, before the rains came. Murder and Assassin would lie in the orange twist trees, after stuffing themselves all morning. Mischief and Arsenic had a berry swatting game where they pretended to swat berries but ended up swatting each other's faces which made them fall backwards laughing soundlessly. As Assassin's son, Arsenic didn't get as much attention as Mischief. Murder lay like a satisfied queen as Torment, Mayhem, Debacle and Scandal paid their respects to their new prince. Arsenic didn't seem to mind. He twittered at everyone who came near him, regardless of whether they'd come to see him or not, and screwed up his little face in delight if anyone touched or petted him.

Death is an ugly thing to watch. Arsenic's courageous crawl through the luminescent saplings was no match for the sinister force slowly killing him from the inside out. He kept scanning the trees, hoping his mother would reappear and carry him to safety. But he was alone, except for the shadow of the video camera, pointed directly at him like the barrel of a gun.

His last cries broke my heart.

Princess knocked at my door.

'Hey,' she said. 'How are you going?'

I was so surprised to see her, for a moment I didn't answer.

'Uh, great. Should be back out in no time.'

'Take your time. I told Diane not to expect you in the field until after vacation.'

Princess talking to Diane on my behalf? I wondered what was going on.

'Thanks. Please, sit down.'

I could sit up easily now, and Princess sat opposite me on the bed with her legs crossed. It was like a slumber party. She was jittery, as though she'd drunk a lot of caffeine. The skin beneath her eyes was swollen.

'Have you been sleeping?' I asked. She exhaled in relief that someone had noticed. I realised why she had come. According to the bitter calculations of Kermit and Summer, Princess had been to the forest a total of two days in the month. She was running away from their accusing stares to another invalid. I felt sorry for her. Ruling the monkey house required a certain indifference towards what other people thought.

'I haven't slept all night. My bladder infection still hasn't got better, and now I have this really sharp pain in my shoulder.'

'It should get better, but you need some rest.'

'I can't. I haven't been out all week. I have to go out tomorrow, but I'm so tired . . .'

She sighed as though the forest was a monster waiting to devour her youth and prettiness.

'You can't possibly go out tomorrow, you'll be useless. You'll just hold everyone up.'

She looked at me gratefully.

'I will, won't I?'

'Definitely. You have to get better first, otherwise you're just wasting everyone's time.'

She nodded, as if that resolved it. Since that was obviously what she came for, I waited for her to go. But she twirled the corner of my bed sheet around her index finger. I marvelled at the lack of dirt under her fingernails. Even I had dirt under my fingernails and I'd been out of the forest for weeks.

'You know that new movie with Steve Martin?' She spoke quickly, as if she was telling me a secret.

'The one in Liberia? Sure, I saw previews for it last month.'

'I know someone in it.'

'No kidding. Who?'

'The young guy. Tom Welling.'

I gasped.

'Superman from *Smallville*? Oh my god, he's *hot*! How do you know him?'

'I was his prom date in high school.'

As she twisted and untwisted my bed sheet, it seemed to me she was reliving another time. When she went to proms on the arms of future movie stars and the whole world was an endless stream of silk and chiffon, house parties and debutantes. How beautiful and distant it must seem to her now as she turned 26, holed up with dirt, resentment and dying monkeys. As if on cue, she said, 'I wish I knew what to do about Carlos.'

'Why don't you get married?'

'That's not going to solve anything. I'll end up supporting us. Emma's husband went over to America and now he works in a kitchen. Carlos wants to start a lawnmowing business, but I'm scared he'll end up washing dishes. He promised to learn English and hasn't. He hasn't saved any money. He can't even afford the plane ticket.'

There were obvious hitches in Princess's fairytale. The damsel doesn't exactly expect her knight to ask for a free ride back to her kingdom, and by the way could she hook him up when they got there. Princess wanted a man who would lay the world at her feet, and in the enchanted garden of Costa Rica, Carlos could. He heroically swung his machete through the perilous undergrowth so she would not be touched by insolent curling vines. He ran through hills and valleys like a puma, so she would not have to quicken her pace. But in America, Carlos would be just another Latin American immigrant, and she would have to do the providing for both of them.

'You know what I really wish he'd do?'

I shook my head.

'Walk the dogs with me. I like to take them out at night after dinner, and I don't like to go alone. Carlos says he'll come, but then he wants to stop at all the bars and talk to people. I just want some quiet time where I don't have to talk.'

'Well I'm not Carlos, but if it's just company you want, I'll come too.'

She smiled. 'Great.'

So it was that Princess and I became friends. Each night, we walked the dogs through Vacas, past the playing field surrounded by its cement wall and barbed wire, past people sitting on their porches watching the last of the day's light.

Each night, she had a new illness. Her shoulder hurt. She had food allergies. She had a migraine. The burden of leadership was breaking down her body, consuming her with a tiredness that had nothing to do with sleep.

I soothed her troubled conscience and lied about what everyone thought. I began to like her. There was a vulnerability about her, a childish happiness that appeared when the cool breeze skipped across our skin to the stars. I was surprised how much she worried about everyone else. She was hurt when Andreas challenged her authority by contradicting her at dinner. She was frantic that Sarah hated her and still ate dinner in her room. She knew about Kermit's nightly habits and was anxious his drinking was the cause of his general hostility. Annie still couldn't recognise the monkeys and Princess was worried it was her fault. And then there was Diane, always Diane, to report to, to soothe, to promise even more of herself than she had given already. She knew Diane loved her, but not more than the data, never more than the data.

I listened as we walked. The dogs jerked at their leads, each wanting to be ahead of the other. Sometimes one of us would be pulled forward as Strider or Tucker chased a chameleon whose camouflage had failed.

I was trapped in the dubious limbo of feeling like I could chase monkeys again, and knowing I shouldn't. I could walk but I couldn't carry anything. My back felt tired, as though it was much older than the rest of my body. Had I been in Australia, I would have started chiropractic treatment or physiotherapy. There was nothing of the sort in Liberia, but I was convinced a few massages would help.

So back I went to the St Augusta clinic. I planned to ask my friendly doctor with the moustache if he knew anything about scoliosis.

'The doctor you saw before is not in,' said the veiled receptionist. 'It is Saturday. I have called our spinal surgeon.'

'I don't need a surgeon,' I said, alarmed. 'I just need someone to have a look at my back.'

'Desmasiado tarde. El viene.' Too late. He's coming.

Dr Juval looked like summer at Club Med. He had a swarthy tan, perfectly set off by a white shirt, ironed to perfection and rolled up to the elbows. His hair was boot polish black except for grey wings at his temples.

'Thanks so much for coming in,' I said, thinking I had pulled him away from lounging by the pool.

'My pleasure.'

He guided me into the consultation room by the elbow and sat me down in a chair. I told him what had happened and he nodded wisely, holding his chin between his thumb and index finger.

'I'm sure it's not serious,' he said. 'But I will have a look. If you could please remove your shirt and lie face down on the examination table. I will be back in a moment.'

I did as he asked. I wasn't wearing a bra. Embarrassed, I lay on my stomach and turned my head to the wall. I heard the door open and footsteps. The drawer of a filing cabinet rolled open and shut. At the sound of breaking glass, I turned my head around. Dr Juval had snapped off the glass cap to an old style medicine vial.

'What's that?' I asked

'Medical lubricant.'

He emptied the contents into his hands and threw the vial in the trashcan. He rubbed his hands together and approached the bed. I closed my eyes. His hands were firm and sure on my spine. They explored my shoulder blades, bending my arm back so he could probe his fingers underneath the bone to the muscle. He rubbed each vertebra, and felt the muscles surrounding them, as though he were making a mental map of the damage. The medical lubricant lost its fluidity and became sticky and viscous. He snapped open another one, and his hands caused ripples under my skin. It was overwhelming to suddenly be free from constant aching, to feel my muscles relaxing for the first time in weeks.

When he pulled down my skirt and my underpants, I was not alarmed. The buttocks, gluteus maximus, are the largest muscles in the body. Many male physiotherapists have hastily explained that knots in the buttocks cause compensation and pain in higher areas. He kneaded them with his knuckles. The muscles clenched around his fist then became smooth and supple. He rubbed my calves, my ankles, my feet. Every coiled sinew, every twisted tendon, came undone. He stroked and moulded until every part of my body purred. He snapped open another vial.

Warmth spread between my thighs. I was becoming inappropriately aroused. I calmed myself down. It was just my oversensitive libido protesting against four months without sex. I kept myself still, telling myself he didn't know. It was my secret.

Hands parted my legs. Fingers massaged the inside of my thighs. Chemical signals shot my drowsiness awake. One finger pushed into my vagina like a fantasy reaching out and grabbing me by the throat.

I wish I could say I got up, punched him in the face and stepped over his body on the way out the door. I wasn't drugged or immobilised. I'd trained in martial arts for five years for just such an occasion. I could have done some serious damage with two well-aimed knuckles to the throat. At the least I could have dislocated his jaw.

Instead, I swallowed a gasp. The finger slid in easily. He pulled it away and again massaged my thighs. I was surprised by how much I wanted it again.

I listened to his breath. It was long and heavy. The hands left my legs and I felt them again on my shoulders. They were stronger now and less gentle. They pushed under my shoulder blades and kneaded out the last of my body's resistance. Against my head which lay at the edge of the examining table, Dr Juval pushed his penis into my hair. I felt his erection straining through his pants, as he rubbed it back and forth over my complete humiliation.

Still my secret leaked through my vagina, so when he pushed his fingers in, three this time, the conquest was complete.

'*Esta bien?*' he asked. Is that good?

'Yes,' I replied, weeping. 'Yes.'

I took the bus home. The world went by very fast while I moved very slowly. My back was sticky with medical lubricant. I saw a white piece of it flaking off my arm, like mould on a fish's tail.

I probed myself very gently, as though I just had an accident and was checking for broken bones. Was I traumatised? In shock? Intellectually, I knew I'd been sexually assaulted. I'd read enough literature to know Dr Juval had totally screwed with his Hippocratic oath. But crouching in the corner of my psyche was the knowledge that I had brought this on myself.

I took a deep breath. As I exhaled, I quickly reconstructed the afternoon's events. I flicked my hair over both shoulders like it was salt. I could lock up the whole affair and never look at it again. No one had to know. Maybe in a few years I could giggle about it to my girlfriends, write to the fantasy section of *Cleo* for 50 bucks: 'My Sordid Sex Secret of Costa Rica'.

But then I realised it wasn't that easy. By encouraging the Club Med doctor to stick his fingers in my pussy, I had set a precedent for all the other white girls after me. He probably thought now that every gringa was begging for it. Diane was recommending people to go to the clinic. What if he did it, or worse, to someone else? That kind of thing could really fuck a person up. My chest contracted into a painful fist.

Everyone had to know.

I started with Princess.

'I was sexually assaulted by the doctor at the St Augusta clinic in Liberia.'

I started crying. She looked at me, stunned.

'I fell asleep while he was massaging my back,' I lied, 'and I woke up with his fingers in my vagina.'

'Oh my god.'

I cried for a little longer, wiped my eyes and stood up.

'Can you tell Diane? She needs to know.'

I had a flash forward to Princess standing up at dinner and telling everyone while I hung my head and looked at my lap.

'Also,' I said, 'I want to tell everyone myself.'

Brad was on the porch with Kermit and Andreas. I grabbed his arm.

'I need to talk to you, right now.'

We had barely spoken since Whimper died. But I needed him now. If I was going to tell everyone, I needed support

from someone who loved me. He followed me into the
bathroom. I took off all my clothes.

'I've just been fingered by the doctor in the St Augusta clinic.'

His mouth fell open, but he didn't say anything.

'It gets worse.' I got into the shower, and scrubbed myself
like I would never get clean. 'I liked it.'

It was the only time I told the whole truth to anyone.
Every other version I told was a lie. I fell asleep. He gave me
a pill. But to Brad, the whole dirty truth poured out like
poison. My wet vagina. The snapped bottles of lubricant that
half filled the trashcan. His erection in my hair.

Raw with the ugliness of it, I waited for Brad to say
something. I could hardly breathe and my legs were shaking.

'Well,' he said slowly, 'at least one of us is getting some.'

For one terrible moment I thought he was calling me
a filthy whore. Then I understood. He was smiling. The
oubliette collapsed, and my Brad was back again. I laughed.

'You stupid faggot.'

'Oh come on. I'd pay to get fingered by a doctor at this
point.'

I kept laughing, in desperation, in relief, in pure happiness.
Brad was laughing too, and I hugged myself in the shower
and laughed and laughed until the laughter turned into crying
then back into laughter. Brad held out my big blue towel and
wrapped me in it, gently but firmly so I wouldn't break, then
he held me for a few long moments until the towel soaked
up all the tears.

I stood up at the end of dinner.

'I've logged all the video. Every tape is numbered and
catalogued on the "video" file in the hard drive. Also, I was
sexually molested today at the St Augusta clinic, so don't
go there.'

I felt the effect ricochet through the group like an atomic blast. They all looked at each other, at the same time avoiding me. No one but Brad could look me in the eye. At that moment, how I mistrusted and hated them all. I knew they wanted every sordid detail, blow by blow. I was like a sexual assault story in magazines that everyone reads with salacious outrage.

'And don't ask me any questions,' I added defiantly. 'Because I don't want to talk about it.'

Rachel came up to me in the kitchen.

'Uh Vanessa? I used to be a rape crisis counsellor. If you ever want to talk about it . . .'

I slammed my plate down so hard on the bench, it cracked. Every ear in the house swivelled towards us like radars. My voice was tight with fury.

'Don't you dare ever mention it to me again.'

I turned my back on her and walked out, satisfied everyone got the message.

chapter 12

Dog star

The volcano was beautiful in the sunset. There was a walk I loved, just outside Vacas, where a white road turned off the highway. It wandered past a tea plantation where hundreds of bushes sloped in diamond patterns down a hill. No one drove down the road except the handful of people who lived in scattered shacks under the shadow of Volcan de las Viejas. On the right-hand side before the river there was a rocky outcrop overlooking a vast plain. Charles kissed me there once. We were sitting on the smooth granite when he pushed me onto a cluster of yellow flowers. As his hand felt up my skirt I turned my head and saw petals flutter like tiny flags in the breeze.

My back was slowly recovering. To prepare myself for a fourteen-hour monkey day, each afternoon I walked the dogs down the beaten white road until I could see the mist playing along the edge of the volcano's crater.

As I turned out of Vacas, I tightened the leashes as we approached a tyre factory guarded by seven ferocious hounds. Every day, Strider and Tucker, safe on their side of the chicken-wire fence, did their best to antagonise them; lunging, barking and snarling until the slobber ran freely on both sides. But this time, there were no dogs in sight. The silence was eerie. I craned my neck to see if there was a canine ambush ahead. The tyre factory was empty.

I heard someone cry out. Horrified a small child might be trapped inside, I hurried towards the sound, mentally preparing myself to leap the fence, rescue the child and get the hell out before we were all ripped to shreds. As I came closer, the cries became more pitiful. I couldn't see anything.

A black bundle the size of my hand came leaping towards the fence, tail wagging.

'Oh no,' I said, backing away instantly. 'No way.'

A man emerged from the factory. He walked over, picked up the black bundle and held it out.

'*Para usted?*'

'No, sorry, I can't take a puppy. I live in Australia. Au-str-a-lia. Very far. Long plane. Strict quarantine.'

The puppy began to whine. The man made as if to throw it away. He shrugged.

'*Lastima.* I have many big dogs inside. I let them out in ten minutes and they will kill it.'

He paused, correctly assessing the limits of my resistance.

'I guess I'm taking the dog.'

The puppy, as if sensing its close shave with death, leapt into my arms. She (I saw it was a girl) squirmed, rolled over, licked my face. Then I saw her fur moving. It was undulating with fleas. They swarmed onto my hand, looking for more blood to suck. I dropped her. Undeterred, she frolicked between my legs, ran up to Strider and Tucker who were completely unimpressed, licked their faces, then ran back to me.

'Look,' I said to the rolling, tumbling bundle of joy. 'I am NOT taking you home with me—comprende? I'll find

you a suitable Costa Rican family. I'll even buy you dog
food. But Australia is absolutely out of the question.'

We continued on our walk towards the volcanoes and passed a little wooden shack. A woman was in the yard, washing her clothes. There was another dog there. It was a little thin, but otherwise healthy looking. The yard was overrun with chickens. A perfect playground for a puppy.

'Excuse me,' I said. The woman looked up and smiled. She had the smooth golden skin of Costa Ricans and the friendliness of people who are glad to see strangers.

'Hola.'

'Hi. Look I found this puppy, but I live in Australia, and I was wondering—would you like her?'

The woman smiled and held out her arms.

Right, I thought. That was easy. I picked up the puppy and made to hand it over. She wriggled in my arms, yapped twice and licked my face. My arms wouldn't move. My body thrust forward as if trying to propel my arms into action. What are you doing, yelled a voice in my head. Give her the stupid dog. Still my arms refused. I sighed and took a long hard look at the fur, fleas making Mexican waves from head to tail. I thought of the dozens of puppies she'd bring into the world to plague Vacas. It's not right to give such an infested gift, I told myself. At least clean her up a little.

'Actually,' I said, 'I'm going to give her a bath to get rid of her fleas and take her to the vet so she can't have babies. I'll bring her back in a few weeks and you can have her.'

The woman smiled and shrugged her shoulders, chickens chasing each other around her feet.

The puppy tripped between my legs all the way back to Vacas.

'It's just a bath,' I said. 'A bath and desexing. Don't get your hopes up.'

I really could not take her to Australia. Australian Quarantine won't even let you bring peanuts from another country, much less a third-world, flea-ridden, tick-infested mutt with a belly so bloated with worms she looked like a malnourished Ethiopian child.

We passed the vet store on the way home and bought some flea shampoo. The puppy's euphoria evaporated as soon as she saw the hose. I sat down and pinned her to my lap. She started to whine but I was merciless. As the water poured over her, the fleas panicked. They flocked to her head then jumped onto my legs. I hate fleas. I hate the way they weave in and out of hair and refuse to die when you pinch them. Hundreds swarmed on my lap and I was beginning to feel sick. I squirted the entire bottle of flea shampoo onto her tiny wriggling body. It was then she really started to scream. She howled and scratched and writhed. Her sharp little claws made razor-blade slits on my wrists, arms, neck and legs. The shampoo got into my cuts and I nearly started howling too. Still the fleas poured off her in an endless stream of dead bodies. They covered my legs and flowed in a massacre onto the floor. When I rubbed shampoo onto her ears she whimpered, and the water went red with blood.

It took 30 minutes of intense suffering for everyone concerned before I was satisfied that every disgusting invertebrate was dead. The puppy was very quiet. Large patches of her skin were oozing blood. Exhausted, I took her out into the sun and sat on the grass while the howler monkeys watched us from the mango trees. I folded back her ears. Her ear canal was choked with the bloated bodies of ticks. I hate ticks even more than fleas, and I swallowed my nausea and yanked them out one by one. I burst their bodies between my nails and soon my fingers were covered in blood.

The puppy lay on my lap and closed her eyes, her skin stinging from shampoo and her ears aching where I'd pulled out the ticks. She looked like she was trying hard to be grateful she'd found a home.

'Darling,' Brad said when he found us together on the porch. 'What is that?'

'It's only temporary,' I said hurriedly to Princess. 'I just have to get her desexed. I've found her a home already.'

'That's okay. She's cute.' Princess had a habit of salvaging kittens from the street. She could hardly object to a puppy. 'Does she have a name?'

'Sirius,' I said proudly. 'I've named her after the dog star.'

'You did not,' Brad retorted. 'You named her after Harry Potter's godfather.'

'Sirius is a dumb name,' said Kermit. 'I think he should be Midnight.'

'A, he is a she. B, Midnight is a fine name for a retro 80s punk band and a stupid name for a dog. C, I found her, I get to name her.'

'I thought you weren't keeping it, so why do you give a shit?' Kermit snapped back.

Kermit and I were having problems. In the aftermath of being 'diddled by the doctor', as Brad referred to it, I was suddenly and intensely aware that Kermit was sexually attracted to me.

'Does Kermit want to fuck me?' I demanded of Brad.

'Er, yes.'

I reeled.

'Oh my god. That is disgusting. Since when?'

'A few months. I thought you knew.'

I exploded. 'I did NOT know. If I had I would have chopped his dick off. Who does he think he is? Let me tell you darling, I've had men jump out of moving vehicles for me. And do you remember the band Take That?'

'The loser boy band Robbie Williams was in before he was famous?'

'Well Jason, the one no one remembers, ran, yes *ran*, after me on Bondi Beach for my phone number. How the *fuck* does Kermit think he would *ever* get into my pants?'

Brad was looking at me as if I had lost it.

'Mischka, it's just a crush.'

What did I care about Kermit's secret fantasies? But I did care, and I was furious. Visions filled my head of Kermit touching me, Kermit orgasming, Kermit putting my hand on his penis. I wanted to put my hands over my ears and scream. It was true, I was overreacting. But after the episode with the doctor any sexual thoughts were like snakes crawling on my skin. I could barely even stand the shame of being naked and took my shower in about fifteen seconds before I hurriedly covered myself up.

In fact, since the St Augusta clinic, I was like a newborn superhero with exaggerated sensory perception for detecting pheromones. I didn't usually pay attention to men on the street but now I sensed every pair of eyes that watched me. I could follow their line of gaze, whether they lingered on my breasts, my ass or the crease between my thighs, and translate it to what they were thinking. It wasn't pleasant.

Kermit was so in lust with me, I could smell it, and it made me want to tear him apart. I screwed up my eyes and spat at every interaction. Eventually, he stopped being hurt and became angry. For every lash I dealt, he had a snide remark to shield himself. If I turned the screw too fast and tight, he'd clench his fists and breathe fast through his nose like a raging bull.

But the evening when Sirius ran back and forth between us, wagging her tail and licking faces, I forced myself to smile at Kermit. Though I meant to give her to a Costa Rican family, secretly I was hoping someone from a land with more lenient quarantine laws, i.e. America, would take Sirius home. Kermit could be an obnoxious asshole all he liked to me, but he was a sucker for animals. I'd often find him curled up in a hammock with one of Princess's salvaged kittens. He was my prime target. So I swallowed my bile and let the argument get buried under pats and coos as the newly washed, de-tick'd, de-flea'd Sirius basked in the attention of affection-starved monkey researchers who spent all day looking at cuteness but were never allowed to touch.

It was coming up to the end of the month and in a week Andreas was leaving. He was going back to Texas to stay with his family for a while before he flew to Germany to see Ada. I was surprised when Brad told me they were still together, but Andreas always kept information like that close to his chest. I was due to film the ancient temples of Tikal for Disney and wasn't supposed to stay for the party, but I delayed my flight because I felt I owed Andreas his final goodbye and I couldn't resist wearing my new halterneck dress with the Chinese buttons and oriental flowers.

Nothing unusual occurred in the first half of the party. Though we were all drunk, we actually made it to Soda Limon, the nightclub in Vacas. I liked watching Ticos dance. The girls all took their dress cues from MTV, with dresses so tight it obviously took some time to squeeze into them. They kept their long black hair tightly pulled back, taking the MTV message that if it wasn't blond, it was best kept out of sight. The boys all wore baseball caps and American t-shirts with English words they couldn't read. The cheap lights flashed red and orange, and the music was turned up so loud it was distorting. The dancers laughed and flung themselves around with careless abandon.

I was in the nostalgic phase of drunkenness and moved to tears that Andreas was going. I bought two whiskeys, served in Styrofoam cups with ice, and sat down with him at a table. After we threw back our drinks, I felt waves of inebriation cloud my vision. From the corner of my eye I saw Annie leaning into Brad and whispering flirtatiously in his ear.

'Darling,' I said to Andreas, leaning close and throwing caution to the wind. 'I'll miss you.'

Andreas carefully and deliberately leant down and stroked my calf.

'I'll miss you too.'

Oh my god, I thought. It was like a high school disco where everyone starts pashing each other. My body tingled in anticipation of crossing over an impossible line. Sexual animation from Andreas. Incredible. Of course I never would have done anything, Brad was my best friend after all and there are strict rules about cutting grass. Still, the old me could never resist conquering the unconquerable, and I was curious if Andreas would try something.

Brad appeared from nowhere and pulled me onto the dance floor. Annie flopped in the chair next to Andreas.

'Hey,' I protested, stumbling. 'I was getting somewhere.'

Even under the lights I could see Brad's face was bloodless. He assumed a tango position and spoke urgently in my ear.

'Annie's going to fuck Andreas.'

'Sweetie, you're delusional.'

'I mean it. She just told me. Sarah's been encouraging her.'

'But Sarah is Ada's friend! She can't be telling Annie to fuck her friend's boyfriend.'

'She did. And do you know what Annie, that cunt, said to me?'

Brad looked like he was about to cry. I sobered up and paid attention.

'She said, "I'm going after Andreas tonight, and if I fuck him, I'll tell you *every single detail*."'

I looked over at Annie. She was sparkling. She wore a green singlet that drew out the green in her eyes, and one strap had fallen from her shoulder. She was laughing at something Andreas said and his eyes were fixed drunkenly on her breasts. She stood up, took him by the hand and they walked out into the rain. I had a new feeling for Annie. Respect.

I checked my watch—3:42 a.m.

'There's no way she can pull it off. There isn't enough time. Besides, she's only slept with two people her entire life, she hasn't had enough seduction practice.'

It was pouring outside. Andreas and Annie sat under a gutter, their arms wrapped around their knees, and their heads leaning together like two swans. A large light illuminated the rain, turning it to streaks of silver.

'Look, they're just talking.'

Brad's lips were a grim line.

'Don't be so sure,' he said, as they stood up and came inside.

'We're going home,' Andreas said while Annie looked down, coyly.

'So are we,' I butted in. Annie gave me a look of death but I ignored her and grabbed Brad's hand.

When we arrived, Sirius was pushing her black nose in between the gaps in the white gate. She made little noises of joy as we walked in and practically jumped into my arms. I tried desperately not to care as I put her down. I couldn't get attached. I just couldn't. We sat on the porch, and Sirius rolled on her back between my feet, wriggling her pink, fat belly for me to scratch. I pushed down on it and each time she gave a little grunt and wriggled some more. People walked in and out of the house, noisily kissing Andreas and getting all sentimental. I stayed on the porch with them, but really, besides Brad, I didn't care about anyone as much as the little black fur ball squirming at my feet.

At 4:20 a.m., I went inside to pack, since I was leaving on the 5 a.m. bus for San Jose to catch my plane for Guatemala. I shot Brad a 'don't worry' look, and gave Andreas a hug. When I came back out to the porch with my bags, there was no one else up. Sirius jumped like a frog around me.

'No, you aren't coming.' But she didn't believe me and kept wagging her bottom in excitement.

'Shit, I forgot my ticket.'

I went back inside the pizza house. Andreas's door was wide open. His bed was empty. Annie's door was closed, and though I tried to shut my ears for Brad's sake, from behind it I heard muffled sounds somewhere between ecstasy and despair.

I slept all the way to Guatemala. I woke as bewildered as Sleeping Beauty without the benefit of a prince to explain a few things. I shied from the seething mass of people crawling like briars over the dirty streets. Street lights flooded the buildings like suns and I felt danger in the alleyways between them. I half expected the cars to fly, driven by people in spacesuits.

I took a taxi to my hotel and lay on my bed, staring at the ceiling. The mattress was springy, and the room was clean and smelt like air freshener. Now that I was alone, safely contained in my peach-scented capsule, the weight of the last month collapsed on my chest. I could barely breathe.

I hadn't told anyone at home about the doctor. I told myself it would just upset them and anyway, I was fine. I hadn't told anyone about my back, because they would be worried and really, I was nearly better. But surrounded by so much empty space, uncluttered by boots and dirt and voices, I felt cut adrift from everyone I loved. When they sent their thoughts of me into the ether, they were misprogrammed. I felt my molecular structure had changed somehow. I wasn't the same Vanessa they knew. They didn't even know I was in Guatemala. I was floating between planets, between comets, and they had no way to reach me.

I'd been trying to cry for a week. My insides were knotted ropes and I thought if I could cry, they'd loosen a little. But besides my semi-fake crying with Princess, and my mutant laughter-crying with Brad, I couldn't do it.

I tried again, lying on my bed, safe from the jungle. I shut my eyes and made low exhaling whines, my mouth stretched in a monkey fear grin. I got up. It was too ridiculous. I took a hot shower, got dressed and caught a bus to the diamond city of happiness—the mall.

I'd always hated shopping malls. I thought they were sterile madhouses full of frantic housewives and bored teenagers. But spending enough time in the opposite—a very *un*sterile forest full of no one—made me appreciate the beauty a mall represents.

Guatemala city had an impressive mall. Not everyone could climb those sparkling steps and pass through the fake palm trees into paradise. The poor, the depraved and the sinister were kept out by security guards with rifles. The floors shone like polished marble. Stars of light twinkled in the ceiling, and a magic wind kept away the hot, damp night.

Gentle music floated through hidden speakers, whispering, love never ends and beauty never dies.

I headed straight for the golden arches and ordered a McChicken, a cheeseburger, French fries, a chocolate thickshake, an apple pie and a caramel sundae. As I bit into the soft warmth of my burger that burst with pleasing artificial flavours, I felt ready to face the reason I had come.

It was my last filming assignment for Central America. I'd filmed two segments on capuchins, one on howler moneys, one on turtles, and one on Las Pumas, an animal refuge near Vacas. True to form, I had done no research and didn't have a clue what was in Tikal besides temples. Disney didn't want temples, they wanted animals, so I was hoping against hope the temples would be crawling with some kind of monkey.

It wasn't until I dug into my caramel sundae that I thought about why Diane had not contacted me about the sexual assault. At the monkey house I had done a pretty good job suppressing my feelings and ignoring what had happened to me but now I was away from it all I wanted to know why my boss had not contacted me to find out if I was alright. I heard through Princess that Diane was worried and wanted to know if I needed anything but why wouldn't she call or even email herself? Did she think it was my fault I had gone and got myself molested?

I felt smouldering ashes of outrage that I was being ignored as if I was an embarrassing family secret. Didn't she feel even a little responsible? Not only because she recommended the St Augusta clinic, but because I was one of her staff? Without thinking, I stormed into the nearest internet café. I wrote her an email that went something like this:

Dear Diane,

About a week ago I was sexually assaulted by one of the doctors at the St Augusta clinic. He massaged my back, and I was so tired I fell asleep. When I woke up his fingers were in my vagina.

I have considered leaving the project, as this has been extremely difficult to deal with without friends and family. I will see how I go in the next few weeks. I would at least like to see if anything can be done as I hate to think of anyone else going through the same thing.

Best regards,
Vanessa

There, I thought. Try sweeping that under the carpet.

Tikal was once a sprawling ancient metropolis, more than 576 square kilometres of ancient Mayan ruins. Mysteriously abandoned more than a thousand years ago, the jungle cloaked the city with its tentacles and buried it for centuries. In 1848, the city was discovered by a tree gum harvester, who saw the tips of the ancient temples over the tree tops.

There were no monkeys on the temples. I climbed hundreds of rickety wooden steps to their pinnacles, but only managed a glimpse of howler monkeys shaking the trees. Resigned to failure, I walked back to my lodge. One the way, a furry four-legged creature appeared on the path. I dove off the path, pulled out my camera and set it up on my tripod.

It was a coati. I usually saw coatis, which are related to racoons, running away from the monkeys. Assassin especially liked to rip the heads off the pups and suck on their necks like popsicles.

The coati sniffed the ground, tail high in the air. The setting sun was behind it, setting its red fur on fire, and insects flew around its head like fairies with golden wings. As the moon was rising through the dusk I did time lapses of the clouds moving across the temples and then just as the last light was extinguished, another coati ran from the top of an ancient astrological star gazer right down the stone steps. Who needed monkeys?

For three days I wandered through Tikal, tickling holes in the ground with grass blades to make the tarantulas come out and stalking turkeys with brilliant plumage that the Mayans domesticated thousands of years ago. I slunk in and out of stone passageways, built for kings and queens of the ancient world, and climbed to the tops of the observation towers where great astronomers had faithfully plotted the course of the stars. I felt gloriously insignificant, as though I never mattered and never would. Me and everything I carried inside me was invisible to the stone giants that watched over this kingdom, I was a dust mote that, unlike them, would soon be swept away.

At night I thought of Sirius. I thought of her months into the future after I'd left Vacas, wandering the streets looking for scraps. I thought of her sick, infested with parasites, bitten by other dogs. She would come back to the monkey house and sit at the gate, waiting for me to come home. I wanted to keep her so badly it was like someone raking their fingernails across my heart. But I couldn't. I'd saved her, kept her fed and warm for a while, but eventually I would throw her back to a life she didn't deserve, not when she loved me so faithfully. Not when she was worth everything I had.

For the first time since I walked out of the St Augusta clinic like a piece of raw meat, I fell on the bed and cried and cried and cried.

When I got back to the monkey house there was an email from Diane. My Guatemala email worked—she was definitely freaked out. Panic leaked from the monitor. I could see her pacing her office, beside herself. Something like this was not good for PR. Something like this could bring the monkey project down. She told me to catch the 3 p.m. bus on Friday for San Jose. She had friends she wanted me to talk to, and they would help me press charges and take the doctor to court. I had no time to lose since I had not reported him to the police straight after it happened, and if I could I should make a statement immediately. I was to call Diane if I had any questions, but otherwise her friends would be waiting in San Jose.

I was dumbfounded. It was a reaction alright, but not the one I wanted. I was looking for acknowledgement, something along the lines of 'I'm really sorry this happened to you, what can I do to help?' I did not want to be ordered to San Jose, to discuss my violation with people I had never met. Neither did I want to make a police statement. I was familiar with the Vacas police. I passed them every time I went to the post office and they never failed to make leering comments and stare at my tits. I could just imagine going into their shack and telling them about being fingered by a doctor in Liberia. Not only would they be jacking off to the tale for weeks, the story would be around Vacas in seconds.

I replied to Diane's email, saying that it had been hard enough to discuss what had happened with her and Princess, much less complete strangers. I didn't want to go to San Jose and I didn't want to go to court. I just wanted to go back to my normal routine in the forest with the monkeys.

I didn't mean to slap Diane in the face, but I guess that's how she took it because a few days later I received her reply, which in essence said that she felt that the decision was up to me, but if she were me, she'd be worried about him doing the same thing to someone else. She added that if I did leave to let her know so that she could replace me as soon as possible. She also added in a snippy little comment that she noticed that I had fallen behind in my data collection and reminded me that she had said I could do the Disney filming as long as it didn't interfere with my work on the project.

By the time I finished reading, I was shaking with fury.

You fucking bitch, I thought. She was throwing feminism in my face, declaring it my responsibility to take up a crusade for women in a country that wasn't mine, where I had no friends besides Brad, and no family for support. She made it clear that every hapless girl the doctor molested henceforth would be on my head. She was calling me a coward. She insinuated I would run, and when I did, I wouldn't be missed. I was only a pipe in the data collection factory through which she gathered information on her precious fucking monkeys. I was completely dispensable and easily replaced. And on top of everything, she was holding the Disney segments ransom. She knew damn well why I was behind on my data and it wasn't because I was busy logging my footage.

She won't sign, I thought. Originally, we negotiated a contract where Diane had the final approval on the capuchin monkey segments and they couldn't be aired without her signature. Disney was already editing the segments and there was no replacing them. I was screwed. She wanted me to leave the project and then she would let the tapes and the approval form sit on her desk until hell froze over. She wouldn't sign.

Oh yes you will, I thought, my insides clenching like they were breaking stone. Oh yes you fucking will.

Murder was carrying the last of the babies on her back. Mischief was once the prince of an entire generation that would have succeeded the old reign of Sin. Now he was alone, carrying the weight of all those little ghosts on his frail shoulders. He knew he was in danger. He didn't vocalise at Mayhem or Scandal when they approached for a friendly sniff. He didn't jump off his mother's back to play with other monkeys. He didn't play at all, not even by himself. He developed a crease between his eyes from frowning all the time.

He clung to his mother and shut out the world by closing his eyes. Murder for her part, stayed far away from Dopey and everyone else. I never thought I'd see her relinquish her throne but she did, without even a last contemptuous flick of her tail. She became invisible. She ate alone and in silence. Even when her own family approached her to check on their prince, she slunk away. She grew thin from constantly running and never stopping to eat. We hardly ever saw Mischief nurse, and he looked as weak as a baby bird.

Dopey scanned the trees for them. He had a deep red birthmark, like a bloodstain, under the right corner of his mouth. When Murder caught him looking, she shivered and slunk away.

Dopey lay down on the branch, waiting for someone to groom him. He kept lifting his head up and looking around as if to say 'Hello? Who wants me?' But though Dopey had miraculously defeated Angel, he wasn't getting any respect from Sin. Everyone was ignoring him. Usually the group took their cues from Murder. If she had sex with the new alpha, he was accepted. If she didn't, he wasn't. But it wasn't that simple anymore.

Brad and I weren't fans of Dopey either. Sin had never been any good in intergroups. With the alpha male changing so often, they could never form a solid male resistance. We were used to the smug crowing of Snow White over the radio about how we'd had our asses whopped yet again (usually from Kermit). But of all the pathetic, slovenly alphas we'd seen, Dopey took the cake. At least the other alphas made a stand, vocalising and threatening so the females and babies could escape. At the first hint of trouble, Dopey ran away faster than the babies. He always had been and always would be a coward.

That morning, when Snow White war cried, Dopey ran from the old quarry of the Gravel Pit, down to the dry river bed of lower SQS and up the crumbling Snuffle mountain. He even outran Whisper, who was usually the first to scat. Everyone was exhausted, and now Dopey had the nerve to look around for grooming.

'Give it up, loser,' I said, catching my breath against a tree.

'Dopey, you suck,' said Brad, leaning against me.

Just then Assassin approached. Brad took out his PSION.

'Assassin, what are you doing here?'

Like every mother who lost their baby in the wet season, Assassin was scrawny and unkempt. But she had a hard edge to her I hadn't noticed before. When Arsenic had fallen, the group passed by the body several times, but Assassin never stopped to check if Arsenic was still alive. She reacted so differently to Whisper, who stood for hours over Whimper, swatting away the flies. Assassin's lips were tightly pressed together as she came closer to Dopey.

'Don't, Assassin. He's not worth it. He'll be gone soon.'

But she turned on the branch, pirouetted and sex squeaked. Dopey looked up, ecstatic. He jumped up and sex grunted at her. She twittered and squeaked while Brad and I watched, horrified.

'Assassin, he killed your baby!'

It was no use. Dopey mounted her, thrusting as hard as he could. She held on to the branch grimly until he finished, then she sat and groomed him. Brad shook his head.

'Assassin, you're more fucked than I am.'

As soon as I left for Guatemala, Brad was sucked into the Andreas–Annie scandal. They were trying to keep their affair secret, even though Sarah, Brad and I knew about it.

'I'm sorry, honey,' I patted Brad on the shoulder. 'I heard them doing it on my way out. How did you find out?'

Brad looked shattered.

'Andreas asked me for condoms.'

'What?'

'After the first night.'

'Are you joking? They had unprotected sex two days before Andreas left for Ada?'

'Yes.'

'Is Annie on the pill?'

'No.'

'Jesus!' I gasped.

'It gets worse. They were being all gooey around me because I knew, and eventually I couldn't stand it and went to San Jose. Before I left, I went to say goodbye to Andreas. I knocked on the door. Annie came out looking flushed and dishevelled. Then Andreas came out of their bedroom and he . . .'

Brad choked.

'He wiped his arm across his mouth.'

'Oh my god.'

'I'll never forget it for as long as I live. He was eating her pussy when I knocked. It was so gross. I nearly threw up.'

'Darling, I'm so sorry.'

'That was the last I saw of him. Then, the night I got back from San Jose, that stupid bitch came to my room, looked me in the eye and gave me a new packet of condoms.'

Brad's hands were shaking.

'I hate her. I hate her so much I could put my fist through her face.'

That month, Brad and I made predictions for the house war. Vicious feelings were circling like vultures and it wouldn't take much before we all combusted. I hated Kermit, who in turn hated me. I hadn't forgiven Rachel for the night she asked me if I needed her counselling, and didn't intend to. Brad now hated Annie, and Kermit who was being an asshole to him. Summer and Annie hated Rachel who wouldn't let anyone ignore her, and would repeat questions, over and over, until someone answered. We ignored Sarah who still frequently had meals in her room. And everyone except Brad and I were still bitching about Princess, who kept contracting one mysterious illness after another.

Brad and I both agreed that if there was a house war, it would probably be me that started it. I was careless with rage. I did nothing to shield my eyes when they were full of loathing and disgust. Andreas, strangely enough, would have kept me in check. While he was around, I had a gentle reminder of a weak and shivering afternoon in the rain, waiting for salvation. But with him gone, I was now the most senior assistant. I had Brad holding me up, Princess trusted me, and the rest of the house was at my mercy.

My one weakness was Sirius. I woke ten minutes early every morning to hug and pat her on the porch before we left. When Brad and I had our day off, she'd run between us all the way to Soda La Fuente, where we kept her under the table and fed her scraps. Every time I came home from the forest, she had a present for me: a leaf she carried proudly in her mouth or a fallen coconut she rolled towards me with her nose.

The rest of the time, Brad and I plotted imaginative ways to kill off everyone in the house. We liked to push Kermit off a cliff, or even better, hack open his head with his own machete. Rachel always got hit by a car, and Sarah caught fatal diseases while she was kissing ass. Annie we just left to crawl under a rock and die, which wasn't too far from reality. Since Andreas left, she sank further and further into depression. Not one spark was left in her. It was her own fault; she chose her alliances unwisely. For some reason Brad and I could never figure out, she wanted desperately for Brad to be her friend, and it was just not going to happen.

'She cried all day,' he said while we lay on his bed, legs spread in front of the fan. Brad had his usual fungus and I had a case of thrush that swelled my vagina lips to twice their size. Annie had it too, from fucking Andreas no doubt, and Brad and I tried to imagine how I'd caught it off her.

'I ignored it for hours, but she just kept snivelling, so eventually I said, "What?" and she burst into tears and told me all about how she was missing Andreas blah blah, and finally I said, "Annie, what did you expect?" and she looked at me like what she expected was sympathy, and I was like hell no, not after the mouth-wiping episode.'

I snarled sympathetically. I had no particular grudge against Annie, but I was happy to bitch because for all we talked about everything and everyone, we never talked about what was really eating me up from the inside. Diane. For the first few days after the email I did nothing but spit vitriol and fury. It spewed in endless streams as I lingered over every line of that fatal email I'd learnt by heart. I called Diane every black name I could think of. I dreamt of ways to punish her and sabotage the project. Then, when I thought I'd collapse with the enormity of it, Brad took me by both hands, and said he couldn't talk about it anymore.

I was shocked. We'd always talked about everything. But I'd been blind to him wilting, battered by the sheer force of my tirades. His eyes begged me not to consider it a betrayal.

'I need her for graduate school,' he said quietly. 'I can't. I just can't.'

There was a moment when I hated him too, when I wanted to tear away and run through the forest until I collapsed. But a moment more and I forgave him. If that was all he couldn't give me, I still had more than most.

So the poison leaked out from other cracks, that ran across Brad as well, and we held hands in the forest and killed them all, over and over.

Not long into the month, Brad caught dengue fever. He lay in his bed, shivering and sweating, for a week. The Costa Ricans call dengue 'breakbone fever' because it felt like someone was smashing your joints with a sledgehammer. Brad was so weak he could barely lift his head.

The doctors misdiagnosed it and gave him antibiotics. He tricked himself into thinking he felt better and against all my protests came into the field. By 2 p.m. his whole body was vibrating with a pounding that started inside his temples and ran all the way to his feet. He was in bed for another week. By then it had been diagnosed as dengue, for which there was no cure. Only bed rest and fluids. We could only hope it didn't turn into dengue haemorrhagic fever, where the blood vessels start to leak and cause bleeding from the nose, mouth and gums, and bruises slowly spread over the body from internal bleeding.

When Brad was beyond my reach, I learned how the others felt. There were no friendships in the house besides ours. It was almost as if the sheer force of our alliance broke everyone else apart. I performed the monkey rituals quietly, and for the first time noticed the quiet of everyone else. I passed the days by watching Murder and Mischief, and planning a future for them despite my forebodings.

Once, before a thunderstorm, I crawled into a large hollow log. When my eyes adjusted to the darkness, I saw three scorpions and a spider with brilliant red markings barely an inch from my eye. I was a little afraid, but as the sky darkened and the rain poured over us in sheets, we made a truce and waited out the storm together.

It was then I decided I needed to make another truce— with Diane. The burden of carrying her around stitched up inside me was becoming too heavy for comfort. I crawled out of the log two hours later, stiff and swollen, mud matting my hair and my clothes absolutely filthy.

When I got back to the monkey house, I called her to make peace but burst into tears instead.

'Hello, Vanessa, what's wrong?'

'You don't think it's my fault do you?'

Her voice softened.

'No, no, of course not. We just want what's best for you.'

'It's happened before,' I sobbed. 'When I was in university I was molested by a lecturer. I just couldn't go through the whole thing again.'

It was half true. In first year, a maths lecturer put his hand firmly on my bottom under the pretence of guiding me towards the lectern.

'Did you just put your hand on my ass?' I demanded. He turned red and backed away.

'No, no, of course not.'

'Good. Because I'd hate to report you to the sexual assault unit and prematurely end your career.'

He hastily apologised. I changed classes and never heard from him again.

I don't know why I brought him up. I suppose I was trying to find a way out for Diane and I. She'd made her feminist stand and said I should prosecute, and now I was divulging information that allowed her to forgive the fact that I wasn't. It seemed to work.

'Oh I'm sorry, I didn't know. Of course you should do whatever you want, whatever you feel comfortable with.'

That wasn't what your email said, I thought. But I kept crying and pushed my advantage.

'And another thing, Diane, my data. I haven't been falling behind because of the Disney segments, it's because of everything else, I'll catch up soon, I just haven't been able to concentrate, I haven't been sleeping...'

'Okay, okay.' She was obviously uncomfortable with raw emotion and wanted me off the phone ASAP. 'As long as you do it soon.'

'I will, I will.'

And that was that.

Princess's genitals swelled so much she could barely sit down. She had no idea what STD she had but she gave it to Carlos who developed a lump the size of a golf ball on his testicles.

Brad was still sick and I was sick of being in the forest without him. In a miraculous deliverance, I developed some kind of genital irritation.

The next day, Brad and I dragged Princess to Canas. It was a small town twenty minutes from Vacas in the opposite direction to Liberia. We had a secret mission. In one of the motels, there was a pool. A blue dream, filled with heavenly, chlorinated water. As soon as we arrived, we squealed and jumped in, splashing around and letting the sun shine on our faces. There were no bugs to worry about, no chiggers, no mosquitoes and no ticks. Only that miraculous pool surrounded by a beautiful garden of concrete.

'You know what we're doing at the end of the month?' I said to Brad who was lying on a banana chair next to mine. Princess was floating in the pool, her blond hair streaming around her like a mermaid's.

'Quitting?'

'No way. We are going on an all-expenses-paid vacation to Nicaragua. On Disney.'

Brad sat up.

'You're joking.'

I smiled. I had tons of money left over from Disney, and all the Central American segments were done.

'We are going to resorts, darling. Resorts with pools and fountains. With arabesque statues and courtyards. And best of all, with airconditioning and cable TV.'

Princess got out and lay on an adjoining banana chair.

'I've always wanted to go to Leon,' she said dreamily, when she heard of our plans.

'You should come! Meet us there.'

We spent the afternoon planning the ice cream and pizza we'd eat, the movies we'd see, the pools we'd swim in.

'Henreike arrives at the end of the month,' said Princess, which between Brad's illness and my consuming rage wasn't that far away. 'We need to have a party.'

'A *Chicago* party!' cried Brad. His mum had sent him the DVD of the musical with Renee Zellweger and Catherine Zeta-Jones. We'd watched it at least fifteen times, and frequently did our own musical renditions in the field.

We dried ourselves off and ran around Canas for the rest of the day. We bought cheap black underwear, fishnet stockings and frilly nightdresses for the girls and wife-beater shirts and boxer shorts for the boys. When we got home to Vacas, I dyed Brad's hair black, and he dyed mine vermilion red.

That night, we practised our dance routine of 'The Cell Block Tango' in the kitchen while we cooked dinner. Annie walked in on Brad bending me backwards in a tango dip. Badly missing Andreas and desperately needing a friend, she rolled her eyes and turned away before they filled with tears.

During dinner, everyone looked a little bitter that Princess, Brad and I, who were supposed to be sick, were so cheerful and suspiciously tanned. Brad and I ignored them and fell into our habit of talking to each other as though no one else was around. 'What are you going to do with our daughter?'

'Our daughter' was Sirius, and it was becoming harder with each passing day to give her up. I'd talked to Angelina's family who said they would keep her but, lovely though they were, I didn't trust them to keep Sirius in perfect health for sixteen years, or however long she lived. I didn't trust them to take her to the vet when she was sick, to keep her in the yard away from cars, or to give her a flea bath every week. Costa Ricans just didn't think about dogs that way. Dogs were more like chickens, but without egg-laying capacities. If I left Sirius with anyone in Costa Rica, I'd never be truly sure she was okay. I could send Angelina's family money, but they would be crazy not to spend it on their own children instead of a mutt.

'I don't know,' I said. 'I told Diane about her, and she said Sirius's new family would have to tie her up until I left Costa Rica.'

My heart clenched at the thought. Poor Sirius tied up, tugging at the leash, trying to follow me home.

'Well,' said Kermit in a snide voice from the other side of the table. 'It's true. They'll have to tie her up for the rest of her life or she'll get smashed up by a car looking for you.'

Tears pricked my eyes as this image took over my imagination. For the past week, I had tried to ignore Kermit being mean to Sirius. He called her stupid in front of me, and pushed her away whenever she came near him. Once he yelled at her for licking his face. I knew I was oversensitive when it came to Sirius, but I also knew Kermit knew it. Whenever he thought I was looking he shoved her with the toe of his boot. Before I could stop myself, the words escaped my lips. I enunciated each syllable and ended each one like a whip.

'Shut up Kermit.'

There was so much malice in my voice that it carried across the entire dinner table. Stunned, everyone stopped eating. There was nervous laughter. I got up, took my plate into the kitchen and threw it in the sink. Everyone was silent as I walked out.

Brad came running after me into my room.

'Mischka, are you starting the house war?'

'You better believe it. Right now, in fact.'

'But wait! Darling, he's not afraid of you anymore.'

'He will be.'

I stormed back into the monkey house. Kermit was taking his anger at me out on Sirius and it wasn't fair. I would much rather he hit me with a baseball bat than even look at her the wrong way. Sirius had become a symbol for me, as though she were a helpless part of myself that I had to protect. Kermit was in the kitchen doing the dishes. Everyone scattered when they saw me coming.

'Kermit.' I kept my voice low.

Every muscle in my body was ready to snap. I was prepared for the old karate technique of conquering your opponent through stark raving lunacy. I let my anger curdle at the base of my throat so that when I started screaming, the whole of Vacas would know about it. Kermit looked up, a stack of dishes in his hands. He looked so miserable and hopeful, the madness slipped away from me. I tried to hold on to it.

'You have to stop being a bitch about my dog.'

'I wasn't talking about Sirius,' he said pathetically. 'I meant all dogs in general.'

'You know what I'm talking about. Don't push the doggy button, Kermit. It's below the belt.'

He looked at his feet.

'I'm sorry.'

The ill will I'd been carrying for him for the past month vanished, and I had the odd feeling of wanting us to be friends. I had a bizarre impulse to hug him. I checked it. Instead he sat with Brad and I on the porch, and when Sirius jumped up and licked his face, he tickled her tummy and told her she was a good girl.

I spent the last week of the month with Carlos and Jesus in Nirvana. They were behaving differently towards me since the sexual assault. Usually they let all the gringos stumble their way through the forest, getting lost, losing the monkeys, and generally making asses of ourselves. But now they kept me close to them, as if they were sorry they hadn't been there at the right time.

One morning we were at our 5 a.m. river crossing. Being the Tarzan jungle-bred Ticos they were, they both skipped across a section where the river was wide and running fast. I stood on the other side, rubbing my bleary eyes and wondering what they had jumped on. Carlos turned and waited for me.

'There're no rocks in this river, Carlos.'

'*Si, Banessa.*' He pointed to a slight rise in the water where a rock was beneath the surface. I tried to focus, but it kept shifting with light refraction.

Fuck it, I thought. Here goes. I closed my eyes and took a leap of faith. And fell in. Normally, I dragged myself out and trudged on but the river was deep and rushing fast. I couldn't find my footing on the bottom.

'*Jesus!*' Carlos cried. '*Banessa, ella fue avec el rio!*' She has gone with the river.

Gone with the river, I thought. She certainly has. Carlos was standing on the bank helplessly, watching me get swept away. I was compassionate of his predicament—he didn't want to watch me drown but he couldn't swim. Water was covering my backpack, and I suddenly stopped struggling and thought happily, 'Diane sure will be pissed when my PSION breaks.'

'*Banessa!*' I saw Jesus up ahead, on one knee with his strong forearm held out. I came to my senses and kicked my way over to the bank. I grasped his hand and held on as I struggled away from the water that rushed like suicide towards Nirvana waterfall.

Another knight in shining armour, I thought, as Carlos came running towards us. Where the hell do they keep coming from?

'*Ay Banessa!*' he cried, sitting beside me as I wrung out my socks. 'I thought you were gone!'

Jesus started laughing.

'*Ella fue avec el rio,*' he crowed, falling on his side.

Carlos joined in. '*Fue! Fue!*' I couldn't help myself. We laughed and laughed until the sun split the leaves into shadows of light and dark.

'Annie falls in every day,' said Jesus. 'I don't like her. She doesn't laugh like you.'

I raised my eyebrows. I had never heard Jesus say he didn't like anything before. He was always so Zen. I felt absurdly pleased.

'I would have given all my money to see her fall in that river. All!'

'We'll bring her tomorrow,' Carlos said.

'Tomorrow!' they cried together. '*Ay Banessa, aii.*'

I put on my wet socks and squelched them into my shoes. They giggled all morning, occasionally chortling, '*Fue avec el rio—heeheeha!*'

We never crossed there again, and whenever we had to skip across rocks, one of them always waited a step ahead, ready to grasp my hand as I jumped.

The night before vacation, we threw Henreike her *Chicago* party. She seemed like a nice enough German girl, but Brad and I hardly noticed her. We were too busy getting dressed and putting our make-up on. Brad wore a white wife-beater and black pants and I wore wide black panties over black stockings, a black bra and high heels. I made like Cleopatra with the eyeliner and pulled my bright red hair back tightly into a bun.

'You look like a slutty ballerina,' Brad cried in delight.

It was the night Brad and I discovered our dancing potential. We obviously couldn't go out into Vacas looking like a Halloween brothel, so we got drunk and danced in the lounge room. Brad used to swing dance in university, but he'd fallen out of practice and out of shape. But now he was in peak physical condition. His muscles rippled from his forearms to his six-pack. I was toned and light, and Brad picked me up as though I weighed nothing. He made me run up and jump and he threw me high above his head while I squealed and hoped to hell he caught me. He swung me horizontally around his body, finishing the move with a twist and a twirl. He dipped me so my hair brushed the floor.

We were having so much fun, I could understand how badly everyone wanted us to break apart. But there was no chance of it that night. We danced until midnight then, claiming we had to have beauty sleep, we stopped the party and went to bed.

The next morning we were on our way to Nicaragua. Our first stop was Managua, against the advice of Carlos and Jesus.

'They cut people's heads off. It's a very dangerous city.'

'You'll return with a knife in your back. *Tiras los ojos.*' Keep your eyes open.

We promised not to go out at night and to catch taxis everywhere.

Brad and I called that vacation 'the honeymoon' as a celebration of our extended marriage. Everyone who met us thought we were a couple, and the old ladies at the bus station selling oranges always smiled as we walked by holding hands.

Once we arrived in Nicaragua, we were shown to our beautiful rooms with two king-sized beds. We turned the airconditioner on full blast and snuggled under the blankets with the TV remote control. We watched three movies in a row, before stumbling out bleary-eyed to the theatre where we saw Euripides's *The Trojan Women* in Spanish. The Nicaraguan Opera House was awesomely designed, with towering granite columns and ceilings four storeys high. We swooned at the enormous chandelier in the foyer.

The rest of the time, when we weren't watching movies, we went to the mall. We ate burgers and bought designer clothes. Everything was so shiny and new. We breathed in the cool white sanitised air as though we were in heaven.

A few days later we travelled up through Granada and Leon, two beautiful historic cities that showed the peak of the Spanish conquistadors. There we reclined by our marble pool with the fountain in the courtyard and lay naked in our respective beds, watching more movies. When we were hungry, we meandered through the narrow streets, stumbling on houses of famous Central American poets like Rivas, and eating in tiny restaurants that had served tapas and conchillas for centuries.

At night we sat on starry terraces and talked about nothing but dreams, drinking our batidoes and eating even more hamburgers.

In total we watched 36 movies in five days. I remember the last one was *The Shawshank Redemption*.

As we packed up our bags and prepared to leave I said, 'Do you ever feel like we're doing time for a crime we didn't commit?'

'Constantly Mischka.'

We hugged, swore eternal devotion and undying love, before we trudged back home to the monkey house.

chapter 13

Temptress too long

mischief was dead.

Murder was nowhere to be found and we hoped she'd gone into hiding. But eventually she reappeared, without Mischief. I hardly recognised her. She was crazed with grief. Her eyes darted around as though she couldn't trust anything they settled on. The side of her mouth with the scar drooped lopsidedly and there was a crusted substance at the corners. She gnawed on her own foot. She picked at her scabs until they bled. When her family came to see her, she stared past as if she couldn't see them. Dopey lifted his head lazily. He'd try to take her soon. Impregnate her with his own demon seed. He lay down again. Time enough for that.

The forest was drying out. Vine tendrils grew a bark shell over their sinews. High above us, leaves began to shrivel. I wondered if Murder felt these things curdle inside her. Alpha males didn't kill babies in the dry season. If she could have kept Mischief alive for another month, maybe he would have made it. But one look at Dopey, the birthmark running from the corner of his mouth like a bloodstain, and I doubted it. He didn't need the cover of rain and saplings growing like magic beanstalks. He would have hunted them under a naked sun.

I stared at Murder's bare back. I imagined Dopey lunging at her with fangs bared, sinking his canines into Mischief and whipping him off her back. She'd been so vigilant the month before—how did he catch her? She must have been tired, so tired, and just closed her eyes for a moment...

Sin should be alive with machine-gun twitters and playful slaps. We should be cursing our way through baby pile-ups like we did in Nirvana where they rolled and tumbled indistinguishable from one another. Instead there was graveyard silence as Assassin sat next to Dopey, a new dark queen in the making.

At 4:40 a.m. I crashed to my knees on a rocky platform and spent the next half an hour trying to straighten my leg. I heard a cry deep within Snuffle and chased the monkeys down the deepest valley in Lomas. I lost the monkeys, found them, lost them again, as they ran through godforsaken thickets as tangled as rats' nests. I had left my machete at home, so I was defenceless against the hardening vegetation. By 6 a.m. I was so feral with mud and vines and thorns, I looked like the monster at the end of a B-grade movie, just before it's killed by the squeaky-clean hero.

At 7 a.m. I slid a hundred metres down Orange Twist on my ass, completely tearing my blue gortex jacket, the only possession I took pride in. By the time I reached the bottom of the dry waterfall, the monkeys were at the top, so I gritted my teeth and hauled myself back up by saplings and roots growing in the rock face. Every now and then I slipped and smashed my jaw shut.

When I reached the top, the monkeys were on the other side of the valley, exactly where I started. I sat down and blubbered like a bona fide lunatic.

Two weeks later, I had a nervous breakdown.

Before Guatemala, I couldn't cry. Since I returned, I couldn't stop. It was as though someone smashed a sledgehammer into a dry well and now there was only water. I cried in the morning as I did my exercises. I cried silently on the walk into the forest, tears making my cheeks cold with the early morning breeze. I cried if I lost the monkeys, I cried when I found them. I managed to hide it from everyone except Brad, in front of whom I bawled until my whole body shook and I couldn't breathe.

I woke up at one or two in the morning feeling like I was drowning. Struggling to the surface from my dreams, I was paranoid I didn't have enough air. I went outside and breathed in the cool night breeze as Sirius pushed her wet nose into my hand.

When the alarm went off, I lay in bed like a cat on the cusp of my ninth life. I wanted to burrow into my mattress so when they came to call me, there would be only emptiness, and a disarray of blankets. But there was nowhere to go. I couldn't bear the thought of Kermit's face pressing at my window, knocking until the glass nearly broke, calling 'Vanessa' with a voice as expressionless and distant as a television commercial.

So I made it outside just as everyone was piling in the car. I cut corners for those extra seconds in bed to coax myself out of it. As a consequence, I always forgot something: my machete, my PSION, my lunch.

The only person in the house who knew what I was going through was Annie. When her misery recognised my red eyes and my dragging feet, the corners of her mouth turned up a little. A crack had formed in the defences surrounding what she wanted most. She became a tiny winged creature and swooped down on Brad with all her might. She brought him small offerings like biscuits or her place in the dinner line. If she annoyed him, she quickly disappeared out of reach of his swatting hand. I was too tired to fight her off, and Brad must have been relieved to find better company than I was.

One night I was doing my laundry and Brad called me over.

'Mischka, we're playing Trivial Pursuit.'

'No thanks,' I said, too tired and depressed for board games. 'I suck at it.'

'I bags Brad as a partner!' cried Annie, her face blushing red with pleasure.

With the last venom I could muster I said, 'Annie, stop pissing on his leg.' But the effort exhausted me.

She sucked her nostrils in. Her eyes were as hard and shiny as glass balls. It won't be long now, they said.

In the forest, the monkeys could have been turning cartwheels in sequined bikinis for all I cared. I wandered away from my field partner, claiming to hear other monkeys or to be searching for the rest of the group. When I was out of sight, I sat down against a tree and stared into the canopy.

The mosquitoes were dying off, but the jungle was not done with its plagues. We began uncovering giant ticks in awkward places; behind our knees, on the pendulous parts of our genitals. When you pulled off their gorged bodies and popped them, they covered your whole finger in blood. Even if you were careful to twist them off so their heads didn't get stuck in your flesh, the bites stayed for months. They filled with pus and itched like crazy until you scratched them. Then they scabbed over and filled with pus again.

The chiggers should have been gone already, but they were making a last stand with a frenzy of breeding as the ground dried up. I must have stopped to rest in one of their evaporated mud pools because the top of my left foot had erupted in more than a hundred small pustules that burned like someone rubbing chilli on an open wound. I scratched them until my foot was covered in a giant scab, weeping pus and blood along the cracks.

On top of everything, Brad and I had been shitting rivers since we got back from Nicaragua. Several times a day, foul yellow streams laced with stomach acid shot from our bottoms. When I finally went to the doctor, she told me I had more amoebas in my stool than she'd ever seen in her life.

The multitude of parasites didn't help my mental state, but neither were they to blame for it. They were just a metaphor for what was nudging me towards the edge. It was Andreas and the taxi driver who finally pushed me over it.

As we walked out of the internet café, Brad looked at me strangely.

'I just got an email from Andreas.'

'And?'

'He said he would have screwed your brains out if you'd given him the chance.'

We sat down on a park bench. The ice cream I was licking dribbled over my fingers and onto my lap.

'That is so . . .' I struggled.

'Dirty.'

'I don't understand. I never did anything, never said anything. You know I wouldn't have . . .'

My voice choked. Of course, I'd always wanted attention from Andreas, but this was too much. Andreas never even talked about sex, much less refer to a fellow monkey researcher as though she were in a porn magazine. For him to have said something so crass about me made it sound as if I was some kind of witch that made men, any men, all men, just want to fuck me like a two-dollar prostitute, and that somehow it was all my fault.

Brad put his arm around me.

'I know, Mischka, I know. It's not your fault, it's not.'

A few days later I picked up Sirius from the vet in Liberia after her desexing operation. Her little belly, fat from food now, not worms, had six tiny stitches. She was so happy to see me, she whined and wagged her little bottom until it nearly fell off. I bought her ten kilograms of the most expensive dog food I could find, as well as some toys and beef-flavoured treats.

In the cab on the way home, the taxi driver pointed a fat finger at Sirius.

'You know black dogs aren't good for women?'

I thought I must have misunderstood him.

'What?'

He leaned closer to me, his eyes boring into my lap, where Sirius was sitting.

'The little black hairs get stuck up your vagina.'

His breath smelt like sour beans. I nearly told him to stop the car and let me out, but we were already on the highway and I had ten kilograms of dog food and a puppy to take care of. I couldn't haul them both twenty kilometres to Vacas.

So I just stared out the window and dug my nails into the leather upholstery so I wouldn't scream.

When we got back to Vacas, I dumped the dog food at home and went straight to the internet café. Fans chopped up the hot air while black plastic bags on the windows tried to keep sunlight from melting the computers. I wrote an email to Heather, telling her everything that had happened.

I can count the number of friends I have on one hand. Heather was my index finger. By the time I walked back to the house, Princess was holding out the phone. It was Heather.

'Darling, how are you?'

'I'm fine, I'm really fine.'

To my surprise, she burst into tears.

'I just can't believe what you've been through you sound so shell-shocked you're like a holocaust victim over there and you aren't fine darling you really aren't and you have to get out of there and come home.'

'I can't,' I said wearily. 'I have to wait until the Disney segments are approved. Diane won't approve them if I'm not here.'

Heather kept crying.

'You have to go somewhere. You can't just stay in that monkey house.'

'I'm going to Boston at the end of the month to see Anna.'

'You go now, darling. You go right now.'

I called Anna in Boston. She was my ring finger. We'd been practically married since high school, then she really got married and moved to Boston with her husband who was studying at Harvard. As soon as I heard her voice, I started bawling and told her everything.

'You're suffering from chronic depression,' Anna was a psychologist in training. 'Crying all day and all night is not normal. You have acute anxiety and you're also in denial. Get your butt over here right now.'

There was one problem. No one went on vacation early. When Tristan's grandfather died and Tristan went back to the States for the funeral, Diane told Princess he would have to make up the time.

I tried to explain to Anna and Heather why I couldn't just leave. For them, it was as simple as filling in a leave form, checking with the boss, then going. For us it was different. Diane already thought she was too lenient on us, with all our Vacas days and monthly vacations. If any of us were going to make it in primatology, nine to five wasn't enough. Even fourteen-hour days weren't enough. Hundreds, even thousands, of hours of data went into each scientific paper. It was like monkey boot camp; it wasn't supposed to be fun, but it prepared you for the gruelling slog that was field primatology. Diane knew any would-be primatologist would kill to be given our opportunity. She received hundreds of applications a year, and here we were, the chosen few, bitching and whining about how we needed more time off.

I didn't want to appear ungrateful, but in my moments of clarity I knew that if I didn't get off the monkey project soon, they were going to have to haul me away in a straightjacket.

I dialled Diane's number. If a grandfather dying and sexual assault weren't good enough, I'd have to think of something else.

Diane sounded wary when I burst into tears, as though she was suspicious of being manipulated. The words were out before I could think about them.

'My father's dying of cancer. I need some time out. I have family friends in Boston and I'd like to see them.'

There was a long pause.

'Don't you want to go back to Australia?'

My story had major flaws. I hadn't spoken to my father in three years. We'd had a major falling out over a psychotic episode he had in Sydney before he relocated permanently to Laos. He'd been in and out of psychiatric institutions and rehab centres ever since I was a child and I finally decided my life was better off without him in it.

I concentrated on making up the next part of my story.

'My father's receiving treatment in Bangkok and won't be in Australia for another four months. There's no point going back early. Besides, I love the monkeys. I want to stay here.'

'We normally don't allow this,' she said. 'And I'd hate to set a precedent.'

Another pregnant pause. 'But you have been through more than most, so I think this once it's okay.'

A huge weight lifted off me as I hung up the phone. I was going to Boston. I threw a travel bag together and ran outside to tell Brad.

'She let me go early,' I whispered fiercely as I dragged him behind the mango tree.

'She did not.'

'She did. I told her Dad was dying of cancer.'

'You *what*?'

'It just came out.'

'Are you brain dead? How do you think you're going to get away with that?'

'I don't care.'

Brad looked at me worriedly but didn't say anything. He knew desperation when he saw it.

At dinner, Annie and Sarah shot me death stares across the table. Annie because she thought I was always getting my way, and Sarah because she'd kill to go on vacation early.

They needn't have been so upset. I was about to learn a very big lesson.

I hardly ever lie about the little things. Lies make my face turn red and my armpits sweat. I never told my teacher my dog ate my homework, I just said I didn't do it. I never make excuses for forgetting birthdays, I just tell people I completely forgot about them on their special day. I can't even lie about how I feel about people; if I don't like someone, it's written all over my face.

But every now and then, when my back is against the wall and there's no way out, I tell an absolute whopper. I got the talent from my father who also only lied about the big and important things, like the times he said he'd never leave me, which he did, twice. The trick is, when you're telling the whopper you must absolutely and totally believe yourself. It's like you zap yourself into a parallel universe where everything you say is true.

Lying to someone you'll see once and never again is fine. There are no consequences. But if you're going to lie to people you're with 24 hours a day, who overhear your phone calls and whispered secrets at night; if you're going to perjure yourself to those who are the jury, judges and executioners of the social hierarchy that confines you; if you're going to bring out envy and wrath with the incredibility of your falsehoods . . . Well, you better hope to hell you don't get caught.

Anna was waiting for me at the airport and I fell into her arms.

'Everyone's dying to meet you, Tarzan.'

'I hope I remember how to hold a fork.'

It was Thanksgiving and Boston was alive with parties. I had sex with someone, not because I wanted to, but I felt like I should. Kind of like physiotherapy exercises for a broken ankle. I wanted to see if I still could, or if I'd break down in the middle and sob as I'd done every night in November. I didn't cry. It hurt a little, being the first time since Charles, but it was mildly satisfying.

Anna said I'd definitely made progress on my mental health and in my pocket I had a list of what I had to finish before I left Costa Rica. It had one name. Sirius. On the other side in much smaller writing, it said Disney.

I stepped off the plane in San Jose a much harder person than when I landed more than six months ago. I thought of who I was then, vain and self-centred, convinced I was the life of the party Costa Rica needed. I didn't think that anymore. I had things I wanted that were bigger than me; Disney would be finished because I said I'd do it, and I was taking Sirius home. I reminded myself of Assassin. Not friendship, nor morals, nor God almighty was going to get in our way.

The woman at Australian Quarantine wasn't very enthusiastic about my plan.

'Ms Woods, do you realise how difficult it is to import animals from third-world countries?'

'But she's adorable,' I said. 'And heroic. Just the other day she saved a child from being hit by a car by barking.'

'Really.'

The woman sent me a bewildering array of forms whose sole purpose was to dissuade you from importing foreign mutts. The only way Sirius could get into Australia was to spend six months in an AQIS approved country, like America or England. She would have to pass a battery of tests for every conceivable disease known to science. Then she'd be locked up in Australian Quarantine for a month. The cost of everything, including the flights, the shots, the vets, administration and her quarantine stay, was $10 000. I gasped. I had nowhere near that much money.

I emailed my mother and asked her to back up my finances.

She rang me yelling, 'Vanessa, of all the stupid ideas you've ever had this is the worst I've ever heard. You don't have anywhere to live. You have barely enough money to look after yourself. Under no circumstances will I give you a cent. I remember you used to try and make me buy fish at the Chinese restaurant so you could throw them back in the sea. Wasting good money. I can't believe you're my daughter . . .'

Anyone with a Chinese relative could have told me my mother would rather cook the dog and eat it rather than spend $10, much less $10 000, on its welfare. I took a deep breath and told my mother about the doctor.

She listened in silence then burst into tears. It was hard on her, harder than anyone. She said she'd fly over immediately, take out a loan and come to look after me. I cried and said I loved her, but that wasn't necessary. I just had to do the right thing. I had to look after my dog.

'Anything, my darling. Whatever you need. I love you.'

Wiping my eyes on my sleeve, I called my stepmother, Helen. She was the second woman to have a disastrous ten-year marriage to my father, and after he dumped her and ended up as a Buddhist monk, she remained close to my sister and I. Helen was nuts about animals. She donated thousands to animal welfare and gave all her cast-off Gucci suits to the Cat Society.

She wholeheartedly supported my freakish plan to bring a Costa Rican mutt into Australia for $10 000. She said she had friends in Phoenix, Arizona, who would take care of Sirius for six months and take her to the vet for all her shots.

I found a pet agency who specialised in pet immigration.

'Australia,' said the woman from Petfly in Phoenix. 'You are a brave one, honey. Well don't you worry, we'll get your doggie home.'

'She means everything to me,' I tried not to cry. 'Please take care of her.'

'Don't you worry honey, I'll look after her like she's made of gold.'

'You are undisciplined and stubborn. I am sending you to a nice family in America. Do you know how many people in Vacas would love to go to America? Everyone. Show me how nicely you can behave, so you don't bring shame on your mummy. Now, stay.'

Sirius was making the transition from nappy-shredding yard dog to upper-class house dog as well as could be expected. The problem was, she wasn't house trained. She was also very excitable, and the last thing I wanted was for her new family to arrive home one day to a house full of rubble and puppy pee. So I asked Princess if I could keep Sirius inside the pizza house to train her. I didn't expect Princess to say yes, but I guess between the sexual assault and my dying father, she didn't feel like she could say no. Princess was doing her best to be good to me in light of our friendship, but I think she understood something had changed in me. We no longer took the dogs for walks together or had cosy chats in her room. Still, she did everything she could to help take the pressure off, giving me easy days and lessening my house chores.

Sirius was a clever girl and learnt fast. She never once peed inside the house and didn't touch a single possession except her blue squeaky ball. She learnt every command within a week, except 'stay'.

She never liked to let me out of her sight.

'I just don't understand why he doesn't love me,' I said for the hundredth time.

'Mischka, are you still talking about Boston boy? Please, he was such a loser.'

Two weeks after sleeping with the nonentity from Thanksgiving, I was having peculiar feelings. I was convinced we were supposed to get married.

'He must have been special. I wouldn't feel this way if we weren't meant to be together.'

Brad spun around and slapped me with his PSION.

'Face it, after you got diddled by the doctor your emotions got all twisted. You can't just have casual sex now, darling. You're in the glory box.'

'I'm where?'

'Oh, you know that Portishead song,' Brad started singing.

I joined in for the chorus and soon we were wailing about reasons to be a woman.

Ecstasy jumped onto Providence and started threatening us. Brad and I were in Nirvana, and I was grateful I no longer had to see Murder's haunted eyes. I was sticking to my new goals, Sirius and Disney. All I had to do was wait out the next three months and I was gone. I gave up trying to please Diane with my data-collecting abilities. Besides, the less data I took, the less I had to clean. And the less data I took, the more time I had to enjoy the monkeys.

Brad and I were in love with the isolation of Nirvana. We transformed the Quebrador into *A Midsummer Night's Dream*, where he was Oberon and I was Titania, and instead of fairies for subjects we had monkeys.

We had magical powers. We were a force to be reckoned with. Nirvana were behaving themselves now the sun was gathering strength. The fruit dried up and they stayed close to the river. They spent hours by the Nirvana waterfall, where

Brad and I would strip off and jump into a pool so deep we couldn't touch the bottom.

Rachel joined our magic kingdom and I steeled myself to exclude her but, to my surprise, she was really sweet. Her awkward social skills when she first arrived were because she was scared of us. I imagined what the monkey people must have seemed like to her—sullen and browbeaten as we were by the Valley of Death. We would have scared anyone. Once Brad and I started acting like normal people, Rachel came out of her shell.

She was from the Jewish neighbourhood of New York. Her parents weren't wealthy and Rachel had the shoulder-shrugging attitude of someone who is used to doing without things. She was incredibly smart and one of those earnest people who really want to know what you think.

As part of our acceptance ritual, Brad and I ordered her to get naked and swim in the waterfall. When she took off those ugly glasses and undid her hair, she was beautiful.

Since Brad was gay, Rachel was a lesbian, and I'd had some lipstick-lesbian experiences, we called Nirvana 'Land of the Queers'. We swished around and made up stories of who we'd send to the gallows or exile in Sin.

'Careful, Dopey will come and get you,' we threatened the babies who were just climbing off their mothers. The picture of peace and perfect harmony in Nirvana was a balm for the senses. When we arrived in the mornings, there was no overlording or vocal threats. Instead they threw us casual glances as if to say, oh you again.

Finally, the recognition I'd been craving all along.

The whole of Vacas turned out for the bull fights. Technically, we were still working, but it was hard not to get caught up in the festive atmosphere. Our ugly town was covered in fairylights spelling crooked words we couldn't read. Bougainvillea crept over every cement structure and burst with pink flowers.

The bull ring was flooded with lights. Around it, amusement park stalls were set up selling sugared pastries and cotton candy. In the spirit of Christmas, which was fast approaching, I tied shiny streamers into all the monkey girls' hair. The boys put on their best shirts and prepared to tango with death.

Women were not allowed in the bull ring so we watched from the bleachers as our boys swaggered around, beers in hand. The bull was let out and it bucked and charged into the ring. Someone threw a life-sized dummy filled with straw in its path. The bull stabbed it with its horns and thrashed it until the stuffing went flying. There was no bull fighting per se, and the objective as far as I could tell was to make the bull charge you then get out of its way. Leaving the ring was a sign of weakness, but if the bull headed straight for you, you were allowed to climb the barricade.

'Hey Jesus,' I called, leaning over the balustrade. 'When was the last time someone was killed?'

'Not this year,' he answered. 'You look pretty tonight. *Labios del puta.*' Lips of a whore.

'Jesus!' I squealed. 'How rude!'

'Labios del puta is a flower. A red flower that matches your lips.'

I was wearing bright red lipstick that matched my singlet that matched the streamers in my hair. I squirmed in pleasure and caught Brad's squinty eyes.

I know your game, he mouthed, wanting to remind me what happened with Andreas. I pouted back, suitably chastised.

When the bull was exhausted, another was let in. This time the bull had someone on top. We watched mesmerised as the bull used every one of its rippling muscles to hurl the rider to the ground so it could trample him. After seven minutes, the bullrider fell and men with horses and lances kept the bull back while the rider scrambled to safety.

I bumped into Angelina's sisters and sat down with them to watch the next bullrider.

'Why would you sit on a bull that doesn't want to be sat on?' I asked them.

'If they can handle a bull, they can handle a wife,' Rosa replied and they all screeched with laughter.

'*Merde*, it's Chad,' said Theresa, 'Billy's old flatmate.' A tall gorgeous blond man was walking towards us. Who the hell is that? I thought. I thought we were the only gringos in Vacas.

'*Senoritas.*' He swaggered over, and his eyes settled on me, the new one. '*Hola. Como estas chiquita?*' How are you, baby?

'Charmed I'm sure.'

He was shocked I spoke English. I stared him down with raised eyebrows and he rapidly made his excuses.

'Oh hi, uh, guess I'll be seeing you.'

'What a jerk,' I said to his back.

A chorus of protests erupted around me.

'How can you say that! Chad is the most beautiful ever!'

'Banessa, how will you get a man if you scare them so?'

'I love him,' said Theresa. 'If only I could make him take me back to America.'

'I'll take you to America, Theresa. You don't have to go with Mr Incredible.'

She looked at me sadly.

'If only you could.'

I squeezed Theresa's hand and felt empty. It was true. What other way did young girls like Theresa have to get to the promised land other than becoming Madame Butterfly?

We watched the bull thrash around the ring, cheering when the bullrider survived a particularly energetic bucking, and booing when he fell off. These girls were all very precious to me. Every time I saw them, I was reminded how women should be with one another. I loved to hear how they saw the world and all their hopes and dreams, and in turn they squealed with laughter at nearly everything I said. They were a stark contrast to the women in the monkey house, with all our hidden agendas and fighting for a place in the hierarchy. Not for the first time, I wished I lived with Angelina's sisters and their mama who smothered them with love.

At midnight, dancing began under a marquee and Brad and I tried the swing-dance moves we'd been perfecting in the field. The Ticos formed a circle and watched in amazement as Brad swung me around his head and flipped me over and backwards from one side to another.

Hours later I crashed into Jesus who was drinking with his friends. He caught me as I stumbled. I hung on his shoulders and wagged my finger in his face.

'Jesus! We have to go home to bed, I'm out with you tomorrow.'

His friends laughed and cheered.

'Not go to bed together, you vaginas.' More raucous cheering. Jesus chuckled.

'*Tranquilate, Banessa.* You sleep in. I'll find them tomorrow morning and you can catch the bus in.'

It was a sacrilegious suggestion. The Nirvana bus left from Vacas every morning at five, and stopped at the entrance of Nirvana highway. No one was allowed to catch the bus unless the car broke down, as it meant you wouldn't be in the forest until 6 a.m.

'I think he loves you,' Brad whispered in my ear. I slapped him. He was just testing me. He knew I was trying to change, and one of my new rules was not to flirt with men anymore just for the sake of it. Jesus transferred me gently to Brad's arms.

'Okay,' I said. 'As long as you promise to find them.'

'I promise, Banessa. Sleep sweetly.'

It was 3:30 a.m. One hour until we had to get up.

When I woke it was 11 a.m. I jumped out of bed and ran into the living room.

'Oh my god I fucked up!'

Princess was at the computer. She smiled wryly.

'You and Jesus both. He didn't turn up this morning. Apparently he got in a fight and someone smashed his nose. So you're staying home today and finishing off the video. We'll let Nirvana go early. It's Christmas, after all.'

Brad and I spent Christmas with his mum and her boyfriend at the resort that was used to film *Temptation Island*.

It was just like Christmas in Australia. We went to the beach every day for a week and ate big lunches and took siestas. The resort had the names of all the people on *Temptation Island* carved into a cactus and Brad and I tried to remember who had cheated on who and who had made it in the end.

On our way home, we walked past a boy who carefully put his pet iguana on a wooden table. He smiled at me as I passed, his bright teeth sparkling. I stopped to stroke the lovely green scales. It lazily poked out its rounded tongue. As I walked away, the boy raised a wooden cudgel and brought it down full force on the iguana's head. The iguana jerked up, blood streaming through its eyes. The boy bashed the cudgel down again and again. Blood welled up under the eyeballs of the iguana and leaked out like tears.

Brad grasped my hand and pulled me along.

Back at the monkey house, Diane was on her way.

chapter 14

Revenge of the bees

'You little motherfucker.'

I slapped my neck and pulled off the bee that came apart between my fingers. I felt around for the poison dart lodged in the tendons of my neck. Now the fruit and flowers were dried to shrivelled husks, Sin was staying close to the river and so were the bees.

The sting barely registered. I was becoming as blasé about them as I was about the killer snakes that were slithering from their crackling logs to curl up by the river.

I flicked the stinger off my finger without looking at it. I should have paid it more attention. It nearly killed me.

'Henreike, wait,' I panted. 'I think I have heatstroke.'

Sin was scampering down SQS valley. We'd just run from Orange Twist where the scanty covering of leaves left us naked beneath the sun. The valley was cooled by the last dribble of water squeezed from the drying earth. As I bent over the swampy stream, I felt swollen and sore as though tight rubber bands were fastened all over my body.

The monkeys ran ahead. I couldn't keep up.

'Henreike, can you keep them for a few minutes? I need to rest.'

Henreike was at the monthling stage of wanting to assert her new skills and flap around a little. She was from Leipzig, Germany, a town in the east full of gigantic people. Henreike was no shrinking violet and was attractive despite her large masculine features.

'*Ja*, Vanessa. No problem.'

I climbed the valley to the Gravel Pit. I figured the monkeys were heading towards Cemetery, and I could head them off before they found their sleeping tree. The sun was out of sight behind the guanacaste trees, and I found a large flat rock that was still warm. I lay down on it, the heat relaxing my muscles.

Just for a minute, I thought. I'm so tired.

'Vanessa, Vanessa, where are you?'

I opened my eyes. It was nearly dark. I tried to take a deep breath and couldn't. There wasn't enough air in my lungs.

'Henreike?' I rasped.

My radio bleeped and flashed red. I tried to pick it up but my muscles were locked into place.

'Vanessa, Vanessa.'

Blood rushed painfully to my head as I sat up. I winced and forced my hand to pick up the radio.

'Henreike?'

She sounded panicked.

'I don't know where I am.'

'Hold on.'

My radio beeped again.

'Mischka?' It was Brad. 'We have the car at the bottom of Gravel.'

'It's Henreike, she's lost. But I—I can't breathe.'

'What's wrong?'

'I don't know. I thought it was sunstroke, but my throat feels like it's closing.'

'Stay there, we'll find Henreike.'

'No, I will. She's scared and I'm much closer than you.'

'If you're not down here in ten minutes, I'm coming up.'

I struggled to my feet. The ground spun to the fading sky. I whooped. Faintly, I heard a response. She was near Cemetery.

The shitty thing about Gravel Pit was the more you went down, the thicker the thorns. Which was fine if you followed a trail. Not so fine if you didn't. Even worse if you did it in the dark. I cut weakly with my machete. Branches slapped my face like bat wings.

'Henreike?'

'I'm here!'

I couldn't see a thing.

'Henreike, I want you to keep calling. I'm heading straight for you.'

I chopped and slashed. My heart beat faster but the depth and frequency of my breathing couldn't keep up. I cut down and sideways and back up again.

Finally, in the darkness, I grasped her pale hand.

'I'm sorry . . .' she looked frightened. 'What's wrong with your breathing?'

'I'm fine, we just have to get out of here.'

I looked around and realised I had no idea where we were. I tried to make a mental map of where we should be but I was too groggy to focus. I felt like I was breathing through a pin-sized hole in my throat. So I did what you're supposed to do when you're drowning. I swam up.

Coughing and spluttering, we made it to the top.

'Vanessa! Vanessa!' Brad's electronic voice sounded worried.

'We're here, we're coming.'

By the time we reached the car, everyone was anxious. Brad held my face in his hands.

'Your face, it's all swollen.'

Suddenly I got it.

'The bee,' I whispered hoarsely. 'It must be the bee.'

'Take her to hospital,' Brad barked at Kermit who was driving.

'Liberia?'

'There's no time. The one in Vacas.'

The Vacas clinic was a cement shack on the outskirts of town. Given my treatment at the Liberia hospital, my hopes for the Vacas clinic weren't high. But suffocation has a way of compromising your standards. We pulled up, tyres screeching. Brad jumped out.

'I'm coming in with you.'

'No,' I rasped. 'Cold. Passport.'

Brad understood. I was shivering, and I needed my passport for identification.

Summer held my hand.

'Shit you look pale,' she whispered. 'Do you want me to stay?'

I shook my head. All I wanted was to breathe again.

I stumbled into the reception. The receptionist barely looked up.

'Nombre?'

My tongue had become an inflated muscle clogging up my throat. I could barely pronounce my own name.

The receptionist looked annoyed.

'Do you have a passport?'

I inhaled the largest rasping breath I could and slammed my hand on her desk. I leant forward so she could smell the rancid sweat pouring through my skin.

'A bee stung me. I can't breathe. I am going to die in your waiting room if you don't. Get. Me. A. Doctor. Now.'

She leaned back and reached for the phone.

'Hola? You better come out here.'

The doctor appeared. I clutched his arm as though he was the resurrected Christ. Tears dribbled down my face.

'Please. Help me.'

He threw a sharp look at the receptionist.

'What happened?'

She shrugged.

'She said she was stung by a bee.'

The doctor quickly led me into a room and laid me down on the bed. I felt protest struggling somewhere. Every time I lay on a surgery bed in Costa Rica, something bad happened. But I was too weary. My eyes were closing. I felt his cool hand on my forehead. Then he slapped my face.

I tried to yell, but nothing came out of my throat.

'Banessa? You have to stay awake.'

My eyes were heavy. Sleep beckoned like a water fairy. I was sure she would lead me to a nice hot bath. The doctor pulled me off the bed and put me in a chair. Then he rushed out of the room.

There was sleep again, with flowing hair, stroking my forehead and humming in my ear. A hand slapped my face, harder. My eyes were glued shut but I wrenched them open and saw the doctor kneeling beside me holding a syringe the size of a sausage with a silver knitting needle at the end. Without speaking he stabbed the knitting needle into my upper thigh the same way you'd stab a knife into the throat of your bitterest enemy. Even in my delirium I felt the needle slice through the tendons and rest somewhere near my bone. He pushed down hard on the syringe and liquid flooded between the sinews into my veins. He drew out the needle and put it on a platter. It was smeared with blood.

'Banessa, can you hear me?'

My head wobbled uncertainly.

'I'm going to wait twenty minutes. If you still can't breathe, we have to put a tube down your throat. Just sit here and try to stay calm.'

I slumped over in the chair and passed out.

When I woke up, I was covered in my red polar fleece I'd taken to Antarctica. It smelled faintly of penguin shit. The doctor came in. He took my pulse and felt my forehead.

'Your friends came. Your passport is at the front desk.'

He frowned.

'Another hour and you would be dead.'

I tried my tongue. It was still swollen but it kind of worked.

'What happened?'

He raised his eyebrows as if I was a very naughty girl.

'If you are allergic to bee stings, why don't you carry adrenalin?'

'I'm not allergic.'

'Are you telling me this is the first time you've been stung by a bee?'

'Hell no. I get stung by bees all the time. Nearly every day. Sometimes by swarms.'

'You have to stay away from them.'

'I can't. I work with monkeys. There are bees in the forest.'

He sighed. I was one of those crazy gringas. He handed me a yellow tube. On one end was a long rectangular piece of metal.

'You need to carry this everywhere now. If you get stung, inject it into your upper thigh. It's pressure operated. Push here, and the needle will shoot in.'

Holy shit, I thought. Needle is an understatement. It was more like a barbeque skewer.

'How long do I have to do that for?'

He looked at me carefully.

'The rest of your life.'

'Are you serious?'

'Banessa, listen to me. You have developed a hyper-allergy to bee venom. Your body has had too many stings and even a tiny amount will shut it down. Every time you are stung, your body will react faster and faster. Your face will swell up. Your throat will close. Eventually you will lose consciousness and die. This time it took a few hours. Next time it will be less. Comprende?'

I nodded, bewildered. I wandered like a sleepwalker into the waiting room where Brad and Summer were waiting.

'What the hell is that?' Brad asked when he saw my yellow barbeque skewer.

'Don't even ask.'

When I walked into the monkey house, Diane was in the living room. She had arrived that day. We sized each other up like boxers in the ring. Then my legs wobbled and I gave up.

'I had an allergic reaction to a bee today,' I said, thinking our common allergy might unite us. 'I nearly died. They had to stick a horse needle in my ass.'

She didn't smile.

'Yes,' she said pleasantly. 'I have a cold.'

Dread clutched my intestines. Apparently, Diane had been rooting for the bees.

I skipped dinner and went to my room, which was now a tent in the backyard. Since Diane had taken the pizza house back, the rest of us were faced with an uncomfortably squashed monkey house. I would happily have moved into Brad's room but, over the next four months, five new people were arriving. That meant fourteen people in the monkey house. Which meant Brad and I would have a room-mate.

The thought of undressing, masturbating and snoring in a room with a stranger freaked me out, so I took Diane's old tent and pitched it in the backyard. I wasn't the only one who didn't like the idea of two room-mates. Kermit moved into the laundry. He cleared out all the junk, boarded up the bars with plywood and cut a few holes for windows and a door. Between Kermit's room and my tent, the monkey house was starting to look like a refugee shelter.

Personally, I preferred the tent. It was tall enough to walk through, with two rooms and a front section. Sirius was allowed in and I'd grown so used to having her in my bed, I couldn't bear the thought of sleeping alone.

As I stumbled into the tent, Sirius followed me, wagging her tail and worrying a coconut husk in her teeth.

'Not tonight, sweetheart. A bee tried to kill mummy today.'

My face was still twice its normal size and I felt like I hadn't slept in weeks. Brad came in after dinner.

'Thanks for bringing my jacket to the clinic.'

'I thought you were going to die.'

'Near-death experiences don't seem to get a lot of street cred around here. How's Diane?'

Even saying her name made my stomach tight. It was obvious our relationship had significantly deteriorated. I knew it was more than the sexual assault. With all my illnesses and issues, I was pretty much useless to the project. She must have seen the negligible amount of data I'd been sending to the States. With all the time and resources she'd put into training me, it must have made her furious. And then, considering her high hopes for me at the beginning, it must have seemed like a betrayal that I turned out to be such a disappointment.

'Well after dinner she put up a chart. One line was the number of follows we've collected over the last three months. The other, higher, line is the number of follows we're supposed to be getting. We obviously aren't Tristans this year.'

'How did everyone take it?'

'Hysterical. They're like Brady Bunch crack whores in there. I had to escape and check you can breathe. Then I'm going straight to bed. Are you going out tomorrow?'

'Like you said, I nearly died. I think I'll stay home and make sure my windpipe is functional.'

'Well gather your strength, Mischka. The next day you're out with Diane.'

Murder was at the bottom of the dry waterfall. Slices of shale stacked on top of each other made a cliff over which I could see her waving her tail in the valley canopy. Determined to be a good monkey researcher, I skidded down the path and stood under her tree. I radioed Diane and Henreike.

'I have Murder down here.'

'We have everyone else up here,' Diane replied.

That was strange. Murder was always the centre of the group. She nibbled on a piece of bark.

'Murder, what are you doing down here? Why isn't anyone following you?'

I hauled myself back up the dry waterfall. Diane was chatting to Henreike and the monkeys were in the Luehea trees. Luehea looked like a star fruit except it was brown and rock hard. The monkeys pounded them on branches for hours then cracked their teeth to extract a few measly seeds.

'Shall we start?' said Diane. It was 6:01 a.m. 'I'll type, you spot.'

It was barely light enough to see the monkeys but I knew it was some kind of test.

'Okay, focal is Calamity. Focal handles Luehea, focal bites Luehea, focal taps Luehea left hand, focal taps Luehea right hand, focal pounds Luehea.'

'Wait a minute,' Diane lowered her PSION. 'What are you calling a tap?'

I felt like a kangaroo caught in headlights. It was a trap.

'Uh, a tap is when they hit the fruit lightly against the branch with one hand.'

'And a pound?'

'A pound is when they hit it harder with both hands.'

'I see. And how exactly would you quantify "hard"?'

'When they use both hands to slam it down.'

'What if they use one hand and hit it hard?'

'It's a pound, but I add the hand they used.'

She looked at me as though I'd dropped a turd in my pants and rubbed it on my face.

'Vanessa, how long have you been recording food data this way?'

The truth was, I hadn't taken any food data. It took too long to clean. I wondered if Diane knew this, and whether this exercise was designed to humiliate me.

'Since the beginning. It was what I was told.'

Diane's look called me a liar.

'You know this means we might have to throw out your data.'

I would rather she slid bamboo under my fingernails. After the stolen sleep, the gruelling hours and the bodily penalties, for your data to be thrown out meant it was all worth nothing. You may as well have been sleeping the whole time.

I kept silent.

'Let's try it again.'

And I was forced to say in a small voice, as Diane knew I would, 'What's the difference?'

'A tap is when they touch it with their finger. A pound is when they hit it on the branch.'

We finished the follow, shame choking me like bee venom.

I excused myself on a toilet break. I went a little up the trail and leant against a tree. So this was how it would go. I'd seen it all before with Billy. There would be no open confrontation. She would calmly and softly pick me to pieces.

I pulled my pants down and squatted. As the hot urine gushed out of me, suddenly I wasn't ashamed. I was angry. I was good, goddammit. I knew these monkeys. I knew every path, trail and shady bower they walked on. I knew who they hated, who they screwed and who they were afraid of. I deserved as much respect as anyone.

I pulled my pants up and made a vow. That was the last time she'd get me. I wasn't going to give her the tiniest excuse to humiliate me again. If she had her alpha status on her side, I had youth on mine. I could outrun nearly everyone on the project. I could definitely outrun her.

Right, I thought as Scandal scampered above my head. Let's play ball.

We didn't stop. Dopey led the group running, like the sissy he was, and we stuck to them like flies to honey, taking data the whole time. As soon as we finished one follow, I found another. Diane and I had an unspoken understanding. We didn't sit down. Henreike, at her low position in the hierarchy, didn't feel comfortable sitting down first, but eventually she was too exhausted to keep going. When she sat down, I sat down opposite her. Diane would not sit next to me. She sat down five metres away on the other side of Henreike. She only addressed Henreike, which meant Henreike had to turn her back to me so she could speak to Diane.

Halfway through the day, I felt something on my inner thigh. Without ceremony, I stuck my hand down my pants and scraped my nails over the itchy area. When I looked under my fingernails, all I saw were a few specks of dirt. How the hell did they get there and why were they itching me?

I looked closer.

'Holy shit!'

Henreike and Diane looked at me.

'They're alive! I have dirt creatures down my pants.'

Diane stood up and handed me some masking tape.

'They're ticks. You have to get them all off.'

I looked closely at Diane. Maybe I was reading the situation all wrong. Maybe she wasn't persecuting me after all. I took the masking tape.

'Thanks.'

I ran behind a tree and pulled my pants down. It was worse than I thought. Hundreds of dirt specks were crawling up my thigh. One had already buried into the soft skin around my vagina. I plastered the masking tape on my legs and ripped it off like wax strips. The ticks were stuck on their backs, wiggling their legs. I pulled most of them off. Then, not wanting to fall too far behind, I caught up with Diane and Henreike.

Half an hour later I felt a needle point driven through my skin. I stripped off the covering layer of clothing and found a dirt speck tick burying into my skin. This happened at regular intervals throughout the day. I thought of asking for the masking tape again, but didn't.

As the day wore on, I kept looking for signs that Diane and I could be friends. I joked about the monkeys. I asked questions about her research at the university. But one thing I learnt about Diane was that however smooth her voice, however politely she laughed at your jokes, and however calm and untroubled her eyes, she had no control over her body language. When she spoke to me, she turned her torso away so she had to twist her head uncomfortably. When Henreike stopped us for a break, Diane would sit as far away from me as possible with her back turned. Soon it would get worse. She would stop smiling at my jokes and would not speak to me at all. But even in the beginning the various contortions of her body spoke with high definition clarity.

So I charged on for fourteen hours. I chased monkeys up cliffs and down ravines. Diane would not follow me when the path was too steep, instead we finished the follow by radio. My last follow was Calamity, number 36. The most I'd ever done was 30. Henreike had dark circles of exhaustion under her eyes and she was soaked with sweat. I was exhausted, but kept standing. So did Diane. We followed the monkeys to their sleeping site.

In the car on the way home, Annie launched into a monologue.

'And then Sleepy swiped Bashful and Bashful screamed—it was so funny.'

I stared at Annie to make sure it was really her. Since when did she give a shit about monkeys? She hated monkeys. I hadn't seen her this animated since . . . since . . . Andreas. But it didn't make sense. Who was she in love with now? Kermit? Then I turned and saw Diane smiling for the first time all day.

'So Diane,' Annie gushed. 'Why would they do that? Why would Sleepy turn on Bashful after he'd been grooming her for two hours?'

'Well, it all depends on who's dominant.'

I felt a pang. It was the same voice Diane used with me a long time ago. The voice that warmly encouraged your blossoming curiosity.

'And Bashful is such a little troublemaker,' Sarah joined in.

This was too much. Sarah would microwave a monkey if she thought she could get an extra half hour of sleep. What the hell was going on?

I cornered Diane on the porch when she was taking her boots off.

'Hi Diane? Can I talk to you for a second?'

She smiled and once again I wondered if I was making the whole thing up.

'Sure.'

I took a deep breath.

'It's been hard here, after everything, and I think I might go home early. Probably in February.'

When I booked my plane ticket from Australia, I thought it lasted for eighteen months. The travel agent probably told me it was a twelve-month ticket but being the non-forward planning idiot I am, I forgot. I found out about the twelve-month limit early on in the monkey project when I tried to book a return flight for August instead of May so I could go to Africa and film the other five segments for Disney.

The ticket was unchangeable, and I needed at least two months in Africa, which meant leaving Costa Rica at the end of February instead of early May. I almost brought it up a million times with Diane and Princess, but people who quit the monkey project early were referred to with a tinge of disgust so I always chickened out at the last minute. It was now January. I had to say something, and the whopper about my dad was the perfect leaving excuse.

'Well, I don't want to force anyone to stay here. Why don't you go home now?'

I wanted to leave so badly I would have run the whole way to San Jose. But the Disney segments were not back yet and I didn't trust Diane to sign them off unless I was right there, watching her.

'There's not much point. I told you before, my father's in Bangkok until February. I don't have a job in Australia so I'd just be sitting around doing nothing. Besides,' I said carefully, 'the Disney segments should be here soon. I'll stay and make sure they haven't done something stupid with them.'

Her eyes narrowed and we understood each other perfectly. She wanted me gone, and I wasn't going until I got what I wanted.

I saw Sarah quickly walking away from the door. I followed her.

'Sarah?'

Things had been tense between Sarah and I ever since I'd left for Boston. She suspected I was lying about my father. Now she knew I was. I told her months ago, when we were friends, that I had to leave in February to film for Disney.

We were no longer friends, and now she was dangerous. She never could keep her mouth shut and eventually it would get back to Diane. I summoned all my powers of persuasion.

'About my dad.'

Her eyes warned me not to make her despise me but I kept going.

'My dad is really sick you know.'

She couldn't look me in the eyes.

'Whatever.'

'Sarah really . . .' I squeezed out a few tears for authenticity but I could have slashed my wrists for all the effect it had.

'I just wanted to let you know. I know you don't believe me, but I'm telling the truth.'

She swept past me into her room, contempt knocking me over in her wake. She didn't care about the lie, particularly. She didn't even care about me leaving early, even though everyone else was scandalised because our contracts were for twelve months and we were told leaving early was 'letting the project down'. It was the other thing Sarah couldn't forgive— keeping a secret. She liked to keep secrets because they made her feel powerful. As her friend, I was supposed to tell her secrets. I'd told her about leaving in ten months instead of twelve, but I had kept two very important secrets from her: Charles, and now what was really going on in this complex web of lies I'd wrapped myself up in.

It was only a matter of time before she punished me.

Dopey walked the branch gingerly, preparing to run at any moment. Murder jumped up as though the devil had arrived and head flagged to Assassin, who was grooming Murder's back. Murder opened her mouth in a silent snarl and kept

flicking her head, urging Assassin to join her. Assassin did
nothing. Murder forgot about Dopey and stared at Assassin.
Assassin coolly walked past her and jumped on Dopey's back.
Together they threatened Murder.

Devastated, Murder ran. Dopey thrust into Assassin,
grunting like a warlord.

The forest was like biblical Egypt; it always had another
plague up its sleeve. The latest was Sloanea. The trees were
stripped bare like they'd been hit by an atomic blast and the
only hint of green was the Sloanea trees that grew by the
river. The monkeys stayed in them all day, eating the grape-
sized fruit that grew by the bushel. I was happy they had
something to eat, but the fruit was covered in fine hair like
tiny shards of fibreglass. The monkeys rubbed the hair off
the fruit any way they could; against a branch, between their
palms, or rolling it between their feet.

Diane was interested in how the infants learnt to clean
Sloanea and so it was our duty to stand beneath the shower
of splinters that rained down like deadly fairy dust. They got
under your clothes and itched all day. They were practically
invisible. As the taxi driver suggested would happen with
Sirius's hair, they got stuck up your vagina.

The worst was when they fell in your eye. Every time you
blinked it was like a needle scraping the inside of your eyelid.
Your eye watered and you held open your eyelid for as long
as you could, but eventually you had to blink. Summer had
one for more than two days. By the time I took her to the
clinic, she was weeping with frustration and lack of sleep.

I didn't get hit that badly by Sloanea because I'd been
taken out of Nirvana and permanently assigned to Sin. Dopey
was afraid of other monkey groups who had moved closer to
the river, so he claimed as his territory the Dead Cow Pond.

Named after the massive carcass Princess and Carlos found floating in it several years ago, time had not softened the stench of the stagnant water. There was no shade here of any kind. The fallen leaves crackled like a furnace. When the monkeys drank from the pond, they tested it with their tongues in case the water was too hot. They lay along smouldering branches, panting and feebly tapping Luehea for the last of the seeds.

I started to think nostalgically of the wet season, when if I wasn't dry at least I was cool. I would have welcomed the hordes of mosquitoes and the pustule-swelling chiggers, just for the relief of clouds passing across the sun.

We had to triple the amount of water we took with us and the extra weight made my back ache painfully each day. Even so it was never enough. Just the sight of the barren trees and panting monkeys was enough to keep us thirsty.

I could have done it. I had just over a month left to go and I was fitter than I had ever been. What I couldn't cope with was Diane.

I was assigned to Diane one day out of three, sometimes two, just as Billy had been. And each of those days I worked like a demon. Diane and I never started later than 6 a.m. and we didn't stop until twelve hours later. As she had with Billy, she made sure we were never on our own. If we were, it might have forced a more intimate interaction between us. Instead there was always a third party whom Diane could address without referring to me directly.

The third party was always a new person. With Billy the new person had been me. With me, the new person was Henreike or Summer. Ostensibly, this was because the new person was less experienced and needed Diane's guidance. But I thought it was so no senior people who were my allies could see what she was doing to me.

As to what she was doing, it was genius. She never said a harsh word. After the pound/tap incident, she never corrected me. She took data unquestioningly as I ran through the dead forest. But at the end of each day I felt crushed. As though she'd whipped me ceaselessly from the moment the sun lit the sky.

The modifications to her behaviour were tiny but effective. We were still having our standing up competitions where neither of us sat down. When Diane did sit down, she deliberately sat ten metres away from me, with her back turned. She never spoke to me unless we were taking data, and communicated all her thoughts and desires through the third party.

It wasn't pleasant for the third party either. Henreike and Summer came to dread the days they were out with Diane and I. Not only was the work exhausting, they had to negotiate the prickly silence.

I knew what was happening. Ostracism is the most powerful form of social punishment. I saw it all the time with Murder and Assassin. When Murder approached, Assassin ignored her. Murder couldn't do anything. Assassin wasn't attacking her. She wasn't aggressively pushing into the alpha female position. With barely any effort at all, Assassin was drilling a psychological needle into Murder's anterior cingulate cortex, the area of the brain that detects social pain.

Both Murder and I were being carefully annihilated.

The competition to be Diane's favourite was hovering between Annie and Brad. Watching Annie rise in Diane's estimation was like watching a pig unfold wings and do double loops across the sky. Annie was without doubt the worst researcher since Billy. She couldn't stand the monkeys, she hated everything about the forest and she still didn't know Nirvana after five months, which was actually worse than Billy.

But Annie's effervescence that so charmed Andreas was doing the same for Diane. It was a tap Annie hadn't turned on for a while, but now it was gushing out in full force. She laughed uproariously about her own monkey stories. If Diane made any kind of statement, Annie would practically slobber in her effort to agree with her.

It made everyone else a little queasy but they played along—they had no choice. Every evening in the car was an exercise in hilarity and monkey fascination. It was a new competition of who loved the monkeys more.

Brad was the more obvious choice for favourite. He had the gift of recognising a monkey by the way it moved, something I hadn't seen since Tristan. He sped through the forest like lightning and only the Ticos could predict monkey behaviour better. He was also the only one on the project who had any interest in becoming a real primatologist. He had the drive, he had the obsession. And Diane liked it.

One night after a bad day with Diane, I reached for his hand in the car. Gently but firmly, he pulled it away. I saw Diane watching us like a cascabel. I turned and looked out the window.

As soon as we got home I rushed into my tent. Brad followed me.

'Mischka, I'm sorry.'

I was already crying.

'So I'm poison now?'

'You know why. I need her for graduate school. She has to write my recommendation. If I don't have it, then this whole year has been wasted for me. You're going to work in television and write books. I'll be chasing monkeys for the rest of my life. I need Diane.'

I sniffled.

'Does she really hate me so much that she'd punish you for being friends with me?'

Brad was grim.

'I'm afraid so. She doesn't know how close we are but she's sussing it out. Today she said, "Yeah, these media people. I don't like them. They just take what they want and leave."'

Despite myself, I gasped.

'She said that?'

'She's trying to figure out who your friends are. How strong you are here so she knows how much force it will take to pull you down. You shouldn't let her know who your biggest ally is.'

I sat down on the bed. Brad sat next to me and put his arm around my shoulders. Sirius crawled onto my lap.

'Is it the doctor? Is she blaming me for what happened?'

'I think it's more than that. You're bringing the world into her bubble; Disney and filming and everything else besides. She's terrified. And no, I don't think being diddled by the doctor helped. You're a loose cannon.'

Sirius was licking the tears off my face by now.

'But you still love me?'

'Of course I do,' Brad snapped, impatient with my histrionics. Then he smiled. 'You're the dark matter blowing her universe apart.' He stopped, thoughtful. 'Dark matter. I like that. My darkling.'

Smoking is a filthy habit. The first time I picked it up I had a gun held to my head on the Ethiopian border. I quit a year later and didn't touch another one until Diane and I got 40 follows without her speaking a single word to me all day.

Sirius and I were chasing her ball in the back garden near the avocado tree when I saw a glowing orange ember floating up and down. I'd never seen a firefly this far from the forest so I stood, watching.

'Hey,' said a voice. I jumped back two metres. It was Kermit. Sirius waddled up to him, tail frantic. He patted her and made kissing sounds. He was sitting on a large log. From it, he could see the light from his refugee window.

'Need a smoke?'

I realised I did. I sat down next to him.

'Rough day?'

'Shit yeah.'

That was all we said. We puffed in silence. Kermit was taking up less space than usual; he'd lost a lot of weight. The last few months of nastiness between us spiralled in a grey column out of sight. I realised his attraction for me was never as focused as I assumed. He didn't want me. He just thought about me the way I'd thought about Andreas or Jesus, someone to idly wonder about as you were sitting under a tree, staring at monkeys. He never deserved the venom I gave him. It was my conflicting vanity and confusion after the sexual assault that were at fault. All Kermit wanted was a girl he could look after. For a moment he might have dwelt on me because he thought I needed looking after most, but it would have passed on its own if I'd just chilled out and let it.

It occurred to me I could have done worse than Kermit. He was sweet and caring and the lucky girl he finally fell in love with would be treated like a queen. I was suddenly flattered I had ever been a contender and sorry I hadn't appreciated it. I wanted to tell him, but couldn't without it sounding like pity. So we finished our cigarettes as Sirius rolled around on her back, slobber dribbling down the ball she held in her mouth.

'Vanessa?'

Rachel stood at the door of my tent, visibly upset. My tent was the new therapy room and Summer, Rachel, Brad and Kermit came singly or in packs to unload.

Rachel had been visiting me even more than Brad lately. She felt out of place in the house, like people were annoyed at her and she didn't know why. I knew why. It was because she looked like the nerd in high school and people were digitally programmed to be mean to the nerd. I never told her because I thought she was great the way she was. She had a strong sense of social justice and right and wrong, and one day, while the rest of us were doing nothing spectacular, she was going to make a difference in the world. And by then what she looked like wouldn't matter. No one bags out Bill Gates for being a computer geek.

So to escape the high school mentality of the house, Rachel hung out in my tent. She liked to sit on the end of my bed and tell me about Israel.

'Rach, what's wrong?'

'It's Annie and Sarah.'

'Those bitches, what have they done to you?'

'It's not me. It's you.'

I frowned. Me? I hadn't done anything to either of them lately.

'I was with them in the field today, and they started bitching about you. Sarah told Annie and me that your dad was a lie. She said you'd made it up, that you told her ages ago you were leaving early. I stuck up for you and said you'd never say anything like that, they were just being mean and then she laughed and said . . .'

Rachel took a deep breath as though the memory was painful.

'She said everything that came out of your mouth was a lie. That you'd never told the truth in your life and you probably made up the story about the doctor so you could go on vacation early. They hate you.' She was shaking. 'They really hate you. I can't believe they said those things right in front of me. I mean, they know I'm your friend.'

Sarah and Annie were particularly mean to Rachel and were always poking fun at her behind her back: her thick glasses, her Jewish New York accent, the way she dressed. I thought about what it had cost her to defend me in front of those two girls, with their matching eyes full of malice. She was so brave. And I didn't deserve it.

'Rachel, thanks. For standing up for me. It means a lot.' She held my hand.

'I want you to know, I didn't believe them for a second. I know you wouldn't lie about your dad. You're not disgusting like they are.'

I reeled and felt despicable. Newton's third law. For every action there is a reaction. It was only a matter of time before I got what was coming to me.

Against all odds, Annie was winning the favourites game. Though Brad excelled in every aspect of monkey protocol, Annie and Diane shared a hatred that fastened them together tighter than spun steel.

Me.

I knew the game was up when Rachel relayed another snippet of conversation. Diane started it.

'Some people just don't dress properly for the forest. I don't know how Vanessa survives in those little tank tops.'

'You should have seen her in the wet season,' sniped Annie. 'She only did up one button of her shirt. And she was NOT wearing a bra.'

Vacation came and went and there was no sign of the Disney segments. I was desperate. After a flurry of emails my producer told me she'd sent the tapes weeks ago. I went to the post office. They told me to go to Liberia who told me to call Puenta Arenas. No sign. I wrote to my producer and begged her to send them again immediately. If I didn't get them, I couldn't go. Every day I checked the mail pile, hoping for a glimpse of a package with Mickey Mouse ears.

I didn't have much time left. The symptoms I had before Boston were returning. I woke up in the middle of the night panting with anxiety. I fell asleep in the forest standing up. I burst into tears at regular intervals. But I couldn't afford the luxury of another breakdown. Because every third day I was with Diane.

Newton's first law: An object in motion stays in motion unless acted on by an unbalanced force.

I wasn't happy but I was cruising, however unsteadily, on autopilot. Then the unbalanced force hurtled into me like a comet.

Brad and I broke up.

* * *

It was brewing for a week before I finally noticed. Brad was withdrawn and sullen. I put it down to his mood matching mine; we usually had synchronised mood swings, right down to PMS. But then I noticed that the nastiness that he usually reserved for stupid people was being directed at me.

I decided to ask him what was wrong on our day off. I planned to draw it out of him gently. Make him understand we were the best of friends and whatever I had done to annoy him, I would fix. I bought him an ice cream and we sat down on our favourite bench in the park in the middle of Vacas. I took a deep breath.

'Why are you being such a prick?'

He sat up as though an electric shock had passed through his body. He did me the decency of turning away before I could see the disgust on his face, then walked home without me.

He didn't speak to me at dinner. At first I was angry at him too. But as I realised the depth and extent of his rage, I became afraid.

As soon as Annie came home, she sized up the situation with supernatural insight. She sat next to Brad at dinner, and when she jostled him in the way that had once caused him to rip her head off, he laughed uneasily. She nudged closer to him and every inch she gained was an inch I lost.

Newton's second law: The acceleration of an object as produced by a net force is directly proportional to the magnitude of the net force, in the same direction as the net force.

In other words, if you push something, it moves.

No shit, Sherlock.

For 48 hours I combed through every memory to find out what I'd done to make Brad hate me. I wondered if he was angry at me for lying about Dad, but then I realised that was ridiculous. Brad had even fewer scruples than I did, and with us both being such drama queens, I think he was a little in awe of my whopper performance. I gave up. I sat on the edge of my bed, crying as usual, and decided I would fake a mysterious illness so I didn't have to go out the next day. Diane could screw herself. I might never go out again. I might sit on the edge of my bed until the Disney segments arrived and then leave the monkey house silently in the middle of the night.

I was warming up to the tragedy of it all and went inside to tell Princess. On the board I saw Brad and I were scheduled the next day in Sin, alone. I perked up. We'd be stuck together for at least twelve hours. That had to be enough time to get to the bottom of whatever was bothering him. And this time, I'd do a better job.

However, Brad guessed my plans and at first light he started his stop watch.

'Are you doing a follow?'

'I've started Murder.'

I crept over like an insect that knows it's going to get squashed.

'Murder bites stick,' I said in a small voice.

He looked inexpressibly annoyed that I even dared to spot for him. He had obviously envisaged the morning as him working alone and me floating uselessly around the periphery like a ghost.

'Can you please speak up? I can't hear you.'

'Murder ingests insect from stick.'

'Can you please refer to Murder as the focal?'

He waited for me to cry, and maybe I should have, but I didn't dare. I spotted for him until the hour-long follow was done. When he started the next follow, I started spotting for him again.

We didn't sit down. We didn't stop. We started one follow after the other, until eventually I started to droop. I could outstand Diane, but not Brad. He was an athlete and his 24-year-old muscles were rippling with testosterone. The pressure on my feet was cutting off the circulation while Brad looked like he was ready to run the City to Surf marathon.

I glanced at him furtively throughout the day, looking for signs of thawing, but he gave none. He didn't let the monkeys out of his sight and I didn't let him out of mine.

'Mani approaches to five.'

'That's not Mani, it's Mead.'

'Mead approaches to five. Focal social peeps.'

'That's not a social peep, it's a food peep. Social peeps are shorter and higher.'

'Focal ingests insect.'

'You missed the bite stick.'

And so he went on, correcting me ceaselessly in a flat, even tone. The sun burned with ever-increasing ferocity but there wasn't enough time for water.

Eventually, I gave in.

'Brad, we have to talk.'

The look he gave me was a good imitation of an SS officer. I kept going.

'Okay,' I said. 'Let's talk. You can't hate me until I leave.'

Without speaking, he made it perfectly clear that he could.

'But I don't understand. What happened?'

'You called me a prick,' he said coldly. 'I *hate* that word.'

'Brad I'm sorry, I didn't know. You were just being so weird all week.'

'I'm surprised you even noticed,' he sneered.

'What are you talking about?'

'You're selfish, Vanessa. And I'm bored of it. All you care about is your stupid Disney filming and then you're just going to pack up and get out. You're always running around thinking about you, you, you. Your documentaries, your book about us when you don't even see us. When you get upset I'm supposed to sit there while you cry for hours, then when I get upset you just ignore me until I'm in a better mood and can listen to you whine again.'

'That's not true! I didn't know what was wrong . . .'

'You didn't try very hard to find out.'

There was a long moment of silence. He was standing beneath a Luehea tree, one hand grasping a lower branch as if he would snap it off. I wanted to run over and hug him, but I saw it was too late. Sorry wasn't good enough either. In the distance between my patch of grass and the Luehea tree, I saw the end of our friendship. The silence between us would harden and crack. Annie would have him as a best friend, and perhaps she deserved him. She paid more attention to him than I ever did. Maybe hers was the kind of loyalty he was looking for.

'They don't mean anything,' I said softly, realising the truth. 'Disney will air my footage for five minutes then throw it in the trash. My books will be published and they'll sit on a shelf gathering dust. I don't really care. It's all just to keep me going, to make me more than the dirt I feel like.'

For the first time, I saw everything clearly.

'In the end, all I'll take from here is you.'

A giant grasshopper the size of a bird leapt from behind me towards the Luehea tree. Its wings were the span of an outstretched palm, coloured blood red and speckled with black. I ran after it and threw my arms around the person who, at that moment, mattered more to me than anything else in the world.

'You're right. I'm a selfish mean bitch and I don't deserve a single friend on this planet. I'm sorry I didn't see you needed me. But I love you. I really really love you and I'm so sorry.'

My tears were honest. I could tell because they burned like peroxide and swelled every blood vessel in my eyes.

Brad's body was rock hard, but then he relaxed and when I pulled back, he had tears in his eyes too.

'God, you're such a drama queen. Besides, you'll always have that stupid dog.'

The monkeys left the place Brad and I from then on called Breakup Tree and followed the trickle of water down the Tinamu rocks. We had that clingy feeling you get after a really big fight and I didn't want to let go of his hand. But the air was clearer between us and I knew everything would be alright. At the end of the day Brad taught me how to piss standing up off a log. As the monkeys settled down in the Sloanea trees over our heads, we straddled our pissing log and sang the song from *Annie* where the sun will come out tomorrow.

It was our favourite song because it was ironic. Little orphan Annie thought the sun coming out was a good thing. She didn't know what a bitch the sun really was.

High in the trees a monkey shook some branches in protest, but then all was quiet as they lay down to sleep.

chapter 15

Waiting
for Mickey

'I've just been screwed by Mickey Mouse.'

Brad read the email over my shoulder and whistled.

Disney's budget cuts had canned my next five segments. My entire trip to Africa was booked, I'd confirmed my arrival with the sanctuaries, and I'd even looked up details I usually forgot about, like whether the whole country was covered in swamp and whether the animals were still alive. Suddenly, in one fell swoop, it was over.

The disaster was Sirius. I needed the Disney money to bring her home. I quickly wrote to every documentary channel I could think of; Discovery Channel, Disney USA, National Geographic and a hundred others. With thinly veiled desperation I told them my flights were covered and they could have all the footage they wanted for a tenth of what they'd usually pay. There wasn't much hope. I had two weeks until I left for Africa. Even I knew that was pushing it.

I staggered towards the porch, already heavier with the weight of $10 000 on my shoulders. It may as well have been a million. My credit card wouldn't cover it. My mother certainly wouldn't. I had no job and no prospects of a job. Essentially, I was screwed.

Sirius bounded towards me with a coconut in her mouth. I fondled her soft ears and tried to ignore the giant price tag on her collar.

'She's quite stupid you know,' said Brad, sitting down next to me. 'I'm sure she wouldn't notice if you gave her to Angelina's family.'

'It's not her, it's me. If I leave her here, I'll never have another moment's peace.'

'Well, think of it this way. It's only money. You'd earn $10 000 stripping in a month.'

I thought about it.

'I'll try waitressing first. If that falls through, I'll look into stripping. Mother will be thrilled.'

The downfall of an alpha female is not like the defeat of an alpha male. There is no quick end, no mercy killing. Female monkeys fight like cocks. They peck off tiny pieces at a time until the ring is covered in blood.

Murder was slowly recovering after Mischief's death but Assassin gained mysterious strength from being Dopey's lover. I chanted to myself that he couldn't last long, that a new alpha would take his place. But it was proving the opposite. Dopey was outlasting everyone.

When Dopey wasn't around, Assassin might groom Murder, although Murder was as likely to groom Assassin. It was outrageous, Murder humbly picking at Assassin's fur, the dark queen crawling through the mud. But if Dopey was close and watching, Assassin might swipe at Murder, catching a wrinkle of skin under her fingernails. Sometimes Murder exploded like a supernova. She lashed out, screaming, arms flailing with the rage of one betrayed.

We took data on Murder and Assassin slowly annihilating each other. Murder's mouth bled at the corner and Assassin limped in an eerie echo of her dead son Arsenic. As Diane muttered into her dictaphone, I sulked behind her, trying to resist the urge to slug Assassin and Dopey with my backpack.

Ziggy, the new recruit, was with us. He had a real name but insisted even before he arrived that we call him Ziggy. Brad and I were expecting a stumpy troll-like character worthy of Nirvana but Ziggy was tall and rather good-looking. Brad insisted I drop the ice-queen act and make friends. I made a half-hearted effort but most of my energy went into surviving the ten day sprint to the finish.

The day ground me to dust. The dry air shrivelled my lungs. Sunlight ran up and down the length of me, burning only a little less than Diane's incinerating silence.

I made it to dusk but only just. When the car pulled up, I pressed my lips together so I wouldn't chew them to bloody shreds.

'Banessa?' Jesus whispered. *'Esta bien?'*

I nodded, touched by his concern. Tears stung my eyes. I turned my face to the window before he could see them.

When I opened the door of my tent, Sirius was sitting on a sea of coconuts. She had dragged them in, one by one and lined them up in the front section of my tent. I fingered the fibrous husks and she wagged her tail hopefully.

'Oh sweetheart,' I held her close and pressed my face into her fur. 'Thank you.'

'Banessa?'

It was Summer. She liked to say my name like the Costa

Ricans. Summer had a massive crush on Jesus and I suspected she'd come to find out what he said to me in the car.

'Oh my god, what's wrong?'

'Hello?' Rachel knocked on the pole near the door. 'What's with the coconuts?'

'Rachel quick, Banessa's crying.'

It struck me as odd that my crying signified some kind of crisis. Then I realised no one but Brad had seen me cry.

'How dare you not invite me to the party.' Brad was at the door. 'Oh,' he said when he saw the state I was in. 'Here we go again.'

Summer and Rachel fussed and clucked.

'What's wrong?'

'Does your back hurt?'

'Did your dad die?'

I shook my head.

'It's Diane. I can't stand it anymore.'

'What did she do?'

I was about to launch into a tirade but the specifics eluded me. 'Ignoring me' was too trite. 'Assaulting me with her body language' was too melodramatic. Instead I mumbled incoherently while Sirius stepped on everyone's laps. Brad looked at his watch. He was so used to me crying on his shoulder it was like brushing his teeth.

'Um, we're going to miss dinner.'

Summer and Rachel looked at him, outraged.

'Vanessa's crying!' said Rachel.

'She's always crying. Now hurry up or there'll be no food left.'

'He's right,' I said, rubbing my fists into my eyes, while Summer and Rachel made conciliatory noises and said they'd skip dinner with me if I wanted. 'I know what I have to do.'

Princess was at the computer, downloading the PSIONS. She had distanced herself from me since Diane had arrived. I understood. I had the mark of Cain, and she needed Diane more than my friendship.

She must have heard whispers from Annie and Sarah that I was lying, but to her credit she never said anything. It must have been hard for her. She could never really have any friends on the monkey project because they would either fall from grace as I did, or they would eventually leave her here to battle it out with a new group of monkey researchers.

My time was up, in every sense, but there had to be something left of those starlit walks past the oval. I knelt like a penitent at her feet.

'I can't go out with Diane anymore.'

Princess leant back, as though I had winded her. Diane days were just something you were supposed to cop on the chin.

'She treats me like a leper,' I said quickly. 'She always turns her back to me. She won't talk to me. She hates me.'

'She doesn't hate you. It's just . . .'

I waited for the answer. The final illumination of why Diane found the sight of me more repulsive than a rotting corpse.

Instead she sighed.

'Okay. I'll see what I can do.'

A vulture perched on a dead tree that forked in every direction towards the sky. The bird gave a cry, like a monkey's lost call, at some trace of meat lingering on the breeze.

I walked along Snuffle. The forest was anaemic in the early morning light, colours and shapes still blurred without the sun. It was hard to keep my eyes open.

The hiss registered in the primitive part of my brain that had not been activated since a lion walked past my tent in Kenya. It was a fierce, deep hiss, like a rice shaker. I jumped back and hit a tree before I knew what my body was doing.

We were supposed to wear polinas, thick straps of leather that cover your leg from ankle to knee to protect us from snakes. From the beginning I refused to wear them, since my lack of coordination made them more hazard than help. The leather straps entwined themselves in vegetation, tripping me up, and every time I fell into the river they tripled in weight, and the wet leather was like lead around my feet.

Charles called me reckless, and I suppose I was. But retribution had arrived. A blue snake. I squinted to make sure I wasn't hallucinating, but there it was, its head and neck standing as tall as my knee. It was the colour of a white opal, shimmering with shadows of topaz and sapphire.

Like a seer, the snake swayed its head from side to side. Its tail poked out of its coils, the rattle still vibrating from its warning. I was transfixed. My body began to move in time to its rhythmic undulations.

I knew I was being hypnotised. It would wait until I was locked in its strange dance then sink its curved fangs into my flesh, leaving two perfect holes like a colon in the middle of a sentence.

I shook myself out of the trance. I had to kill it. It was dangerous, lying on the path like that. Someone was going to get bitten. Someone could die.

I pulled out my machete and held it, an unsteady knight in the face of my dragon. How does one go about killing a snake? Especially with its head standing up like that. I knew Carlos could slay it instantly, but I had no idea. In Uganda I once tried to kill a giant rat that was eating our food supply.

After an hour of pathetic hit-and-misses, the cook took over the execution with one swift swipe.

I stepped closer and firmed up my resolve. Somewhere along the way, I'd lost the conviction I was immortal. I knew now I could die. Any one of us could.

The snake cocked its head at my foot pressing into the ground. It lifted its nostrils and flickered its tongue. I stared straight into its eyes. They were milky blue like the rest of it. Its head swung from side to side.

Suddenly, I understood. It wasn't trying to hypnotise me. It was blind. Beside it lay a crumpled heap of patterned brown skin. It must have shed just moments ago, its vision becoming cloudy as it pulled its old skin over its head. I had caught the snake naked, and only then had it dared to make a sound almost extinct in Costa Rica.

I took a long stick and nudged the snake as gently as I could. The snake uncoiled as though I'd caressed it with my fingertips and slithered into the bushes, leaving its old skin as a parting gift.

It wasn't until my heartbeat slowed down that I realised I was holding my breath. I leant against a tree trunk, gasping. This was bullshit. Rocks, bees, and now snakes. My heartbeat crept up again. I dug my fingernails into the bark. If I pulled hard enough I could rip them off. Saliva flooded my mouth and drooled between my teeth like I was a rabid dog. I kicked the base of the tree. My toes slammed into the metal cap on my boot sending shockwaves up my shins. Rage leaked from the corners of my eyes and dribbled into my ears. If I'd had a razor blade I would have drawn it in a perfect slit across my skin. I was parched for blood, my blood. I wanted to smear my fingers through it, taste the metal and grit in it at the back of my throat.

Then, as abruptly as it had come, the rage left me. I sagged to the ground and tilted my head back against the tree. In the flawless blue of the sky, the vulture turned in a wide arc back towards the valley, the heavy swoop of its wings as terrifying as an angel's.

That was the last fucking straw, I said to myself. I'm going home.

When I got back to the monkey house, the package with Mickey Mouse ears was waiting.

Brad cocked his head as I busted into his bedroom with the tapes in my hand.

'What are they?'

'Disney.'

'You're kidding. What are you waiting for?'

'You. I can't watch them on my own. I have a feeling they're going to be terrible, like Disney's got the monkey gnawing on giant pandas or something.'

If there was a mistake, any mistake at all, there would be no time to get them sent back, corrected and returned. Brad and I sat down on the couch, my camera trembling on my lap. I took a deep breath and pushed play.

A bright blond ponytail jumped onto the screen.

'Helloooooo there!' she chirped. 'Today we're going somewhere different—the wilds of Costa Ricaaaaaa.'

Television wise, it was great. It was full of colour, the monkeys were photogenic, and the editing was flawless. Science wise, it was awful. Disney had put in a poisonous grasshopper for monkey food, as well as an apple, which didn't grow anywhere in Central America. Worse still, the capuchin monkeys, Diane's monkeys, were introduced with the Disney presenter standing in front of a spider monkey. Black filled the screen. I felt like I was going to be sick.

'She's going to hate it.'

'Yep.'

'There's no way she'll approve it.'

'No way in hell.'

I clutched my camera tightly and ascended the stairs to the pizza house like they were steps to the guillotine. Diane answered the door.

'Hi!' I said brightly, as though she'd been waiting for this moment her whole life. 'The Disney segments have arrived.'

She let me in and we sat down. My sweating fingers left a smudge on the play button. I clamped my tongue between my teeth to stop myself apologising for every outrageous misdemeanour. I saw her lips tighten when the apple came on, heard her sharp intake of breath at the spider monkey close-up.

'Well,' she said slowly. 'That presenter is frightening. I wouldn't want my child watching this program.'

'Yeah, Denise is a bit over the top,' I said cheerily, 'but people in kids TV are like that.'

There was a long moment when I was sure she would say no. They're ridiculous. Send them back. At the very least get the monkeys right. Lightning crackled in her fingertips. She was the controller of my destiny.

We locked eyes. I thought of the blue snake, at its fiercest when it was naked and blind.

'They're fine,' she said. 'Go ahead.'

Maybe it was an act of remembrance for a time when we respected each other. Maybe it was payment for what I'd been through. Or maybe she just wanted me the hell off her project and was prepared to do whatever it took to get me on the next flight out.

The days passed in a flurry of activity. I had three days to take Sirius to the vet, call her new family who was keeping her for six months in Phoenix, organise my data, ship my stuff back to Australia, and spend as much time as I could with Brad. There was also something else, something I'd been dreading.

It was time to come clean. I didn't want to be the kind of person who lied to her friends.

'Rachel, I have to tell you something.'

Her eyes were clear and blameless. Her integrity was a rare and beautiful thing in a world full of cheaters and scammers like me.

'My dad's not dying.'

She frowned, unable to absorb deceit of such magnitude.

'He's not even sick. I lied about him so I could go home early.'

Her face sunk inwards and her mouth slackened in distress but, to her credit, she didn't condemn me. She just hung her head, the way kids do when you tell them fairies don't exist and Santa Claus is a hoax. It was the most effective punishment my conscience could hope for.

Summer had seen enough of life not to take it too hard. I was grateful for her maturity.

'I guessed. You kind of got fucked up here, didn't you.'

It wasn't a question.

'I'm sorry. I didn't want to lie to you but once I started I had to lie to everyone, you know?'

She took my long fingers in her tiny ones and did her best Crocodile Hunter accent.

'No worries, mate. We caught ourselves a big one, ay.'

There was only one person left to make peace with. Early one morning, when no one was up, I dialled Laos.

'Hello?'

'Dad, it's me.'

'Honey.'

Though I hadn't heard it in three years, it was the same voice that scattered a thousand monsters from my childhood bedside at night. He was the same man who rescued Cambodian street kids and screamed abuse at his daughters. He taught me there was nothing to fear from crocodile-infested waters then gave himself the flu so he could drink alcoholic cough medicine. He promised he'd always be there but then he wouldn't stop leaving.

I got so caught up in pretending he was dying, I started to think about what would happen if he really was dead. There was so much I had to say to him. What would it be like to live with the knowledge that you could never speak to someone again? I decided three years was long enough. Fathers aren't like boyfriends. You can't just dump them and move on.

'Honey, are you there?'

'I'm here.'

'Are you in trouble? Do you need me?'

Manic depressives can do that to you. One minute they're throwing chairs against the wall and the next minute they unlock you, giving you everything you've ever wanted. Every vicious word I'd kept for him evaporated. Instead, I was five years old again, standing on the pathway between the road and the house, watching him walk out on my mother.

'Why did you do it, Dad? Why did you hurt us like that?'

'I don't have an answer sweetheart. I went mad, just mad.'

I told him everything. The doctor, Diane, trying to pay for Sirius when I had no money, the unbearable heat, the rotting stench of rain, chasing dreams you weren't allowed to touch. It poured out, on and on until the sun blinked over the trees and people in their rooms began to stir.

He didn't say a word, just listened, and for once I felt I had a father after all.

When I was done he said, 'You'll have people hate you all your life, sweetheart. Because you're beautiful and strong and they won't ever have the guts you've got. Don't worry about the mutt, you'll find the money somehow. And as for the man who touched you, I could catch a flight right now and blow him apart with an AK-47. Plenty of those over here.'

It was an empty threat, of course. But I felt better. Because somewhere out there I had a knight in shining armour, even if it was my crazy old man who hadn't shot anyone since Vietnam.

Then I confessed that I had told everyone he was dying so I could go on vacation early.

He chuckled. 'Well, at least I'm still good for something. I hope you had a nice time.'

By the time I hung up and dried my eyes, the rest of the house was up. I only had one Vacas day left to type in my dictaphone data.

Annie was using the dictaphone machine. I was very polite.

'Annie, would you mind if I used that today? I have to clean my data before I go.'

'I don't think so.'

I stood stunned. Did she actually say no to me?

'Annie,' I said patiently like I was speaking to a stupid two-year-old. 'I am leaving in three days. Diane wants my data. I have to transcribe it. I have six tapes. I really need that machine today.'

She pursed her lips and raised her eyebrows.

'It's not my fault you've been messing around with Brad on all your days off. You should have been more organised.'

Something in me snapped.

'Annie,' I said softly. 'Get off the machine, now.'

She stuck out her chin.

'No.'

I moved very fast. Within a second I was an inch away from her face. I slammed my palm on the table. She jumped back as though I had hit her.

'ANNIE YOU ARE SUCH A FUCKING BITCH YOU DRIVE ME UP THE FUCKING WALL!'

There were people milling around the house. Princess was making coffee in the kitchen, Kermit was in his room, and Ziggy was at the washing machine. They all froze. I stormed outside and slammed the door so hard I nearly broke it. I breathed hard. I was losing it. I was going over the edge.

I straightened up. It didn't have to end this way. This was her choice, not mine, and I wasn't finished with her yet. I stormed back inside the house.

The blood drained from her face. Her hands were shaking as they rested on the keyboard. I kept my voice low.

'I'm going to ask you one more time, and then I'm going to pick you up and throw you out of that chair. Let me use the dictaphone.'

She didn't move. I was so angry I could have thrown someone twice her size across the room. I stepped forward.

'Vanessa!' Princess called sharply. 'I have another dictaphone here. Use mine.'

Annie and I typed close enough to strangle each other. After a few minutes she rushed into her bedroom, quietly closing the door.

'Darkling,' Brad said as he vigorously scrubbed his crotch. 'Was it really necessary?'

I was sitting butt-naked on the toilet seat. We didn't have much time alone these days, so our sacred time extended to evenings in the shower where we knew our nudity would discourage intruders. It also meant, as long as one of us got in first, we always had our showers before everyone else.

'She asked for it. I had to do my data and she knew it. She was just being spiteful.'

The truth was, I couldn't handle an iota more than I was dealing with already. I was so close to the edge I could spit over it. If Annie didn't have the sense to stay out of my way, that was her problem.

'Well, I had to put up with her today in Nirvana. Oh my god, it was the post-Andreas days all over again. She moped and sulked and finally I had to ask her what's wrong. Then she told me she vomited in the morning. I asked her if she was pregnant, she said no. Sick? No, crying. Then she just looked at me. Like because you were my friend it was my fault. Then half an hour ago Sarah told me Annie's been crying her eyes out all night and that some people, meaning you, should be ashamed for causing the poor girl such distress.'

'Oh please. She has her own claws.'

'Well I don't see why I have to be responsible for your vendettas. She was so miserable today I nearly had to hug her. Which would mean touching her.'

'Did you?'

'No way. But for god's sake, the next time you're going to do something like that, can you make sure I'm not out with her the next day? And give me some warning so I can avoid Sarah. She's like a big fat bird that's caught someone stepping all over her eggs.'

'Deal. Besides, you're with me the next two days and then I'm out of this mental home.'

'Yes, but if I know you, darkling, that's just enough time for you to do a lot of damage.'

It was true. I solemnly promised Brad and myself that I would make it to the end without losing my temper.

Dear Vanessa,

I've looked over your filming proposal and find the offer too good to pass up. I've spoken to Disney Australia and I've decided to commission you to film four segments on the conservation projects Disney supports in Africa. These include most of the sanctuaries on your filming itinerary.

Please call me to further discuss.

Looking forward to working with you,
Sophie Hastings
Manager, Conservation Programs
Disney USA

And just like that, everything was alright.

On my last day, after running us up Snuffle for old times' sake, Sin crept to the bottom of the dry waterfall and lazed on Sloanea branches overhanging the stream. Assassin ripped the head off a baby bird, right in front of me.

I waited for some kind of closure. I thought because my time here was over, there would be some kind of resolution. Assassin and Murder would make up or break apart. Angel would stride in and claim Sin once again for his own. Snow White would storm in and finally take over. But nothing extraordinary happened. Dopey lay, unevicted, Assassin on one side and Murder watching them.

There was one new beginning at least. Torment was pregnant. Soon all the females would follow. I stared at Dopey and wondered, unlikely hero though he was, could he see the next generation grown? I lingered over faces that were burned into my memory. My monkey blindness was cured. They would never look identical again.

Brad and I sang all the Broadway numbers we knew, performing a special rendition of 'Big Spender' for Calamity, who was now brave enough to scowl and shake a branch.

When the monkeys lay down for their noon-time nap, I looked over their faces as fondly as a mother might. They stretched out on their shadowed branches, the dappled sunlight as gentle as warm kisses. I loved these monkeys. I was afraid for them, just as I was afraid for myself. I shivered that a scream might pierce the afternoon air. That they would be driven to run and run until night swallowed their enemies and they could rest for a moment in darkness. Day was not always the bringer of relief, and sometimes night had the least to hide.

But for now they closed their eyes to the murmur of the stream running over the pebbles, and enjoyed their unbroken peace.

There was a tradition on the monkey project. As you were leaving the forest on your last day, you turned and looked behind you. Whoever you saw, you carried with you forever.

The monkeys slept in the huge Guanacaste tree on Toledo. It was where Diane and I had found them the first day I'd arrived. I remembered how unsure I was then, how afraid, even before the worst had happened. I had nothing more to fear from the forest. I was starting again, and again I was afraid.

Every new place is a jungle, with its own sets of parasites, disasters, and monkeys of good and evil. With all I'd been through with this one, at least it was familiar. I had lost the immortality of youth. Somewhere in the jungle I'd become very aware that I could get hurt, that I could die. It was the most frightening feeling I'd ever had, that the worst was still out there waiting for me.

But I decided to savour that moment of peace as I walked out. Surviving is its own kind of triumph.

As I left them for the last time, I looked over my shoulder. I could barely make out her features, backlit by the fading dusk. Then she flicked her tail and tossed her head.

Murder.

A young woman knelt in front of a little girl, peering into her tiny cupped hands. The woman's long dark hair fell over her knees. I stood still because I wanted to remember how beautiful they were, spears of sunlight surrounding them in a golden cage.

The woman stood up and called to me.

'Banessa!'

Sirius cocked her head. She knew someone was calling my name, but didn't know who it was.

'Angelina!' We ran down the road and threw our arms around each other.

'It's so good to see you! What are you doing here?'

'We came back for your party.'

We stood there, looking at each other. I didn't have the words to tell her what it meant that she had come all the way from Panama to see me.

'You look wonderful,' I breathed instead. It was true. She was glowing like someone who had been given a new chance.

'I'm so happy.'

Linda and Sirius jumped around us.

'Banessa! Banessa!'

Manuel was lounging by the side of the road, talking to Carlos. He gave me a bear hug that crushed the air from my lungs.

'I missed you so much,' I said. 'Nothing was the same after you left.'

'We couldn't miss saying goodbye, chiquita.'

Angelina's mother came to the doorway, wiping her hands on her tea towel, just as I had seen her nearly a year ago.

'Querida, it's been too long.'

Linda took Sirius by her ear and dragged her off to play. The rest of us went inside and I sat in the chair of honour covered with the pink cloth. Sophia and Flora squealed when they saw me, and we made plans to meet at Soda Limon later that night.

'Your mother will be happy you're going home.'

I thought of my mother and realised I couldn't wait to see her.

'Mothers should never be too far from their children.'

I wondered if this was the secret to the smiling faces I saw all over Costa Rica. Most of them lived below the poverty line with barely any access to education, employment or any of the opportunities we took for granted. And yet they seemed happier than the whole western world put together.

I realised I loved Angelina's family not because of what I didn't have, but because of what I missed. My mother, my sister and I were not the house full of laughter that this family was. In fact, we were quite dysfunctional. There was no male figurehead to guard and guide us, my mother worked twelve hours a day, and my sister and I were hardly the squealy joy of sisterly love that Angelina's sisters were. Then there was my brother who I didn't meet until I was fifteen because he'd been living with zebras in Zimbabwe—a whole other story.

But they were my family and I loved them. I ran halfway around the world looking for myself, but perhaps the only people who could tell me who I was were right back where I started.

Manuel and Angelina came back to the monkey house with me; Linda ran ahead, holding on to Sirius by her collar. I took down my pink mosquito net and ripped it in pieces. Using a red cord, I made two tutus, one for Linda and one for me. I twisted a coat-hanger into fairy wings. They hung a little lopsidedly on Linda's slender shoulders but she ran around squealing in delight. When we were all dressed up and ready, the party began.

I thought of all the monkey house parties, each one a last dance for someone: Tristan, Manuel, Charles, Andreas, and now finally me.

I looked at everyone, drunk and happy on the dance floor. We understood each other in ways we would never be understood again. We'd picked off parasites together and discussed our genital infections. We talked all day about nothing: who we really wanted to be when we grew up, instead of who we were now; the shape and colour of our favourite penis. I always thought those spiralling hours amounted to nothing, but shards of detail slipped through, so precious they were unknown to even family and lovers.

Kermit did a boogie woogie with Summer while Rachel looked on, laughing. Brad shook his butt in Rachel's crotch. Linda had Angelina's giant sunglasses on and was fluffing her pink tutu as she danced. Manuel had his arm around Angelina and she tenderly nuzzled his neck. I smiled as Brad pulled me over and gave me a sweat-drenched hug.

These people hadn't always been my friends. I thought of the impatience and judgement I had greeted them with and was ashamed. They had always been these people, warm, wonderful, and willing to share who they were. It was me that had changed. Something of the pompous, self-centred, judgemental person I was when I arrived had vanished, so I could see them all now, as friends. And for that I was really, truly, grateful.

I felt alcohol-fired breath on my neck. A hand brushed my ass. I spun around to face Ziggy who was hungrily staring at my breasts. I figured he was desperate to find out how I had ignored his good looks all this time. As he got drunker he must have decided my coolness towards him was just a facade and really, I'd be so much better off if I gave him a blow job.

'Don't touch me.'

He stood with his mouth open, as drunk men do when you repel an advance they think has been charming and polite. His face turned red and ugly. He tossed his head wildly and saw Jesus watching. He stepped away from me.

'*Esta es basura,*' he said in perfect Spanish. This one is trash.

Then he staggered upstairs to his room. I knew if I followed him I could make it right. Soothe that bruised male ego and he'd come back to the party. Then I remembered my first two weeks with Tristan. How angry and confused we were, and how all we had in common was desire. I was different now. I had people here who liked me for who I was, not because they wanted to screw my brains out. I didn't need that kind of validation.

Jesus and I walked towards each other. He shook his head and I knew Jesus would never call Ziggy a friend.

'So, Banessa. You will be home soon.'

'Yes. Home.'

'That is good. You should write to me some time.'

I was touched. Jesus was not the emailing type. He had too much faith in the natural order of things to bridge gaps of time or distance.

'What can I send you from Australia?'

He smiled dreamily, the way only Jesus can.

'I've always wanted one of those hats. You know, that Crocodile Dundee wears.'

'I'll send one to you. I promise.'

Around midnight we went to Soda Limon, where Angelina's sisters and Theresa were waiting. They cheered when I arrived. I felt like I belonged. We sat around, smoking, drinking and talking until 3 a.m.

I was having a wonderful time, until all the fun went cold. It was as though I'd been emptied out from the bottom. The flashing lights and distorting music were suddenly too much. I took Brad's hand.

'Let's go,' I whispered.

He followed me and we sat on our park bench.

'What's wrong?'

'I felt so strange all of a sudden. Overwhelmed. I just wanted to be with you.'

He put his arm around me and I rested my head on his shoulder. The stars shone through the trees and spun around my head. I told Brad what Ziggy had said. Brad whistled.

'He called you trash? That's so intense.'

'I seem to have that effect on men.'

'Darkling, your panties were showing through your pink tutu.'

'No way!'

'In a cute fairy kind of way. Face it—you drive them all a little crazy.'

'I don't want to drive them crazy. I want to have a meaningful relationship. I want to have children and a nuclear family. Complete with white picket fence and a husband who's a banker.'

Brad snorted.

'While you're screwing the pool boy.'

'I won't. I really won't. I'm over all that now. Like you said. I'm in the glory box.'

The music pulsed from Soda Limon in time to the flashing lights.

'I don't mind being alone,' I said suddenly. 'I don't want to make the same mistake my mother did, marrying an alcoholic, and yet I keep almost making that same mistake. Falling in love with men who drink, I mean. I feel like I should lock myself up until I'm ready. Until all my issues are gone and I'll finally be fixed and ready for the right person.'

Brad snorted.

'You'll be dead before that happens. Don't worry,' he said as my face crumpled. 'We're all the same. The best we can hope for is someone who loves us, inspires us, and makes us laugh. Then you fix each other.'

'I may just have a baby via a sperm donor. That takes all the uncertainty out of it.'

'Well yes, if you want your nether regions glued shut. Darkling,' he said, fluffing my tutu. 'You'll find someone. One can only hope he'll be as fabulous as me.'

chapter 16

Blue

We had half an hour of sleep before Brad and I took our bags, Sirius and her doggy carrier to the bus station to wait for our taxi. In typical Vacas fashion, the taxi didn't turn up and the man standing outside the bakery had to call his brother with a pick-up truck to drive us to the only hotel in San Jose who didn't hang up when I said I wanted to keep a dog in the room.

Sirius was plastered against my legs the whole time. She'd never been outside Vacas. She did not like her pet pack and resisted all the habituating exercises I tried, like putting her dinner inside it or throwing in her blue squeaky ball.

She slept, as always, on my bed, her long warm flank down the length of mine and her wet nose nuzzling my neck. She had strange dreams and whimpered all through the night.

The next morning at 7 a.m., we caught a taxi to the airport. I had an awful ache filling me like an ocean. Not one part of me didn't hurt. The noise of plane engines made Sirius cower between my legs as we went from office to office, filling out customs forms and making sure her papers were in order.

She did not want to get inside her doggy carrier.

'Come on, baby,' I said brokenly, tears pouring down my face. 'Please get in.'

She whined and pushed herself into my arms. Her whole body was shivering. It took Brad, the customs man and the taxi driver to get her inside. I cried out for them to be careful of her head, not to hit her legs too hard.

When she shoved her nose through the wire, I panicked. The Chinese believe if you show you love something too much, the spirits become jealous and take it away. It was one of the reasons my mother always called me ugly and stupid.

I had not paid enough attention. Everyone from the baker to the garbage man in Vacas knew how much I loved that dog.

Brad took me by the shoulders.

'Come on,' he said. 'You'll see her in six months.'

But with the premonition that is buried and scorned in each of us, I knew I never would. As it turned out, when I first pinned her squirming body to my lap, one of the ticks I pulled out of her puppy ears had esclerosis. She would pass every test with flying colours, but two days before her flight was to land in Australia, quarantine would call me and say they couldn't let her in. I would cry. I would tell the sympathetic man on the phone about how I found her whining like a child in the tyre factory, how she'd filled my tent with coconuts when she knew I needed it most. But it was no good. Sirius had to stay in Arizona. She was going to a good family, but that didn't make it hurt any less.

Brad led me away, the emptiness growing between the carrier and us. I bawled and bawled, harder than I'd ever cried, and for more reason. I was leaving my heart in that pet pack, the best and most precious thing I ever had. If it hadn't been for her, the jungle and everything around it would have broken me. Looking after her gave me more than happiness, it gave me grace.

For the very first time, I heard her howl. They were long, unbroken sounds, and they carried across the gravel tarmac and resonated more deeply than any anguish I had known. Just like Lot's wife, I looked over my shoulder, and the sight of her shaking pet pack as she scratched at the door turned my whole body to salt. If Brad hadn't been there I wouldn't have been able to leave. He held my quivering shoulders and firmly pushed me towards the cab. He didn't let go until we were in Nicaragua.

The sun was gentle on the sands of the Pacific. The water lapped without violence at our feet. A tribe of young boys kicked a pink soccer ball, while long-legged girls adjusted their bikini straps self-consciously.

We drifted around like the salty air. In and out of the cabanas for food, internet cafés for news of the world, but mostly we were pulled to the ocean. Hours passed as we sat together, inscribing the sand with profound thoughts.

There was nothing to remind us that this was goodbye, except we hardly spoke a word. And it was in that silence that I knew how far we had come together and how long it would be before I found this closeness with someone else.

I knew if he had not been with me, through everything, through all of it, I would taste bitterness each time I swallowed. The measure of greatness is how you change other people.

Brad's greatness shone brighter than every star in the Costa Rican sky.

I flew out of the monkey house like a bat out of hell. I threw everything in my rucksack and bolted with Brad to the bus shelter. I knew Diane would be back from vacation at any minute and for a reason I couldn't explain, the thought of seeing her twisted my gut into knots of panic.

The hurried kisses I gave to Summer and Rachel hurt them. They wanted more from me, a pledge of friendship, a leisurely goodbye. But I'd hit the ground running and couldn't stop.

I just made the bus. I gave Brad a hurried peck on the cheek, as though I'd be back later that day. There was no time for anything else, not with the jungle snatching at my heels. If I didn't escape while I had the chance, it might swallow me forever.

I arrived in San Jose feeling peculiar. I was no longer of the monkey house. I checked myself into a hostel, then lay in my bed looking at the cracked yellow walls. I shook the vines from my shoulders, the invisible mud from my hair. I never had to hear an alarm at 3 a.m. again. I was leaving for good.

I ate *gallo pinto* one last time in front of a Spanish soap opera. I read my book and tossed in my bed restlessly. I made it until 10 p.m. until I called Brad.

'Hi Darlene,' he said when he heard my voice. 'It's great to hear from you.'

I heard him shuffle into his room, close the door and turn on the CD player.

'I guess I'm Mrs Voldemort—She-Who-Is-Not-Named?'

'Diane didn't lose any time. She flayed you alive. You've kicked off Billy and are now officially the worst researcher of all time. Annie and Sarah have obviously been feeding her information, Diane spat out how you used to go swimming, how you were a bully and a bad influence, how your data was appalling, and she just went on and on until she nearly cried. It was freaky. Darkling, I'm so glad you're out of here. You made it just in time.'

When I hung up the phone I wondered if Diane's rage could hunt me down like a heat-seeking missile. For the thousandth time I wondered why she hated me so much. It had to be more than the sum of swimming and gossip. Months later my mother and I sat on her veranda. The wisteria twisted up the poles like jungle vines and we cradled jasmine tea in our mugs. When I told her about Diane, the silent treatment, the ostracism, her venom on the night of my departure, she said, 'But can't you see it, darling. Diane was in *loco parentis*. She was responsible for you and she sent you to a clinic where you were sexually assaulted. You jeopardised her project.'

It made sense. It explained why she was so desperate for me to prosecute, her coldness towards me when I wouldn't, and her refusal to have any written warning to future field assistants about the St Augusta clinic.

But I think, looking back, it was more than that. Brad was right: we create a world for ourselves in which all we do is true and just. I brought something else into her world; I contaminated it. She worked so hard for her monkeys. Every one of the million hours she spent watching them was so the world could understand her monkeys and love them as she did. Then there was me, who could have scattered her dreams like a pack of cards. Of course she wanted me gone, it was only human.

At around midnight, I drifted into sleep.

At 3:30 a.m., I was wide awake. It was a habit I'd have for years. Without an alarm, without even a shred of light, I hear the call of the monkeys, and the soft chug of the monkey mobile in the driveway. Clanging in the kitchen and shuffling feet warn me I'll be late. I feel Sirius's wet breath on my neck and I reach to fondle her ears. By the time I struggle from my spider-web dreams into my own bed at home, it's too late. So I pace the house, clean the bathtub, or lie perfectly still, anxiety closing my throat.

When I return to Australia, my mother thinks I've turned manic depressive like my father. My closest friends tear up when they see how thin I am, how hollow. When I stumble into my psychologist's office, a woman I have known for a long time, she tells me gently that I have post-traumatic stress disorder. Ironically it is what my father was diagnosed with after he threw hand grenades at children in the Vietnam War. My psychologist recommends industrial-strength antidepressants.

I am tempted. I wistfully think about a world where I am numb with bliss. Where I don't lean over the sink, up to my elbows in dirty dish water, and sob until I slide to the floor. A world where I don't seize up with anxiety in the middle of the street, clenched, short of breath and unable to move. Where I don't wake up at 3:30 a.m. exactly, reaching for something I'll never hold again. But I figure this world will come of its own accord, and if it doesn't, well, the monkeys have to live with it don't they? I thought of Murder watching Dopey and Assassin through slitted eyes. I hoped her world would correct itself too, and one day we would both be whole again.

I boarded the plane with a photo pressed in my pocket. It was a black-and-white photo of Brad and I. He has his right hand over my nose, and I have my left hand over his nose. It's called hand sniffing. The monkeys sit in this position for hours, their eyes closed in rapture. Brad and I tried it.

With his third, long finger pressing on the bridge of my nose, the third eye as the Hindus call it, I smell the acid on his skin and strangely it calms me. The heat from our bodies enfolds each other. Not the ravaging heat of the sun, but gentler, more welcoming.

Even in my most intimate, frenzied moments, I have never felt closer to anyone.

I tucked away the photo and boarded the plane, knowing we would always be friends.

Off the coast of Tanzania in Zanzibar, the giant Aldabran tortoises crawled over Prison Island like prehistoric beasts. A sultan had brought them from the Seychelles in the nineteenth century, and they survived the rise and downfall of his dynasty.

In Capetown, the jackass penguins arched their necks to the sky and called for their mates who were dragging a belly full of fish up the rocky shores. The stench of their shit washed over me with memories of glacier mountains and a sun than never slept.

In Kenya, I interviewed Cynthia Moss, the elephant lady, and saw Echo, the famous matriarchal elephant with her two crossed tusks. A producer asked if I wanted to be Ralph Fiennes's assistant in a new movie they were shooting, *The Constant Gardener*. I pictured myself bringing coffee to Ralph's trailer late at night in my negligee. I declined. I had work to do.

Then there was Uganda. I had come full circle to the place I'd begun my travels four years ago, when I was an arrogant brat, full of scorn for things I knew nothing about.

I'd learnt so much. I hadn't entirely thrown off vanity and spite, but I knew my demons now and I would work to get rid of them—or at least beat them down to a respectable level. I'd lost my sense of immortality, but it takes so much more courage to face life without it. And I hoped courage would make me more like the people I admired: my mother, Angelina, her mother.

At least I wasn't alone. Family never disappears, no matter how much you want it to. And good friends, real friends, survive everything. They accumulate, just like wrinkles, and that was something to look forward to.

Now I was in Uganda, and once again I would be meeting old friends. Debby, the woman who'd fought wars for her chimpanzees, who first taught me what people were capable of if they were determined enough.

I ached to see Baluku, the chimpanzee I cradled in my arms for a month after he was brought to the sanctuary with his groin torn up where the rope had tethered him. I remember he used to rock back and forth in the night like a traumatised child. I wondered if he would recognise me, whether we would recognise each other.

But Baluku was not the first to greet me. Instead, I stumbled into the chimp house and fell into the startled blue eyes of the man I would marry.